Praise for TEACH MUSIC CHANGE LIVES

"Glory St. Germain has composed a masterpiece for music educators uniting passion, purpose, and profitability in perfect harmony. This book is more than a guide. It's an invitation to step into your power as a teacher, entrepreneur, and leader in the world of music education."

— **Jack Canfield,** Coauthor of *Chicken Soup for the Soul*®
and *The Success Principles*™, and a featured teacher in *The Secret*

"The greatest mentors often show up with the title of Teacher. But if teachers can't afford to teach, their impact is lost. Glory St. Germain lays out a clear roadmap to teach both effectively and profitably. The world needs great teachers and music and *Teach Music Change Lives* lights the way to a world transformed through education and song."

— **Nick Nanton,** 22-Time Emmy Winning Director,
Broadway Producer, Award-Winning Songwriter

"Music is a language of the heart and the teachers who share it are powerful agents of transformation. In *Teach Music Change Lives,* Glory St. Germain honors music educators as the world-changers they truly are. This book is a profound reminder that teaching music is not just a job, it's a calling to uplift, inspire, and heal through sound, soul, and service."

— **Marci Shimoff,** #1 NYT Best-Selling Author of
Happy for No Reason, Chicken Soup for the Woman's Soul
and a featured teacher in *The Secret*

"*Teach Music Change Lives* is a reminder that music education is about more than just notes and rhythms, it's about voice, access, and opportunity. Glory St. Germain champions the transformative power of teaching through her students' stories. This book affirms what we at El Sistema USA® know to be true, that music can break down barriers, foster belonging, and build a more just and inclusive world."

— **Elizabeth Moulthrop,** Nonprofit Leader, Music Educator, Violinist, and Executive Director of El Sistema USA®

"Glory St. Germain shatters the myth of being 'just a music teacher' and reveals the extraordinary power within you to change lives. Open these pages with an open heart and watch your teaching, your business, and your impact transform lives."

— **Sage Lavine,** CEO & Founder, Women Rocking Business, Best-Selling Author of *Women Rocking Business*

"Music brings healing, hope, and beauty into the world and so do the teachers who share it. In *Teach Music Change Lives*, Glory St. Germain honors the vital role of music educators and offers a powerful guide to building a life and legacy of profound impact. This inspiring and practical book empowers teachers to become transformational leaders nurturing creativity, growing thriving businesses, and making a lasting difference in the lives they touch."

— **Ocean Robbins,** CEO of Food Revolution Network, Best-Selling Author of *31-Day Food Revolution*

"Music teachers have the power to shape their students' confidence for life. Yet many passionate educators leave the profession too soon because they don't treat it like a growing business. In *Teach Music Change Lives*, Glory St. Germain brilliantly shares how music teachers can succeed, thrive, and scale using her holistic approach. By blending mindset, practical strategy, and creativity at its core, this book becomes an inspiring blueprint that empowers educators to leap forward with confidence."

— **Tiamo De Vettori,** Keynote Concert Speaker, Mentor, Multi Award-Winning Songwriter, Author of *Joy First*

"As both educator and musicians' coach, Glory St. Germain draws from a deep well of experience in this insightful book. With warmth and clarity, she uses familiar musical concepts to guide teachers in turning their skills into a successful business."

— **Patrick Worley,** Classical & Nashville Session Musician, M.M. Music Education, Former University Faculty (UNLV & Utah Tech)

"Glory St. Germain's newest book is more than a resource for music educators; it's a powerful guide for leaders of all kinds. Her stories are inspiring, heartfelt, and practical, drawing a clear truth: teaching is leading. Whether you're a teacher, entrepreneur, or growth-minded individual, this book reminds us that when we teach with intention, we lead with purpose and change lives."

— **Kevin D. St.Clergy,** Author, *Beyond Blind Blaming*; Podcast Host, Keynote Speaker

"*Teach Music Change Lives* is a refreshing and empowering guide for music educators who want to make a meaningful difference. Glory St. Germain shares twelve insightful principles that help teachers align with their values, elevate their impact, and build lasting success in their teaching careers. This book is practical, heartfelt, and a joy to read, and it's a valuable companion for any teacher on a mission to inspire through music."

— **Jennifer Foxx,** Music Educator Resources and Foxx Piano Studio

"*Teach Music Change Lives* is a timeless resource filled with wisdom, inspiration, and practical tools for music educators. Through authentic storytelling and reflections from her *Power of WHY Musicians* series, Glory St. Germain's passion and purpose shine through every chapter woven with Divine guidance, heartfelt stories, and creative vision."

— **Kamara Hennessey,** UMTC Elite Educator, AEFC (RCM), B.Mus.(Hon), RMT (ORMTA/CFMTA), Author & Musician

"*Teach Music Change Lives* is more than a book; it's a blueprint for music educators ready to lead with both heart and strategy. Glory St. Germain beautifully harmonizes passion, pedagogy, and entrepreneurship into a clear, inspiring path forward. Whether you're a seasoned teacher or just starting, this book will empower you to transform your studio, your students, and yourself."

— **Gillian Erskine & Paul Myatt** co-founders Forte School of Music, pioneers of Whole Body Learning, Educational Directors at Piano Teaching Success & Best-Selling Authors

"This book is a symphony of inspiration and practical strategies for music teachers. Glory St. Germain empowers you to create meaningful connections, nurture student growth, and build a thriving, purpose-driven studio, one that leaves a lasting legacy."

— **Dr. David Friedman,** Syndicated TV/Radio Host, #1 Best-Selling Author of *Food Sanity*

"As a music studio owner, implementing Glory St. Germain's strategies transformed my business. Her clear, practical, and inspiring approach elevated my teaching, my business, and my impact. *Teach Music Change Lives* is THE Ultimate Music Teacher's Guide."

— **Joanne Barker,** UMT Certified Elite Educator, International Best-Selling Author of *The Power of WHY Musicians Anthology Series*

"Glory St. Germain's book empowers music professionals with both practical tools and soulful inspiration grounded in her deep love for music, family, and her devoted husband, Ray St. Germain. A must-read for anyone serious about music and meaningful teaching success."

— **Buffy-Pearl Handel,** International Speaker, Cultural Educator, Author, and Indigenous Performer & Designer

"*Teach Music Change Lives* isn't just a book, it's a lived experience. The 12 strategies helped me rebuild my studio with confidence and realign my teaching with purpose. If you're ready to lead with clarity and heart, this book will meet you there."

— **Shirley Wang,** Award-Winning Operatic Soprano, Educator, Best-Selling Author, Podcaster & Speaker

"*Teach Music Change Lives* feels like sitting down with Glory herself; wise, passionate, and endlessly encouraging. She's poured everything she lives and teaches into these pages. This book is practical, powerful, and a true gift to music educators. I'm grateful for the years we've worked together and the passion she continues to share with us all."

— **Sam Reti,** CEO of Muzie & Hiyve, Educator, International Best-Selling Author and Entrepreneur

"I wish I could turn back time and gift myself this marvelous book at the start of my teaching journey. Organized, inspiring, and filled with practical wisdom, Glory's insights are laser-focused on what it truly takes to succeed. A must-have for anyone aspiring to teach music and change lives."

— **Ann M. Mracek,** Award-Winning Author, Unpacking the Attic, Composer, Music Educator, B.M. & M.M. in Theory/Composition, University of Kansas

"Celebrated author Glory St. Germain has done it again! *Teach Music Change Lives* not only empowers educators to make a greater impact with their students, but it also provides a success blueprint for entrepreneurial musicians to build the career they've always dreamed of. We wish we had this decades ago, but we're over-the-moon grateful to have it now to guide our way."

— **Vincent James,** Co-Founder of Keep Music Alive and Co-Author of 88 Ways Music Can Change Your Life

"*Teach Music Change Lives* is what happens when business brilliance meets musical purpose. Glory St. Germain gives music educators what most creatives are never taught: a proven framework for building a thriving studio and meaningful career. Her strategies are clear, powerful, and rooted in passion. This is the book I wish every musician-turned-educator had at the beginning of their journey."

— **Michael Walker,** CEO of Modern Musician, Touring Artist & Entrepreneur

"Successful music teachers continue learning, growing, and evolving with their students. Every professional music educator should read *Teach Music Change Lives*. With a deep love for music and a gift for inspiration, Glory shares powerful stories and transformative business strategies that help educators elevate their craft, grow thriving studios, and demonstrate how music changes lives to create lasting impact."

—**Noreen Wenjen,** Internationally Recognized Piano Teacher, Keynote Speaker, Author of Two-Year Waitlist; An Entrepreneurial Guide for Music Teachers, Musical Journeys®, and co-author of The Power of Why 21 Musicians Created a Program

"*Teach Music Change Lives* is more than a book. It's a baton for music educators ready to lead with vision and heart. Glory St. Germain weaves soulful storytelling with actionable insights to help teachers cultivate impactful, mission-driven studios. For anyone who's ever questioned their path or potential, this book is a powerful invitation to dream big and teach with purpose."

—**Dr. Heidi Kay Begay,** Flutist, Podcaster Flute 360, Serial Entrepreneur, Red House Productions, and J&K Productions

TEACH MUSIC
CHANGE LIVES

Also by Glory St. Germain

International Best-Selling Author

THE POWER OF WHY MUSICIANS BOOK SERIES

THE POWER OF WHY: Why 21 Musicians Created a Program

THE POWER OF WHY: Why 23 Musicians Crafted a Course

THE POWER OF WHY: Why 25 Musicians Composed a Legacy

THE POWER OF WHY: Why 27 Musicians Captured the Lead

THE POWER OF WHY: Why 29 Musicians Climbed to Superstar

THE ULTIMATE MUSIC THEORY BOOK SERIES

Ultimate Music Theory Beginner Workbook Series

(Beginner A, Beginner B, and Beginner C)

Ultimate Music Theory Rudiments Workbook & Answer Book Series

(Prep 1, Prep 2, Basic, Intermediate, Advanced, and Complete Rudiments)

Ultimate Music Theory Supplemental Workbook & Answer Book Series

(Prep Level, Levels 1, 2, 3, 4, 5, 6, 7, 8, and Complete Level)

Ultimate Music Theory Exams Workbook & Answer Book Series

(Set #1 & Set #2: Prep, Basic, Intermediate, and Advanced)
(Level 5, 6, 7, and 8)

TEACH
MUSIC
CHANGE
LIVES

12 KEYS TO UNLOCK
THE ULTIMATE MUSIC TEACHERS
SUCCESS STRATEGIES

GLORY ST. GERMAIN
INTERNATIONAL BEST SELLING AUTHOR

The intention of the author is to share information of a general nature
to support and inspire you on your journey to teach music and
change lives through music education with passion, purpose, and
profitability.

For permissions or inquiries, contact: Gloryland Publishing
info@UltimateMusicTheory.com

ISBN: 978-1-990358-23-4

Library and Archives Canada Cataloguing in Publication

**Get your Ultimate Music Teachers
FREE Bonus Workbook.**

Go To: UltimateMusicTeachers.com/guide

UltimateMusicTeachers.com

Dedication

I dedicate this book to all the musicians and teachers around the world who carry the passion and heart to teach music and in doing so, leave a lasting legacy that contributes to a more beautiful, harmonious world.

I dedicate this book to my amazing clients, whose unwavering commitment to building their music teaching businesses continues to inspire me. You've joined me in implementing these 12 Key Strategies to teach with passion, purpose, and profitability and you are becoming the visionary leaders our industry needs now more than ever.

And I lovingly dedicate this book to my late husband, Ray, to our five incredible children, Chrystal, Catherine, Ray Jr. David, Sherry and grandchildren Jeff, Jordon, Catie, Cody, Eva, Jay and Gemma, and great-grandchildren who have all inspired me by sharing their voices and spirits with the world of music.

I love you all.

Teach Music Change Lives

Be Blessed.

TABLE OF CONTENTS

Foreword by Sage Lavine xv

Introduction 1
Welcome to Your Ultimate Music Teaching Success Journey – *Motif*

Part 1 — SETTING THE STAGE TO **19**
        TEACH WITH PASSION

Key Strategy #1 21
From Dreams to Destiny - *Melody*

Key Strategy #2 43
What You Think, You Create - *Tonality*

Key Strategy #3 67
Being Seen, Heard and Understood - *Articulation*

Key Strategy #4 91
Your Passion-Based Teaching Formula - *Dynamics*

Part 2 – TEACHING HOLISTICALLY TO **109**
        DISCOVER YOUR PURPOSE

Key Strategy #5 111
Simple Steps to Compound Connection - *Rhythm*

Key Strategy #6 141
Engage in the Cooperative Learning Theory – *Tempo*

Key Strategy #7 165
L-E-A-R-N Techniques for Teaching Mastery - *Harmony*

Key Strategy #8 191
Your Purpose-Driven Teacher, Coach & Mentor Triad - *Structure*

Part 3 – GROWING YOUR BUSINESS TO .... 213 UNLOCK STRATEGIC PROFITABILITY

Key Strategy #9 215
Financial Planning to Create Your Freedom Lifestyle - *Pitch*

Key Strategy #10 239
Playing the Symphony of Your Work-Life Balance - *Texture*

Key Strategy #11 253
Teaching Business Money Mindset Blueprint - *Form*

Key Strategy #12 275
Your Profit-Focused Ultimate Legacy - *Analysis*

Ultimate Music Teachers Academy 297

Giving Back With Gratitude 298

Acknowledgements 300

About the Author 302

Connect with Glory 303

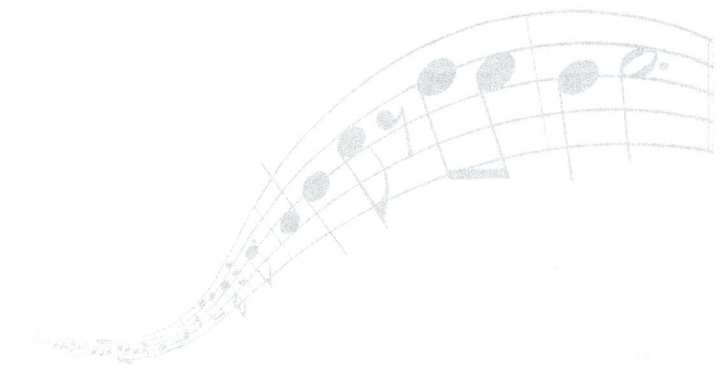

FOREWORD

by Sage Lavine

The first time I saw Glory St. Germain, she was glowing.

It was a Zoom square on one of my virtual events, but somehow, despite the little screen and hundreds of faces, Glory's light leapt out. Her smile. Her sparkle. Her presence. It was undeniable.

At the time, she was a stay-at-home piano teacher with a vision. A woman with a side hustle, teaching music teachers how to build their businesses online. But what stood out even more than her ambition was her heart, so deeply rooted in service. So clearly on fire for music and the people who teach it.

Then life threw her a curveball.

When her husband Ray became ill and was diagnosed with Parkinson's disease and could no longer work, Glory became the sole provider for their household. A moment that could have sent many women into fear, into hiding, into playing small. But not Glory.

Instead, she did what only the most powerful women do: she turned *toward* the pain and let it activate her purpose. She saw the heartbreak of underpaid, undervalued music teachers, and she made a vow to uplift them, to guide them, and to help them create thriving businesses doing what they love most: sharing the power of music.

That vow became a movement.

What followed was nothing short of miraculous. Glory launched her own virtual events, stepped into the spotlight as a speaker, and within weeks made $12K. Then $24K. Then $150K. Then millions. It was like she was timeline-hopping. Defying gravity. Channeling something divine.

But make no mistake: this isn't just a story of financial success. This is the story of a woman becoming a vessel for something much bigger than herself.

Glory allowed herself to be sourced by the magic of music and moved by a mission to heal a world in desperate need of harmony.

Even after losing her beloved husband, Glory never stopped serving. She never stopped showing up for her community of teachers. She never stopped leading with heart.

That's why *TEACH MUSIC CHANGE LIVES* - **12 Keys to Unlock The Ultimate Music Teachers Success Strategies** is so much more than a book. It's a revolution in print. It's a lighthouse for music educators who are ready to claim their worth, rise into leadership, and build a life of freedom, creativity, and impact.

Inside these pages, Glory hands you the exact blueprint that's helped thousands of music educators across the world unlock their entrepreneurial potential. Her 12 Key Strategies will walk you step-by-step through turning your passion into a profitable, purpose-driven business.

If you've ever felt like "just a music teacher," this book will shatter that belief.

Glory knows the truth: you are a changemaker. A healer. A guide. And the music inside you deserves to be heard - loudly, confidently, and unapologetically.

I love Glory deeply. She remains one of the most inspiring leaders I've ever had the honor of mentoring. Her devotion is unmatched. Her strategies are proven. Her heart is pure gold.

This book is a gift. Open it fully. Let it change you. Let it change your students. Let it change lives.

Because when you teach music, you really do change the world.

With love and admiration,

Sage Lavine
CEO & Founder, Women Rocking Business,
Best-Selling Author of *Women Rocking Business*

INTRODUCTION
WELCOME TO YOUR ULTIMATE MUSIC TEACHING SUCCESS JOURNEY
Motif

"The motif you create directs the melody of your life's journey."

~ Glory St. Germain

What do Bach, Beethoven, Elvis, Pavarotti, Taylor Swift, Beyoncé, Michael Jackson, and Kodi Lee all have in common? A desire to play music, determination to learn, and above all, they each had one thing that accelerated their musical genius: dedicated music teachers who not only shaped their talent but ignited a lifelong journey of purpose, creativity, and legacy. They didn't just teach music, they changed lives.

And now, so can you. Whether you're teaching a child their first scale or helping a student prepare for their final exam, you are holding the baton that can conduct brilliance, confidence, and change. Because music teachers don't just shape prodigies they shape *people*. Every student you teach, from the shy beginner to the confident performer, is transformed through music. With every lesson, you are wiring their brain for stronger memory, faster learning, and deeper creativity. You're guiding them to discover self-expression, confidence, emotional healing, and even leadership. This is the power of teaching music, not just to create stars, but to empower every student to shine in their own extraordinary way.

Welcome to *Teach Music Change Lives.*

What does it take to be a successful music teacher? Not 'just a music teacher' but a passion-based, purpose-driven, profit-focused, music teaching entrepreneur? What do the top music teachers, those who excel in teaching, relationships, and financial freedom, do differently to achieve success? Is there a secret strategy that we can all unlock to help us succeed? In fact, there is. For the past thirty years, I have made it my life's work to connect the artistry of music education with the science of business growth, creating a movement of empowered music teachers changing the world.

Teach Music. Change Lives.

My teaching journey began at 16 years old. I didn't just start a teaching career; I launched a full-scale Christmas extravaganza. My motive was clear: put on the most spectacular Christmas recital my tiny studio had ever seen.

The setting? A picturesque winter wonderland, with snow swirling outside like I had stepped into my very own magical snow globe including a piano at center stage. The goal? To instill a love of music in my students (while proving to my parents that teaching piano was a far more lucrative career choice than babysitting). I'll never forget that first recital.

My mother sewed a beautiful blue sequined jumpsuit just for me and let me tell you, I felt like a rock star. The kind of rock star that plays Beethoven *and* insists on perfect posture at the piano. That first performance wasn't just about the music; it was about setting an intention, embracing curiosity, and taking the first step into my journey as a music educator. Of course, my early motives weren't entirely selfless. I had pressing financial responsibilities, important ones, like expanding my sheet music collection, indulging in chocolate snacks, and acquiring just the right amount of glittery accessories (priorities, right?).

Teaching music wasn't just a job; it was a brilliant financial strategy. At five times the pay of babysitting, it was a no-brainer. And let's be honest, I had zero interest in spending my weekends wrangling screaming toddlers. Little did I know, motherhood would later require a whole new skillset, including negotiating with tiny humans while changing diapers in record time.

Looking back, I realize that what started as a simple motif, teaching piano lessons, became the score of my life's symphony. Every decision, every note, every student I taught embellished that original motif, shaping it into something greater than I could have ever imagined.

What I didn't know then, but would come to learn over decades of teaching, training, and building a global community is this:

- **Success in music education isn't accidental, it's intentional.**

- **Passion is powerful, but strategy pays the bills.**

- **And the best news? You don't have to do it alone.**

Whether you're just beginning your teaching journey or you've been guiding students for decades, this book is your backstage pass to what works.

Inside these pages, you'll find the 12 Keys that unlock *The Ultimate Music Teachers Success Strategies*. These aren't fluffy ideas or one-size-fits-all shortcuts. These are real-world-tested, heart-centered strategies that help music teachers teach with purpose, lead with confidence, and grow with joy both musically and financially.

So, if you've ever asked yourself:

- **How do I find more students (and the right students)?**

- **How can I teach theory in a way that's fun, effective, and actually profitable?**

- **How do I build a business that reflects my values and supports my lifestyle?**

…then my friend, you're in the right place.

This book is more than a guide, it's an invitation.

An invitation to step into your full potential as a music teacher.
An invitation to claim your role as a *musicpreneur.*
And an invitation to change lives, starting with your own.

Just as a *motif* guides the shape of a symphony, your vision as a
teacher shapes the lives you're meant to impact.

A *motif* (also called a motive) is a short musical idea: a repeated
pattern that may be melodic, rhythmic, harmonic or a combination,
that is reproduced and varied throughout a composition. One of
the most famous *motifs* comes from the opening four notes of
Beethoven's Fifth Symphony, the first steps into the journey of his
classical masterpiece. You probably already hear the opening notes in
your mind, but I invite you right now to listen again, this time with
wonder. How can a simple four-note *motif* become so memorable?
Just as *motifs* in music are repeated through variations, so are the
words you say, the things you do and the lessons you teach.

A teaching *motif* is a term that is an idea or concept that repeats itself.
A *motif* gives clues to a theme or reinforces ideas that you want to
emphasize in the overall topic. Have you ever heard a repeated *motif*
in one of your lessons? "I can't play that. I can't read that. I can't
memorize that." Yes, if you are a music teacher, you've heard that
repeated *motif* more times than you want to count.

What's your *motif,* your personal repeated pattern?

"I'm just a music teacher. I don't have the skillset to be a business
owner." "I don't have the confidence to charge what I'm really worth."
"I've always wanted to teach group lessons, but I don't know where to
start."

Yes, these are all messages with a common *motif* that I hear from
music teachers around the world. It can be a lonely business being
a music teacher. They know they were born to teach music, but they
don't know how to develop strategies to elevate their income, impact
their teaching and grow their expert music teaching business. Music
is the universal language that impacts us in a deep and profound way.

Music can nurture your soul at the darkest times, lift you up when you need healing and alter your mood as it shifts your inner thoughts. Music is a powerful tool that can transcend you into celebration, relieve you from devastation and guide you towards motivation.

As a music teacher, there is a great deal of responsibility that comes with being a thought-provoking educator (a musical guide of sorts), to ensure music lessons provide students of all ages with the tools they need to express themselves, share their creativity and develop their musicianship skills to become lifelong learners through the joy of music.

Except that, this journey is not always joyful, I know, because I've lived it.

I've been a music educator for more than fifty years (time sure flies), and I've had many learning and growing pains along the way. I struggled to overcome the overwhelm, imposter syndrome and self-doubt in my teaching abilities and limiting beliefs that sometimes held me back from reaching my full potential.

I believe each one of us has a *motif*. It can be a productive *motif*, one that has your life signature on it, or it can be a frustrating *motif*, if you let your tendency to allow limiting beliefs to guide the way. In other words, the most important thing is that you know you always have a *motif*. It's a matter of being conscious of what *motif* you're sending out most of the time. And that the conscious *motif* is the difference between passion vs. depletion, purpose vs. aimlessness, profitability vs. just squeaking by.

Through the years I've discovered the strategies and systems necessary to become an Elite Educator, Author, Course Creator and Music Teachers Business Coach.

My journey has been filled with ups and downs, joy and frustration, from lonely days of endless hours filled with determination in practicing piano to achieve my professional teacher's diploma from the Royal Conservatory of Music (ARCT), to many more days of researching and writing my 60+ Ultimate Music Theory Books, Music Teacher Training Courses and presenting my TEDx Talks.

All of which led me to proud moments of achievement when those 10,000+ hours of intensive dedication to achieve mastery in my goals all seemed worth it.

Each goal started with an idea, a *motif,* the first step in the journey towards my destiny. And this kind of *motif,* the one that is as memorable as the opening of Beethoven's Fifth, that's the one that defines the journey. If you're here to learn how to teach with passion, or maybe you're a passionate teacher but you don't feel on purpose, or perhaps you've been teaching for many years but you're not making the money you deserve and are ready to finally be profitable in your music teaching business - you're in the right place.

FOUR MISTAKES MUSIC EDUCATORS MAKE AND TIPS TO AVOID THEM

Four Mistakes Music Educators make in trying to grow their business are NOT having:

#1 Clarity of Vision – generate focus to achieve goals, facilitate learning, understand the emotional needs of students and the financial needs of business. Not having Clarity of Vision leads to lack of motivation, disappointment and unfulfilled desires.

Creating clarity of vision requires "think time". So often it is "busy work" that dominates our time with constant interruptions and seemingly important deadlines that hold us back from the all-important priority of "think time" to reflect on our past objectives and determine what action steps we can take to achieve our goals easily.

UMT Tip: Block off one hour per week for "you time". This "you time" may be for meditation, going for a walk, taking time to listen to new music, going to a concert, or whatever will rejuvenate your thinking process. You may want to simply sit quietly with your thoughts and take time to write in your journal freely without limitation while listening to 'focus music', which I highly recommend. I always think and write best while listening to focus music.

#2 Plan of Execution - implement strategies with a positive mental attitude to assess teaching results with compassion, developing skill sets and a mindset of abundance. Not having a Plan of Execution can lead to overwhelming, repetitive activities that fail to produce meaningful results.

Processing a Plan of Execution requires commitment with a stick-to-it attitude along with a solid set of proven strategies that will help you grow as a music teaching business owner. It all starts with your mindset, that little inner voice that often deters you from moving forward. It's often a difficult and lonely journey when thinking about your plan.

UMT Tip: Connect with an accountability partner, preferably one who is like-minded and aligned with your goals so you can support each other, acknowledge each other and celebrate each other's accomplishments to help you stay on track. Plan SMART (Specific, Measurable, Attainable, Relevant, Time-bound) Goals.

Create a SMART Goals working document or spreadsheet where you can record your weekly goals and see the progress of achievement. Then take time to analyze what worked and what didn't so you can implement a "reframing" exercise to get you back on track if needed.

#3 Systems that Work – enforce policies, processes and procedures that are effective and repeatable to save time, money and effort to take business to the next level. Not having Systems that Work leads to financial stress, exhaustion, lack of students or even worse, students quitting because lesson structure is not effective.

Understanding systems that work can be a game-changer for you and your business. Teachers often find themselves spending hours of "not getting paid time" doing lesson planning, rescheduling students, scrambling to market for new students while finding themselves not being profitable. It's time to get paid what you are worth.

UMT Tip: Invest in NEPD - Never Ending Professional Development. The world of technology and teaching platforms is evolving so rapidly that in order to stay current in the ever-changing trends, professional development is essential.

One system that can help students learn faster is the Ultimate Music Theory Flashcards System (MusicTheoryApp.com). This powerful system correlates to the Ultimate Music Theory Workbook Program. We partnered with Brainscape to develop the most efficient way to learn music theory. With over 11,000 flashcards covering all concepts in music theory for each level, this app helps students learn easily.

#4 Coaching for Confidence - develop successful thought leadership skills to move forward quickly with efficiency and understand belief patterns for prosperity. Not having Coaching for Confidence leads to self-doubt, loneliness, confusion of direction and an endless search for unanswered questions.

Empowering coaching for confidence is the fastest way to improve your skillset, mindset and teaching business. Think of yourself as a music coach. Your student's success depends on your ability to educate and motivate them to expand their skills and ultimately achieve their goals. Coaching is the essential ingredient for achieving your goals faster.

UMT Tip: Successful educators work with coaches to develop core leadership skills at every stage of their music business. Developing new opportunities for next level communication, self-awareness and influence will help you become a confident thought-leader in your industry. In the Ultimate Music Teachers Membership, coaching is one of our core principles for helping teachers execute goals, create commitment, unlock potential and build trust in their abilities to succeed. Coaching provides a structure for reflection in learning and growing your music teaching business.

In fact, I attribute all my accomplishments to the many coaches who have guided me on my journey to success in my business.

"A journey of a thousand miles begins with a single step."

~ Lao Tzu

It's time to begin with a single step to create your plan and learn the strategies that will help you achieve your ultimate goals. You might wonder, what's the difference between a plan and a strategy? I wondered the same thing and here's what I discovered. In short, a plan maps the path, and a strategy drives the destination.

A PLAN is an outline that defines your objectives for achieving your goals. A plan maps out a pattern or program for a definite purpose. Think of creating a lesson plan for the purpose of being an effective educator as you move through a music curriculum, with the purpose of successful completion of each music level.

One of the most important lessons I've learned the hard way (not a method I'd recommend) in growing my business is the necessity of taking time to plan for success.

What's your success plan for your music teaching business?

A STRATEGY is a blueprint designed with a clear set of plans and actions to accomplish specific unique goals that outline how you can achieve success. A strategy is a set of directions and various elements necessary to attain your desired result in the future. Think of creating a blueprint for the purpose of being a profitable educator as you fill your music studio with students excited to learn from you (and committed to practice, do their homework and don't reschedule, yes, it's a real thing), such as teaching Ultimate Music Theory Club Classes with the purpose of financial growth in your business. I wish someone had told *me* that 20 years ago when I first made the decision to grow my business. How to implement strategies for teaching success, cost reduction, effective marketing, policies and procedures to make processes more efficient while increasing my income.

What's your success strategy for your music teaching business?

OVERWHELM OR OPPORTUNITY The choice is yours.

The good news is, I have uncovered the 12 Key Strategies that helped me take my UMT business to the next level and I'm about to share this detailed strategic planning process with you, so you don't have to take twenty years to learn it the hard way.

Why? Because as a music educator, you know that your students' success depends on your teaching success and your students' willingness to learn. Your success as a music teacher comes from your NEPD and your willingness to learn. I am forever a student willing to learn.

"When the student is ready, the teacher will appear."

~ Lao Tzu

As a young child, running my fingers across the 88 black and white keys of my piano, I often wondered why the keys were in groups of 12 distinct keys that repeated up the keyboard. Each key moved to the next creating a pattern of 12 half steps (also called semitones).

My first teacher, my father, taught me about the importance of understanding the elements of music. He said 12 was a magical number. After all, I was about to turn 12 years old, I was born in the 12th month (December) and I dreamed of teaching 12 doll 'students' in my music theory class learning about the 12 keys. What's so special about the musical 12? A 12-tone musical scale moving by half steps (semitones) from one pitch to the next creates a chromatic scale. Each of the 12 individual pitches is the basis for Major and minor tonality.

To showcase the 12 Major and 12 minor keys, J. S. Bach composed his works of 24 Preludes and Fugues in each of the 12 Major keys and 12 minor keys (in fact, he did it twice.). Bach's highly influential 48 Preludes and Fugues (The Well-Tempered Clavier) is monumental in the transformation of western classical music. J.S. Bach created emotional dimension showcasing the significance of tonality in each key of the preludes and fugues as he used harmonic design and symbolism of melodic and rhythmic *motifs*.

The 12 Key Strategies in this book follow a simple step-by-step planning process, a *motif,* to help you set your intention and focused direction on the impact and growth of your business so you can teach with passion, purpose & profitability.

5 Challenges Teachers Often Fear

#1 Lack of Confidence - What if no one signs up for my music lessons?

#2 Imposter Syndrome - What if they come and I fail them?

#3 Not Qualified - What if I don't know how to teach higher levels, or music theory?

#4 Judgement of Fees - What if people say I charge too much, I'm not worth it?

#5 Overcoming Overwhelm - What if I can't manage things and my students quit?

Here's what I've learned and how you can avoid these fears. FEAR is often described as False Evidence Appearing Real. First, you are worthy. Say that out loud (yes, the teacher in me is showing up), repetition is the mother of all learning.

I'll repeat that: You are worthy.

"You are worthy of love and respect. You are beautiful, gifted, and intelligent. Don't let the storm make you forget it."

~ Russell T. Davies

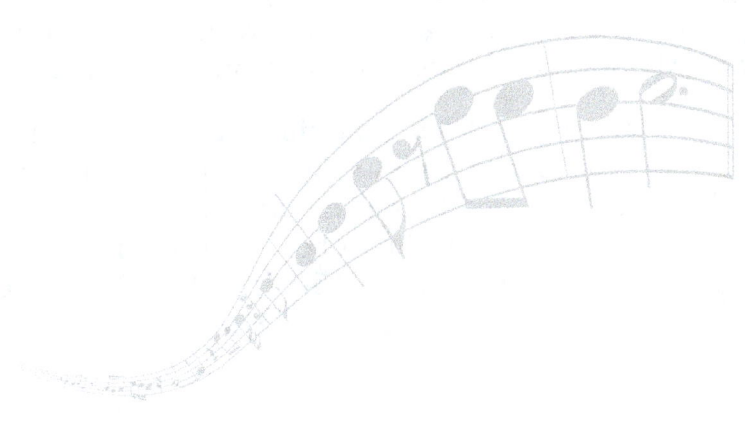

Case Study:
UMT Certified Teacher Shelagh McKibbon–U'Ren

"Why can't you play that? You played it wrong again. Why don't you understand this?" Questions teachers ask impact learning. How did your music teacher make you feel? The negative talk we use with children becomes their inner voice. One of my clients, Ultimate Music Theory Certified Teacher Shelagh McKibbon U'Ren from Canada, heard those words. Her inner voice thought only perfection was good enough, anything less was failure.

Shelagh suffered deeply as no one believed that sometimes it physically hurt to practice the piano. There were times when the music notes on the page simply became black dots all jumbled up. In her late twenties she was diagnosed with depression, anxiety, panic attacks, and dyslexia, but her passion for learning and teaching music drove her to explore different ways she could learn.

Shelagh came across my Ultimate Music Theory Workbook Series and reached out to say that she was finally able to understand music theory with clarity and teach with confidence. I invited Shelagh to become my editor in the Second Edition of the Ultimate Music Theory Series as I realized there were other teachers and students who struggled too and with Shelagh's vast knowledge, we could ensure that the UMT Series could work for all learning styles and abilities.

There were times Shelagh felt like quitting because her 'not good enough' voice popped into her head. But this time she turned it into teachable moments to educate and help others. Shelagh changed her 'not worthy' voice echoing in her head into her superpower of positivity. She eventually joined the Ultimate Music Theory Team as my editor, co-author and examiner of the UMT Certification Course.

We have now written over 60 books together and our journey continues as we explore the world of music education.

Read Shelagh's inspiring story in *The Power of WHY Musicians* 5 Book Series.

This series includes 125 stories from musicians who created a program, crafted a course, composed a legacy, captured the lead, and climbed to superstar.

Discover your WHY and put your creativity to the test. Dream Big and transform your musical mind into a musical masterpiece. It's my deep desire to share my passion for music to help you learn the beautiful language of music to express yourself, because you are worthy. Now it's time for you to take action steps in your own journey to enhance your life as an educator.

The world needs music. The world needs music teachers. And the world needs you. Stepping into your role as an empowered music educator isn't just about teaching notes on a page, it's about embracing your purpose, owning your impact, and making the conscious decision to build a business that serves both you and your students.

Every great composition starts with a *motif* defining idea that shapes the entire piece. Your journey as an educator begins with your own *motif,* your motive to become the best at what you do, to inspire, and to create a lasting impact.

Success doesn't happen by accident it happens by commitment. And that journey begins with one powerful choice: saying yes to yourself, your students, and your dream.

Does your dream seem impossible? It isn't.

You are here for a reason. You are reading this, because perhaps it is your destiny to take the next steps in your journey, right now. I'm going to show you exactly how you can create a thriving music teaching business and take your dream to your destiny too.

YOU CAN DO IT

You might wonder, can a teacher like me, with just a desire to teach music actually make money and grow my business?

Yes.

Can those of us that have felt like imposters in our ability and our confidence as professional educators really build a successful business and make a lasting contribution to music education and make money?

Yes. If I can do it, you can do it.

What you are about to experience in *Teach Music Change Lives* is a roadmap to the Ultimate Music Teachers Guide that has helped thousands of musicians ignite their passion, amplify their teaching skills, and build thriving music teaching careers.

It's time to take your dream to your desired destiny. Your dream and your impact on the world of music begins with the first note. It's time to commit to taking your teaching business to the next level and give you the wings to soar. Trust the Process.

Over the past thirty years, I have invested thousands of dollars in my own business training and built three successful businesses. Now I want to show you the step-by-step playbook of how you can begin changing lives and making money in your business too.

I've helped clients put their teaching programs together, whether teaching online or in person, teaching private or group or both. In this book, I'll share the very best of what I teach my clients in our music teaching business training programs.

Teach Music Change Lives will provide you with the Ultimate Music Teachers "how-to" guide, a master blueprint with exercises and real teacher case studies that you can apply to your own music teaching business.

Ultimate Music Teachers Commitment Contract

I'm so excited to have you on this music teaching business journey with me.

Complete your UMT commitment contract. Post it where you can see it and read it out loud. Congratulations on saying YES to your dream, your students and your income.

I, (your name) _____ am committed to planning my successful journey with a positive attitude and articulating clearly my success plan.

I commit to myself, my students and my ultimate music teaching business.

I commit to working through the step-by-step plan in the 12 KEYS outlined in this book, with determination and dedication, resisting self-doubt and overcoming overwhelm to focus on my true desire by taking one step (even a half step) at a time.

I commit to taking responsibility for my results and taking massive action with purpose and clarity, even when the road gets bumpy, knowing that the final destination is my ultimate destiny. I am worthy of success in all aspects of my life.

Signature: _____

Date: _____

TEACH MUSIC CHANGE LIVES

Let's do this together.
With Passion, Purpose & Profitability, Glory

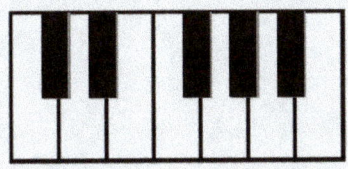

The world needs compassionate teachers (problem solvers), to build their entrepreneurship through music education and implementation of strategies to create successful learning in the lives of their students.

As you read this book, you will:

- **Discover the secret to teaching with passion and not burning out so you can keep moving forward towards your goals.**

- **Learn how to use effective systems for impactful teaching so you can teach with confidence and connect on a deeper level.**

- **Clarify your teaching business, offers, and purpose so you can have a system that works for you and your lifestyle.**

- **Choose a marketing strategy that delivers profitable results so you can have a full teaching studio, make the income you deserve and enjoy the process.**

- **Build your success plan easily from dream to destiny by implementing the action steps and key strategies mapped out for you.**

With the Ultimate Music Teachers 12 Step-by-Step Strategies, you'll have a solid plan that you can implement as you grow and develop your music teaching business.

As each chapter unfolds, I will reveal the strategies that may be holding you back from building your music teaching dream business.

It's time to take the building blocks of your own melody to create the symphony of your life. Your students are waiting for you.

How to get the most VALUE from TEACH MUSIC CHANGE LIVES

You will get the most value by reading this book cover to cover, examining each Key Strategy in order. As you apply the strategies from each key, there will be implementation exercises to help you clarify your dreams and desires.

Your life changing success depends on how willing you are to follow these strategies and embrace the action steps with determination and dedication to step into your destiny.

The people you are meant to impact are counting on you to take action.

Music teachers have a calling and you're here because you've answered it. Teaching is a dream many musicians hold, and if you're reading this, you're already living it.

I believe in you. I'm going to show you the way to score success because your students are waiting for you. To support you in Your Teaching Journey, I invite you to join our community in the **Ultimate Music Teachers Facebook Group** to learn, plan, teach, and grow alongside other passionate educators.

TEACH MUSIC CHANGE LIVES

It's time to implement your 12 Keys to Unlock the Ultimate Music Teachers Success Strategies to Teach with Passion, Purpose, and Profitability.

PART 1

SETTING THE STAGE TO TEACH WITH PASSION

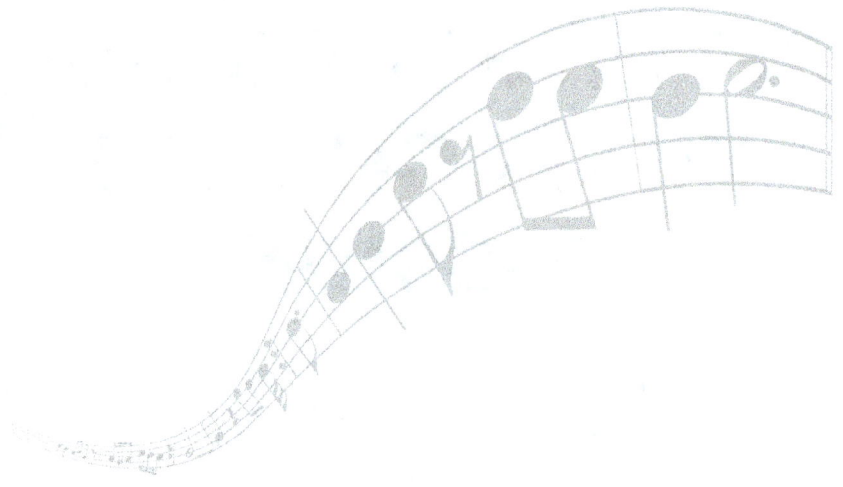

Key Strategy #1
FROM DREAMS TO DESTINY
Melody

"When you see the vision of your dreams with desire, determination and dedication, you will step into the melody of your destiny."

~ Glory St. Germain

What's the melody that lives in your memory? You know the one, the first few notes play and suddenly, you're there. A place. A moment. A feeling. Music has that power. It captures our stories, our dreams, and sometimes, our hearts.

From the moment I heard Ray St. Germain sing *The Girl from Ipanema*, I was captivated. It wasn't just a song; it was an experience. The moment his voice carried the melody through the air, it felt like he was singing directly to me. Just 19-year-old me. No one else. As the smooth bossa nova melody swayed through the room, I was no longer where I stood. I was transported barefoot on a warm sandy beach, the golden sun dipping into the horizon, the scent of the ocean filling the air. I *became* the girl from Ipanema. The melody painted a world so vivid I could feel the breeze on my skin.

Not only did that song become *my* song, it became *our* song because I married him. Ray came as a package deal that gave me three beautiful stepchildren, Chrystal, Cathy and Ray Jr., who would all follow in their father's footsteps as professional singers.

That's the power of music. A single melody can transport us through time, awaken emotions, and make an ordinary moment unforgettable. It imprints itself in our memories of where we were, who we were with, what we were feeling. And just as a simple *motif* blossoms into a full, rich melody, so too does our life's passion evolve into our calling. For me, that calling was teaching music. But stepping into that role wasn't always easy. My path, like any great melody, was filled with highs and lows, unexpected turns, and moments of uncertainty.

The Journey from Motif to Melody

A melody consists of two key elements: a sequence of musical tones (rising and falling, shifting in distance and direction), and rhythm (the heartbeat of sound and silence that gives music its pulse). A melody often starts with a simple *motif,* an idea or a spark, but as it develops, it guides the listener through a journey of emotion, tension, and resolution.

The melody of my journey as a music teacher wasn't always harmonious. There were dissonant moments, challenges testing my resilience, doubts questioning my abilities, and times I wondered if my dreams would ever fully unfold. Although I had always dreamed of teaching music, deep down I often felt like an imposter.

Yet, teaching has always been part of my story even as a young child. At six years old, I carefully lined up my dolls in a semi-circle around our brown wooden piano, ready for their "music lesson." That piano was the heart of our living room, surrounded by my father's collection of guitars, mandolin, banjo, bass, harmonica, and accordion, alongside my mother's cherished violin. These instruments weren't expensive; most were treasures from second-hand shops. But they were loved deeply, forming the soundtrack of our family, our friendships, and our community.

That old brown piano was my best friend. Even then, I felt genuinely excited about "teaching" my very first music theory class. With great seriousness, I introduced my doll-students to the fundamentals of music as best as I understood them. My mom even captured it in photographs, proof that my passion for teaching was ignited long before I taught my first real student.

It Starts with Middle C

Every music lesson needs a starting point, and for me, it always began with Middle C. Let's be honest, what's the big deal about Middle C anyway? Well, it sits neatly between the Treble Clef and the Bass Clef on the Grand Staff, on its own special ledger line. Middle C is also famously known as key number C4, since it's the fourth C when counting upward from the lowest C on an 88-key piano. This one simple note serves as a central anchor for both Treble and Bass.

In my imaginary teaching world, Middle C wasn't just a note, it was "Captain C," the most important white key on the piano. Captain C was the star of the Grand Staff, often leading the way in the popular key of C Major. To me, Captain C was clearly the boss (well, next to me of course).

But my beginner doll-students didn't seem to appreciate Captain C's significance. They slouched and scattered about, unimpressed, silently asking, "Who cares about Middle C?" Undeterred, I passionately explained melody and rhythm, the two elements of music I valued most. Yet, my baby dolls, sitting neatly in their fancy dresses, rolled their eyes with boredom as if to say, "Really? Seriously?"

Determined, I continued by demonstrating dynamics, proudly singing loudly in forte (always my favorite, despite Mom's gentle hints that softer piano singing suited me better). Even then, my teenage Barbie dolls in their glamorous outfits huddled together, completely disinterested, high heels refusing to tap along. Their attitude clearly said, "We're not listening."

But music was my passion, and with my mother's encouragement to keep teaching, I carried on.

My Dream - Becoming a Music Teacher

My dream of becoming a music teacher came true at sweet sixteen when real live human students replaced my dolls. But there was a slight hitch: these students weren't listening either. Like my floppy dolls, they seemed uninterested and bored. Why would a shy sixteen-year-old girl who struggled with piano and theory exams (my scores were too embarrassing to reveal) and lacked confidence dare to teach others? Simple, I needed money to buy a car, a VW Bug. And I did it for just $100 cash. At the time, I thought I'd made it big. Little did I know this humble start would introduce me to the magic of music and teaching techniques that would transform my life.

Reflecting on those early lessons, I remember lining up my dolls, tall ones proudly standing at the back, fancy dolls in pretty dresses in the middle, and the floppy, uninterested ones scattered off to the side. Who knew those childhood "lessons" would become my life's work, teaching students of all learning styles the joy of music?

Music lessons were part of daily life in my musical family, as routine as brushing teeth, but lessons didn't come easy to me. My father emphasized music theory, but my teacher's approach, handing me a theory book and saying "memorize this" left me lost. Why did chords have different names? Why did a V chord lead to a I chord? Why did major keys have relative minors? And what were those letter names at the top of a mysterious "lead sheet"? I had no clue, and it shook my confidence deeply.

Despite years of trying to master effective theory teaching (and investing thousands in books and courses), I struggled. Although I ran a piano studio, my theory-teaching confidence was shaky, holding back my growth as an educator. But I've always been someone who sets and achieves goals even if my theory exam scores barely squeaked by with 61%. (Don't judge, we're friends now, I still passed, right?)

I Almost Gave Up

I vividly remember sitting at the piano, overwhelmed by frustration. My own theory learning had been limited to a tiny blue book and blank staff paper, no guidance, no clarity, just confusion. Have you ever hit that wall, wondering if things could ever turn around?

Then my student bounced through the door with a huge smile, excited and certain I was "an amazing teacher." It hit me like lightning: if this student believed in me so wholeheartedly, why couldn't I believe in myself? In that moment, something shifted inside me. Years of self-doubt, imposter syndrome, and feeling "not good enough" erupted into a determination for change.

I realized then it wasn't just about what I was taught; it was about how I chose to teach. My approach was my responsibility. I no longer needed to live with imposter syndrome. It was time to rewrite my story.

My Life Changed That Day

That day sparked a shift, not in the melody written on the page, but in my resolve to transform how I taught, so my students would never endure the frustrations I had faced.

I dove into research, studying how to write books designed for effective learning. I explored innovative methods to help students grasp, retain, and recall knowledge with remarkable accuracy. I crafted engaging drills and fun exercises to boost retention and enthusiasm. Let's face it, music theory can sometimes be a drag. As teachers, we know theory is essential but how can we make it exciting?

I devoured countless books, tried humor, creativity, anything to spark engagement. But discouragement still crept in, whispering negative thoughts. Maybe I was destined to be a boring teacher. Maybe success wasn't meant for me.

Little did I know, this was only the beginning of something extraordinary.

The AHA Moment

My life changed dramatically when I experienced my "AHA Moment": the realization that fundamental teaching principles apply to every student, regardless of their instrument or voice. Just like composing a melody, a simple *motif* expands into something greater, guiding you forward on your musical journey. In that moment, I knew that if I couldn't find an engaging, effective music theory program, I needed to create one myself.

That was the turning point. I began writing my own music theory books. Each day, I'd rise early, often writing through the night, fueled by coffee and determination. My family affectionately called me the "pink robed writer" after my favorite writing robe, which always got me into the creative zone. At first, I thought simply starting to write would solve everything. But soon, I realized there was much more to learn. I needed advanced training, structured systems, and deeper insights into how students learn differently.

Despite these challenges, I stayed committed. With each obstacle, I saw an opportunity to grow. My mother's wisdom echoed in my ears; "It's not overwhelm, it's opportunity."

My Dream of Becoming an Author

My dream of becoming an author was finally becoming a reality. I'm not sure which moment thrilled me more, selling my first yellow *Basic Rudiments Workbook* or celebrating when my student achieved 100% on her theory exam using the *Ultimate Music Theory Workbook Program.*

Determined, I reached out to music dealers, inviting them to carry the three UMT Workbooks I'd written (Basic, Intermediate, and Advanced Rudiments). Thankfully, they said yes. As a self-published author, I welcomed their feedback and suggestions. Self-publishing wasn't initially my plan. I faced rejection after rejection from traditional publishers who politely but firmly said, "No thanks." It was devastating. After pouring my heart and soul into writing, I felt dismissed, like an inexperienced newcomer being told, "Go away, little girl." Imposter syndrome resurfaced. Should I quit?

Instead, I pressed forward, investing my life savings and borrowing the rest to print my books. My only trusted resource was Miss Google. I felt like she was part of my team.

Then, magic happened. Bob Kohl, the head print music buyer for Long & McQuade Music, a national chain with over 100 stores in Canada, called me. Bob quickly became a mentor, guiding me in building relationships with dealers. His advice echoed a teacher's wisdom: listen, ask questions, learn, and implement.

I'll never forget Bob's valuable feedback: "Glory, may I suggest placing your book title at the top of the front cover? It helps people identify your book immediately instead of seeing just a yellow cover among many." Then he added, "By the way, teachers love your books, we'd like to place another order."

That phone call marked a turning point in my journey as an author.

My Dream of Becoming a Publisher

My journey into publishing brought joy and a bit of embarrassment. How could I have missed something as simple as putting the book title at the top of the cover? After all, I was the CEO of Gloryland Publishing with three books. I still have that first printing; it seems so obvious now. But it was an invaluable lesson.

Bob Kohl continued mentoring me, generously offering feedback and guidance before I printed future books. I remain deeply grateful for his expertise, friendship, and unwavering support, including the opportunity to present numerous masterclasses at Long & McQuade locations across Canada.

Looking at the back of that iconic "yellow" book, I smile at the two other book covers, green and purple, labeled only as "Book 1" and "Book 2," hinting at future publications still unwritten.

Then, something amazing happened. A music teacher named Shelagh McKibbon-U'Ren reached out to me after purchasing those first three books. "Hi Glory," she wrote, "I'm a music teacher in Ontario, and your books have helped me finally understand modes after years of confusion. Your explanations are clear and simple. I had that AHA moment, and I'm grateful to have discovered your materials."

Wow, my first super fan. It was that moment when you realize your sleepless nights and hours of hard work truly made a difference in someone else's teaching journey.

But Wait There's More

Shelagh's message continued, "If you're open to suggestions for your three books, I'd love to send you some ideas." I eagerly replied, "Yes, please." I anticipated a few helpful sentences, maybe a paragraph at most. But Shelagh sent fourteen pages filled with corrections, insights, and ideas. Thankfully, she agreed to become my editor.

Together, we named the green and purple books *Prep 1* and *Prep 2*, created answer books, and held enthusiastic UMT Writing Camps in my basement writing room. We still laugh about those initial fourteen pages. I am deeply grateful for her generosity and invaluable input.

I discovered a powerful lesson; approaching the music industry with an open mind, ready to both learn and share, can profoundly impact your students, colleagues, and your own growth. Over time, my confidence soared, and so did the *Ultimate Music Theory Program*. Shelagh not only became my editor but also my co-author, contributing to over sixty music theory workbooks and five international bestsellers in *The Power of WHY Musicians Anthology Series*.

That marked the beginning of our UMT Dream Team. Together, we've helped thousands master music theory more effectively. This journey inspired me to continuously develop new teaching tools and study resources to accelerate learning.

Through my experiences, I identified what I call the **Three Essential Ds** success principles guiding us toward our dreams. Life's melody has its crescendos and diminuendos, but how we reach our destiny is entirely up to us.

Three Essential Ds in the Success Principles

The first Essential D is DESIRE.

When I started writing the Ultimate Music Theory Series, it began as a simple idea, just a few worksheets. But soon it grew into a powerful vision, a desire to create resources that would genuinely help students learn music faster and with joy. My vision expanded to include the best music theory certification course, empowering teachers not only to master theory but also to live their teaching journey with passion and ease.

As a teacher, my deepest desire was to play piano, not because I loved practicing (definitely not that) but because I cherished expressing myself musically. My beloved walnut-finish piano was always there, inviting me to create and explore. However, my journey was far from smooth. Lack of confidence in music theory kept me from composing and improvising freely. However, despite confusion and frustration, my burning desire kept me seated at the piano, determined to find clarity.

Ask yourself, what is your heart's desire? When our excitement and determination become contagious, others can't help but be inspired.

Tired of feeling inadequate, I desired to teach with confidence. Investing in professional development transformed my skill set, boosted my income, and allowed more family time including a dream vacation to Disney World. That powerful, burning desire led me naturally to the next essential step: Determination.

Reflect for a moment. Is your desire truly a burning desire? Whether your dream is visiting Beethoven's birthplace, performing and receiving standing ovations, or building a thriving music business, what stops you from reaching it? Remember, desire isn't just wishing. True desire sparks unstoppable action.

The second Essential D is DETERMINATION.

My burning desire to write the Ultimate Music Theory Series and create the Ultimate Music Theory Certification Course became reality through sheer determination. "Never Give Up", words my mother often shared, still echoing clearly in my mind. As both a mother and teacher, I've repeated this advice countless times, recognizing that desire alone isn't enough. Without determination, our good intentions remain just wishes.

Determination means taking consistent, intentional action. When my family passionately decided to make our Disney World trip happen, determination pushed us forward. We created vision boards, planned budgets, and found creative ways to save. Yes, doubts surfaced, but children dream without limits and their enthusiasm inspired me to dream big, too. Back then, without today's online resources, determination alone fueled our step-by-step progress toward achieving our dream.

Channel your determination into concrete steps. Schedule your goals clearly, use your calendar, journal, or vision board with deadlines and accountability. Dedicate your time and energy consistently. Stay true to your desire by pairing it with unstoppable determination and passion.

The third Essential D is DEDICATION.

Having a Desire ignites our dreams, Determination fuels our actions, but it's Dedication, the unwavering commitment to a purpose, that ensures we reach our goals. Reflecting on my journey from endless hours practicing piano and immersing myself in music theory, to stepping into teaching and eventually creating the Ultimate Music Theory Program, I realized every note and challenge was driven by something deeper than dedication alone.

It was my profound love for teaching, sharing knowledge, and empowering others that shaped my purpose. Now, passing this passion to you is my greatest joy, enabling you to achieve your own success through the Three Essential Ds.

Dedication means fully committing to your vision. Once you embrace your role as educator and entrepreneur, your dedication naturally inspires students to reach their next level of learning.

You might wonder, did the St. Germain family make it to Disney World? With burning desire, fierce determination, and joyful dedication, we arrived just in time for Christmas and my 35th birthday. As a Christmas baby, it was an unforgettable celebration.

Even when a power outage moved us from Disney World to oceanfront cabins, creating unexpected adventures like watching Santa drive a 4-wheeler on a sandy beach, it became a treasured memory. Despite setbacks, small gifts, and a tiny Christmas tree brought in a suitcase, our celebration surpassed our wildest dreams.

Success builds upon itself. The Three Essential Ds of Desire, Determination, and Dedication guided my growth as a wife, mother, teacher, author, and course creator. Let these principles guide your dreams to reality, too. And now, a Bonus D from my mother Rosabel, who wisely said: "Glory, Always Have a Dream."

The Bonus D is DREAM.

Dream and DREAM BIG, my fellow educator.

My mother Rosabel lived this principle daily. Her accomplishments stretched beyond music (playing violin, accordion, and singing in the choir). She was also an entrepreneur, running several successful dress shops and retail stores. Above all, she was a fabulous grandmother, mother, sister, and dear friend.

After her passing, I discovered a poem she had treasured, pinned carefully on her apartment wall. It is my constant reminder of her wisdom, her vision, and her unwavering belief in the beauty of dreams. The poem is called Always Have a Dream. I cherish it deeply, returning to it often to feel close to her spirit, and now, I'd love to share its timeless inspiration with you.

Always have a Dream

Forget about the days when it's been cloudy,
But don't forget your hours in the sun,
Forget about the times you've been defeated,
but don't forget the victories you've won…

Forget about mistakes that you can't change now,
but don't forget the lessons that you've learned,
Forget about misfortunes you've encountered,
but don't forget the times your luck has turned…

Forget about the days when you have been lonely,
but don't forget the friendly smiles you've seen,
Forget about the plans that didn't seem to work out right,
but don't forget to Always have a Dream.

Author ~ Larry S. Chengges

I had a dream to take my family to Disney World. During that trip, I realized something profound: it was my music teaching business that made this family dream a reality. Embracing the 3 Ds of Desire, Determination, and Dedication shifted my mindset, showing me what's truly possible when we focus on positivity and action.

Think for a moment: what is your greatest dream?

- **Do you want a thriving business that provides financial freedom and the flexibility to travel?**

- **Do you envision teaching online group classes, creating recurring revenue and community impact?**

- **Perhaps your dream mirrors mine, taking your family on unforgettable adventures like Disney World.**

Maybe your goals are more personal:

Is it improving your health? Years ago, my unhealthy habits left me exhausted, overweight, and struggling to teach. It took a wakeup call, a dedicated trainer, and months of training, but eventually, I completed a full 26.2-mile marathon. That proud moment taught me the importance of prioritizing my health because we only get one body and one life.

Is it about deepening your relationships?

I discovered that communicating more meaningfully with my students, family, and friends significantly enriched my life. By listening deeply and openly, I built stronger connections and created lasting positive impacts.

Or perhaps, is it about expanding your musicianship and growing your teaching business?

My journey began with one book and evolved into many, always setting new goals and dreaming bigger. This passion for continuous growth led me to write this book for you, my fellow music teacher.

Right now, you have an incredible opportunity to shape your life, your dreams, and your impact. This is your moment to make a difference, not only in the lives of your students but also in your own life. Teach Music. Change Lives.

Whatever your dream, Dream Big. Embrace your Desire with unwavering Determination and fierce Dedication with support from family, coaches, colleagues, or mentors. With the 3 Ds guiding you, your Ultimate Destiny awaits.

You can achieve anything. Teach with Passion and Dream Big.

"Whether you think you can, or you think you can't —
you're right."

~ Henry Ford

Case Study:
UMT Certified Teacher Dr. MaeRuth McCants

This is a story about "The Song That Never Stopped Playing." Some melodies are unforgettable. They stay with us long after the music stops, shaping our dreams and calling us forward, even when the path seems impossible. For Dr. MaeRuth McCants, music was never just an interest, it was a calling. But the journey to answering that call? It wasn't a straight path, it was a symphony of persistence, detours, and a deep-rooted melody that refused to fade.

Her story begins in the 1950s, in a vintage Midwestern house where winter demanded that the family closed off sections of the house because it was so cold. And yet, nestled in the corner of the stairwell, in the coldest part of the house, sat a piano, her first love. It wasn't fancy. In fact, some keys were permanently stuck, and the ones that worked produced deep, foghorn-like tones. But to young MaeRuth, it was pure magic. She would sit there, bundled in her thick coat and gloves, determined to make music despite the freezing room. That "foghorn piano" became her first companion in music, a steadfast friend that ignited a passion no hardship could silence. At age seven, the melody of her dream grew stronger. Her second-grade teacher saw her enthusiasm and, in an act of profound generosity, offered her piano lessons in exchange for housekeeping work from her mother.

When MaeRuth first set eyes on her teacher's grand piano, she had an out-of-body experience, with its smooth keys, its rich sound, its sheer elegance. It was nothing like her old piano, but it felt like destiny. And so, her musical journey began, not in a music conservatory, not with expensive lessons, but in a tiny classroom, with an unwavering desire to play. Even then, life threw its challenges at her. She was forbidden from crossing the street alone, so instead of watching her cousins play boogie-woogie on their piano, she listened intently from a distance, training her ear and figuring out the music on her own. Without realizing it, she was developing improvisation skills, an early lesson in adaptability and resilience. But then came the day she had to leave her beloved piano behind. When her family moved, the old upright wasn't coming with them. The loss was devastating.

For years, she hoped to return home one day to find a new piano waiting for her, but it never happened. Until she turned sixteen. The mother of her boogie-woogie-playing cousins made her an offer: "You can buy this piano for the number of years that you are old." With sixteen dollars saved from summer work, she finally had her own piano.

But a piano is only part of the equation. Without formal lessons, she faced an uphill battle. No teacher. No structured practice routine. No clear roadmap to progress. Years passed. Music remained in her heart, but without guidance, it became a scattered rhythm and a dream she couldn't fully grasp. Then, at twenty-seven, she turned the key to a new chapter. A graduate student in education and psychology, she took a bold step: she rented a new piano. But as soon as she sat down to play, doubt crept in.

Could she really do this? Did she have the ability? Would she ever be able to play the music she longed to express? Her self-doubt played a louder melody than her piano at times. She wanted to play everything, yet she had to start from scratch. But just as the melody of her childhood had never left her, neither did her determination.

Decades later, she finally understood something profound; the inner child she had been trying to silence for years, the one who had fallen in love with the foghorn piano, who had trained her ear from across the street, who had scraped together sixteen dollars for a used piano, that child was never meant to be ignored.

That child held the key to her true musical destiny. She didn't just return to music, she embraced it fully, earning a music school degree and creating a teaching philosophy rooted in holistic learning, emotional connection, and the belief that music lives in everyone.

Today, Dr. MaeRuth McCants is a testament to the power of perseverance, passion, and belief. Her Ultimate Music Theory

Certification was not just another credential; it was the bridge between her lifelong love of music and her ability to help others unlock their own melodies.

She now teaches with a deep understanding of both the struggle and the triumph, inspiring her students to see beyond limitations and listen to the music that has always been within them.

Because some melodies are destined to play forever. Some journeys are meant to be walked alone, but the most profound transformations happen when we have a guide who has traveled the road before us, stumbled, learned, and emerged stronger. Dr. MaeRuth's story is proof that with the right support, persistence, and passion, we can turn our dreams into reality.

Read Dr. MaeRuth's inspiring story in *The Power of WHY Musicians* 5 Book Series.

But what about your journey? What if there were a way to navigate the path ahead with confidence, clarity, and a roadmap that keeps you from getting lost in the overwhelm?

THE JOURNEY TOGETHER

I promise to provide you with a success formula for reaching your students in a way that is authentic to the way you teach. I will provide you with the road map: a balanced plan that gives you the freedom to envision your dream lifestyle and what you want your music teaching business to look like. How do you achieve success easily? After all, we all feel overwhelmed sometimes, and we don't always have a clear plan of how to get started.

⌢ *Fermata* (Pause to Ponder): Three Steps to a Personalized Teaching Plan

Being a teacher simply requires that you regularly take part in your own professional development. What's the hardest part about teaching? Having a solid success plan and sitting down to map it out.

You can have the greatest ideas in the world, but if you don't take time to implement these strategies they will simply float about in the world of wishful thinking and your dreams will never become a reality. Just like any student, your success lies directly within your attitude of achievement - it may sound simple, but it's not always easy. Complete your success plan this week.

Step #1 Start a success journal.

You may want to go buy a fancy special journal or just notate it on your computer. But writing your success plan is the first step to achieving it. This process is mapping out your desire, your vision for your business.

What's holding you back? What fear will you let go of to achieve your desire?

_____

_____

What action steps will you take this week to live and teach with a positive attitude?

_____

_____

How will you articulate your message more clearly in all areas of communication?

_____

_____

Step #2 Write a creative title.

Title your teaching goal with a deadline. Some ideas might be "My Amazing Weekly Teaching Plan", "My Music Theory Class Map", "My Winning Week of Performances"; your title will get your creative thinking in motion.

What needs to change for you to achieve your outcome this week?

_____

_____

What is your Teaching Goal title and strategy for this week?

_____

_____

What is the deadline for completing your action plan?

_____

_____

Step #3 Commit to blocking off time.

Put planning and professional development into your weekly calendar. Look at all your commitments to see where you can fit in Your Planning Time (even if it's only 15 minutes). Plan, commit, stick to it week after week.

What days of the week will you commit to planning?

_____

_____

What time and how many minutes will you dedicate to designing your week?

_____

_____

What would you like your ideal weekly schedule to look like for maximum productivity?

_____

_____

"Failing to plan is planning to fail."

~ Benjamin Franklin

Teacher planning requires time. When you take the time to plan, your success is so much closer. Are you ready to implement your commitment to planning your week? Awesome. Simply fill in the blanks of your daily progress and adjust your time as needed. Planning to complete this exercise every week will create the habit of planning, and that's the way to score success.

Our purpose as music teachers is to help our students learn by sharing our knowledge with a positive attitude and clearly articulating the lesson. It is also to build relationships so our students can learn effectively to become lifelong learners. As teachers, we fill a complex set of roles. We often become our students' coach, motivator, disciplinarian, visionary, role model, mentor, confidant, cheerleader, and the list goes on and on as our relationship with our students moves from one level to the next.

Teaching music is more than just passing on knowledge. It's about inspiring, guiding, and shaping the next generation of musicians. With every lesson, every breakthrough moment, and every note played, we are actively creating a legacy of learning.

Teaching is a skill that can be refined, a business that can be structured, and a passion that can be transformed into a sustainable, profitable career.

That's where strategic planning comes in. When you approach your teaching with clarity, intention, and purpose, you set the stage for growth, not only for your students but for yourself as an educator and entrepreneur.

♪ Your Coda Notes ♪

_____

_____

The 12 Key Strategies include online Ultimate Music Teachers Bonus Resources.

TEACH MUSIC CHANGE LIVES
From Dreams to Destiny

Dive deeper into **KEY STRATEGY #1** - get your
Ultimate Music Teachers
FREE Bonus Workbook to shape the melody of your
teaching business.

Go To: UltimateMusicTeachers.com/guide

 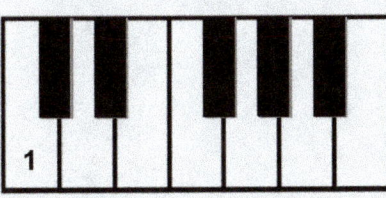 

Key Strategy #2
WHAT YOU THINK, YOU CREATE
Tonality

"Your mindset, thoughts and inner voice can change the results of the tonality in your outside world."

~ Glory St. Germain

What's the tone of your inner dialogue when you teach? Is it calm, confident, and creative or does doubt sometimes sneak in? As music teachers, the tonality of our thoughts shapes the rhythm of our results in our students' success and our own joy. Some days our inner voice sounds like a soothing symphony, and other days more like a toddler with a tambourine - enthusiastic, off-beat, and oddly loud.

As a young mom, I vividly recall listening to my children, David (age 6) and Sherry (age 4), practicing their piano, organ, banjo, and guitar instruments. Occasionally, they mastered the art of "creative interpretation," composing their avant-garde versions on the spot. If you've ever heard Jingle Bells mysteriously shift into a minor key, you'll understand my amusement and occasional frustration.

They often transposed songs into higher or lower keys, sometimes to simplify singing, other times simply to test my patience. I suspect they secretly competed to see who could create the most bizarre tonality. Silent Night in a minor key? Haunting. Twinkle, Twinkle, Little Star in atonal chaos? Unexpectedly dramatic. Yet, despite my initial irritation, I realized something profound:

David and Sherry weren't changing the music; they were exploring it.

They discovered how tonality shifted the emotional impact of a song. Little did I know they would become accomplished musicians, singers, songwriters, and producers, just like their dad, Ray. They listened to understand, and I learned to embrace their creativity, both musically and in life.

Tonality isn't merely about key signatures; it's about the tone of our communication. A song can feel inviting in a major key or dramatic in a minor key, similarly, our tone, inflection, and delivery shape how our messages are received. As a mom, teacher, and business owner, I quickly understood that my tonality could make or break conversations. My children, students, and parents weren't just hearing words; they felt my tone. A misaligned tone meant crossed arms and eye rolls that no amount of theory flashcards could remedy.

I needed to shift my mindset about tonality, not just in music but in communication. When you change your tone, you transform your results.

Musically, tonality refers to relationships between notes, chords, and keys that establish the emotional direction of a piece. Music can be tonal (major/minor), atonal (keyless, exploratory), or modal (based on modes). Similarly, tonality in communication involves relationships between volume, tone, and expression. It sets the emotional context of interactions with ourselves and others, profoundly influencing rapport and effectiveness.

The tonality of our inner dialogue shapes our self-belief and confidence, while our outer voice shapes interactions with students, family, and friends. Changing just the tone can alter the meaning and perception of our message, influencing others' willingness to listen.

I believe our success hinges on attentiveness to our inner voice's tonality. The words and tone we choose in conversation with ourselves ultimately determine our outcomes. Many musicians, composers, and educators share common challenges, not merely needing sharper pencils or blank staff paper, but often lacking belief in their full potential or available resources. Remember, our thoughts create our reality.

Shift your thoughts. Shift your tone. Shift your results.

Unstoppable: Connor Derraugh's Symphony of Courage

I want to share a story that profoundly changed how I listen, learn, and teach. It's not about me, it's about my student, Connor Derraugh. Through Connor's journey, I realized how powerfully our inner thoughts shape our outer world.

But first, let's pause. Smile. A big, bright smile, like you've just won the lottery. (Go ahead, show those teeth.) How does that feel? Happy? Joyful? Think about a child's smile, genuine and infectious, shining even in sleep. Children smile with their whole heart, effortlessly radiating happiness.

Now picture that student, the one who bounds into your studio, a huge smile lighting their face, excited to see you. That was Connor. From age seven, Connor's bright smile and infectious enthusiasm marked every piano lesson. He wasn't just talented; he was extraordinarily gifted. Connor eagerly explored multiple instruments including piano, guitar, and saxophone, always ready to dive into new musical adventures. He passionately endorsed the benefits of learning music theory (and yes, a shameless plug here for Ultimate Music Theory Workbooks).

By age twelve, Connor had already recorded two CDs for family and friends (I still have my copies). At thirteen, he received awards and performed his own tribute piece honoring legendary Canadian jazz pianist Oscar Peterson, earning his first standing ovation. His precision in melodic lines, tonal quality, and emotional expression was remarkable. Connor's life revolved around music; it was more than passion; it was his obsession.

As his teacher, I cherished every lesson, convinced I was learning even more from Connor than any formal teaching course could offer.

He was invincible in his musical world, thriving in composition and performance. Teaching Connor was pure joy.

As Connor was preparing for his Level 8 Piano Exam, just weeks away from inevitable success, he suddenly missed a lesson. I waited, puzzled. Then came the news that shattered everything.

THE UNIMAGINABLE HAPPENED

On May 12, 2010, just three days after Connor's 15th birthday, his parents delivered heartbreaking news:

"We regret to inform you that Connor's routine septoplasty surgery went horribly wrong. The bone from his nose pushed into his frontal lobe, causing severe brain trauma. Connor is paralyzed on his right side. He may never play music again."

My world stopped. This brilliant young musician, weeks from mastering his exam, now faced unimaginable challenges. The injury had affected Connor's motor skills, problem-solving, and memory. How would he ever learn again? How could I possibly teach a student who had once been so extraordinarily gifted but now faced profound physical and cognitive barriers?

Everything changed in one moment.

ONE MOMENT

That one moment changed Connor's life, and mine, forever. As he lay in the hospital bed, his right hand motionless, his parents brought his music, computer, and a roll-out rubber keyboard, accepting the heartbreaking possibility that Connor might never play music again.

Connor faced a daunting road ahead, relearning basic skills like walking and reaching for that one butterfly hanging from the hospital ceiling. After a month, he returned home, and finally unwrapped the new keyboard intended as a celebration gift for passing his Level 8 piano exam. Sitting at the piano, Connor struggled to produce any sound with his right hand, leaving him devastated. Yet, he declared with fierce determination, "No matter what, I will play the piano," stubbornly practicing with only his left hand and even attending jazz band camp at the University of Manitoba.

Music was Connor's life, his passion, purpose, and identity. Faced with the choice to give up or adapt, Connor chose resilience.

TWO HANDS

Time passed, and Connor yearned to play with two hands again. To rebuild neural pathways and improve his motor skills, he creatively combined activities by playing video games on his iPad with his left hand while improvising jazz pieces on the piano with his right. Progress came slowly, yet magically.

Grade 10 began at a new high school renowned for its music program. Initially feeling scared and isolated, Connor found refuge in the school's music room. Remarkably, his jazz teacher saw Connor's potential and advanced him to the Grade 12 Jazz Band, where he played throughout high school. It was there Connor found friendship when the band's drummer, Cole Ediger, welcomed him warmly and became his dear friend.

THREE YEARS

Connor maintained a Positive Mental Attitude (PMA), and over the next three years, he mastered the saxophone (finding its keys softer and easier), while steadily regaining piano skills. Musically, intellectually, and physically, Connor grew tremendously, eventually graduating from the University of Manitoba with a Bachelor of Jazz Studies, double majoring in piano and saxophone. As a professional musician and inspirational speaker, Connor shares his journey to inspire others, teaching the power of positivity, determination, and music through his multi-media presentation, 'Music Healed Me.'

Connor learned that composing music can't be forced, it must flow naturally. Before his injury, composing came easily; afterward, it was challenging and unpredictable. Tragically, inspiration returned following the sudden death of his close friend, Cole Ediger.

Overcome by grief, Connor sat at the piano, and a song poured from his heart in one emotional session. This experience unlocked his musical creativity once more.

Connor not only dedicated that deeply personal piece to Cole but created an entire album, Connor & Cordelia *'Acceptance'* channeling grief into positive action. He continues to write music, proving that heartbreak can give rise to beauty and healing. Connor's resilience taught me profound lessons about life and music. He shared that music saved his life, almost magically.

Today, Connor Derraugh is a performing musician, composer and inspirational speaker.

Inspired by Connor's journey, I developed the Ultimate Music Theory Certification Course and UMTC Elite Educator Program. Though I was his teacher, Connor taught me invaluable lessons about focus, vision, and perseverance. As educators, we carry the responsibility and opportunity to listen deeply, not just to our students but to our inner voices, propelling us toward our goals and inspiring others along the way.

Teach Music. Change Lives.

MINDSET for Transformation and Business Growth

Mindset is defined as an established set of attitudes held by someone. What's your mindset? Did you bring your PMA today? PMA is a Positive Mental Attitude that focuses on the positive side of thinking, and one expects positive results. Yes, having a Positive Mindset can often be challenging (I know, I speak from experience and sometimes that annoying little inner voice is just too loud for any of the other voices to be heard. Shhhhh... let's carry on.) The truth of the matter is you can spend your entire life running around trying to please everyone, chasing one problem after another trying to fix everything and never succeed in living your life to the fullest or realizing all your dreams until one magic thing happens, and that is... you change.

You change your mindset. It's time to think about yourself first. What is your mindset, so you can become the best version of yourself? Think about this, primarily there are 2 Mindsets: Fixed and Growth. You may often wonder how you are the same person getting different results in different situations in your life. It all comes down to mindset.

What are some of the Mindsets you struggle with?

One of the Mindsets I often hear is a lack of confidence, in teachers saying: "I can't charge that much for lessons. I don't feel I'm qualified to teach group theory lessons. No one will sign up for that." In one of our Ultimate Music Teachers Coaching Calls the discussion was about 'Imposter Syndrome'. Thinking you are not qualified or good enough to truly elevate your income. The truth is you are good enough and through altering your mindset, you can alter your results.

Why do you often feel you are not profitable or underpaid? What do you feel you are worth as a Music Teacher as an hourly rate?

As a Coach, I often hear how many of us feel like we are underpaid, not confident to charge what we are worth, or even worse, afraid that our students will quit.

We are scrambling for students and desperate to feel fulfilled as music educators. How do you cope with failure?

Let's define Your Mindset.

Dr. Carol Dweck, Author of *Mindset - The New Psychology of Success* states that: In a Fixed Mindset you believe in your fixed traits. Your goal is to prove yourself. In a Growth Mindset you understand your abilities can be developed through effort. Your goal is to learn and grow.

What's Your Mindset – Fixed or Growth

A Growth Mindset leads to an incredible learning model, by predicting how each decision you make will play out. A Powerful lesson in communicating messages about success and failure.

Have you heard or used any of these statements?

1. **"You learn so quickly, you are so smart."**

2. **"Listen to that. You are the next Beethoven."**

3. **"You're brilliant even with just a little practice."**

How does that make you feel? Do you hear these as supportive and esteem-boosting messages? Listen more closely. Can you hear another message?

The message children hear.

1. **"If I don't learn quickly, I'm not smart."**

2. **"I shouldn't play anything hard, or they'll discover I'm no Beethoven."**

3. **"I better quit practicing, or they'll think I'm not brilliant."**

After seven experiments with 100's of children, Dr. Carol Dweck's research showed that praising children's intelligence harms their motivation and performance.

Children love praise but the minute they hit a snag, their confidence goes out the window and motivation hits rock bottom. If success means they're smart, then failure means they are dumb and that's the Fixed Mindset.

What is the alternative? Praise the process not their intelligence.

Stimulate a growth-oriented process on what they accomplish through practice, study, persistence and strategies. How does this affect you and your mindset as a music teacher when you hear these statements:

1. **"Listen to that musical performance. You are the next Clara Schumann."**

2. **"You teach that so easily; you are so smart."**

3. **"You are a brilliant teacher; you are amazing even when you don't bother to prepare anything."**

What is the language you use with yourself? How do you build confidence in your teaching? Some teachers say: I have lots of students, I make lots of money, others say: I don't feel confident, I feel that I'm not good enough.

In Dr. Carol Dweck's 4 Step Journey of Mindset she states:

Step 1: Embrace your fixed mindset. We are all a mixture of growth and fixed mindsets. Acknowledge and be aware of how we can move into our growth mindset.

Step 2: Be aware of your fixed-mindset triggers. When does your fixed mindset persona show up? Thinking about a big or new challenge? Your fixed mindset may whisper "maybe you don't have what it takes". As you understand your trigger, don't judge it, just observe it.

Step 3: Give your fixed mindset persona a name. Mine is "Nervous Nellie". When there is self-doubt and Nervous Nellie shows up to say, "Who do you think you are Glory?" I acknowledge Nervous Nellie and let her go.

Step 4: Take your fixed-mindset persona on the journey with you. Educate it. The more you become aware of your fixed mindset triggers, the more you can begin to identify your mindset for transformation. What will you name your fixed mindset persona?

YOUR MINDSET

Accept the fact that you have both mindsets. We need to learn and recognize what triggers our fixed mindset. What does your mindset make you think, feel and do?

You can learn to remain in a growth mindset, despite the triggers, as you travel on your mindset journey for transformation. Ask yourself: when, where and how will I design a plan to maintain a Growth Mindset to continue to evolve as an elite educator?

One of my greatest challenges was mindset and shifting from Fixed to Growth.

Imposter Syndrome

I thought, who am I as a woman in business to compete with the entrepreneurs on the global stage, and think that I can become a thought leader in the international industry of music education? How did I overcome my imposter syndrome? Growth Mindset, Professional Development and Coaching has led me to become a Music Educator and Business Expert. And Nervous Nellie was with me all the way.

In 2012, I asked myself a powerful question: "How can I help teachers teach theory?" Nervous Nellie showed up right on cue, whispering, "You don't know anything about course creation." Yet, my desire to help teachers like you teach music theory effectively and profitably was stronger than my fear. That desire inspired the creation of the Ultimate Music Theory Certification Course and Elite Educator Program for Teachers, providing you with the tools to shift from a fixed mindset to a growth mindset. Since then, our Ultimate Music Teachers around the globe have achieved remarkable results.

> *"Change can be tough, but I've never heard anybody say it wasn't worth it."*
>
> ~ Carol Dweck

Case Study:
UMT Certified Teacher Heather Revell

You're not really who you think you are Heather. What? At the age of thirteen, Heather Revell's world shattered in an instant. One of her classmates leaned in, eyes full of intrigue, and whispered, "I know a secret about you." After relentless coaxing, her friend finally revealed the truth. Heather was adopted.

Boom. Bombshell.

Everything she thought she knew about herself suddenly felt like a lie. The foundation of her identity crumbled, leaving behind confusion, anger, and heartbreak. And in those moments, she found her only solace in the one place that had never betrayed her, and that was her beloved piano.

Behind closed doors, she played out her emotions. Some days, the keys were pounded with rage, frustration spilling into every note. Other days, her touch was soft, and delicate, as she poured her sorrow into the melodies. The music became her voice, the piano her confidante, and the act of playing became her saving grace. Heather's journey wasn't a straight path; it was a winding road with sharp turns and unexpected challenges. Her love for music led her from piano lessons at age seven to an invitation from her school Music Master to learn the double bass and tour with the orchestra to Fiji. At just fourteen, she seized the opportunity. Music had given her a place to belong. By fifteen, she was teaching piano. Did she feel qualified? Not at all.

But her love for music and her deep desire to share it overpowered self-doubt. She stepped into her calling as a teacher, building a music program that would later become her career and her purpose. But just when she thought she had found her path, life threw another unthinkable challenge her way.

The Accident That Changed Everything

It started as an ordinary day in the school gymnasium. Heather had her electric piano set up, the sound system ready, and her music stand in place, preparing for a junior choir rehearsal.

And then, chaos. Unbeknownst to her, some students were moving a large, portable basketball hoop behind her. The base had not been filled with water or sand to weigh it down. As they struggled to control it, the entire structure tipped. The steel pole came crashing down. It struck Heather directly on the head. She hit the cold, unforgiving gym floor, her head split open. She didn't remember a thing.

What followed was a battle that no musician, no teacher, ever expects to face, a complete loss of ability. Just like Connor's story, Heather found herself in a grueling rehabilitation process. She had to relearn everything, how to walk, how to think, how to balance, how to concentrate. The pain was relentless. But what broke her heart the most? She couldn't play. Her hands knew the keys, but her brain wouldn't cooperate. Playing the piano was impossible. Blowing into her clarinet or saxophone? The pressure alone made her head spin.

Do You Quit or Do You Fight

In the darkest moments, the question loomed: Do I give up? Would she let the accident define her? Would she let go of everything she had worked for? For three years Heather struggled with the fear that she would never return to the music she loved. But then, she made a choice. She refused to let her circumstances define her. Mindset is one of the most powerful strategies in moving from feeling stuck in a fixed mindset to thriving in a growth mindset. Years later, Heather would come to understand that her ability to adapt, to push forward, and to find meaning through music was the very thing that would shape her destiny.

The Power of Mindset

Three years after the accident, Heather came into the UMTC Elite Educator Program and shared with me why this program was so important to her. It all came down to one thing: mindset. She said it once. She said it twice. And then she said it again. Mindset.

Heather's story is proof that while we can't always control what happens to us, we can control how we respond. Her commitment to a growth mindset helped her rebuild not only her musical abilities but also her confidence, her teaching career, and her life. Because when you change your thoughts, you change your results.

Heather Revell said, "I struggled with my mindset. Coaching with Glory has increased my sense of self-belief and given me the confidence to take my teaching to the next level.

A lot has changed since joining the UMTC Elite Educator Program. I now believe I can grow my business. This program has helped me in setting goals with tools and encouragement to believe in myself."

I'm proud to say that my client, Heather Revell from New Zealand, is now an Ultimate Music Theory Certified Teacher who implemented the growth mindset strategies she learned inside the UMTC Elite Educator Program and went on to become an international best-selling author.

Read Heather's inspiring story in *The Power of WHY Musicians 5 Book Series.*

How did that happen? When you shift from a fixed, "not confident" mindset to a growth mindset, bringing "Nervous Nellie" along on your journey, you open yourself to continual learning and growth.

Two of the most powerful skills elite educators possess are belief in themselves as ultimate music teachers and confidence in the strategies, systems, and materials they use as effective teaching and learning tools.

To succeed as a music teacher, you need to:

Believe in Yourself. Embrace a positive belief in yourself that you are good enough.

Believe in Your Students. Support your students by believing in their "can do it" abilities.

Believe in Systems. Implement effective teaching techniques and trust the process.

As an author, I too, had to overcome self-doubt. Develop the belief I could write effective learning and teaching materials to share with not only my students, but thousands of students around the world. I did so while also supporting teachers to believe in themselves as elite educators to take their music teaching business to the next level.

What belief do you hold about yourself

The beliefs we hold about ourselves, our students, and our community shape our destiny. Who we become, how we teach, and the way we serve others is a direct reflection of our mindset.

The Ultimate Music Theory Teachers Certification Program was created to empower you with confidence to provide the absolute best music theory education for your students. Because when we believe in our ability to make a difference, we truly do.

One of our most powerful relationships is our connection with music. And if you're musically inclined, you might assume I'm referring to tonal relationships, major and relative minor keys, dominant chords resolving to the tonic. But no, I'm talking about our personal relationship with music itself. Let me tell you, my musical journey has had all the drama of an epic movie soundtrack. There have been moments of passionate love, deep frustration, bitter disappointment, exhilarating triumph, and even soap opera-level heartbreak. Let's be honest, haven't we all encountered that one impossible piece that made us question our life choices?

Yes, I'm talking about Rachmaninoff with those giant hands capable of chords most pianists only dream about. And let's remember his own journey of overcoming adversity. His first symphony was considered a complete disaster, plunging him into a creative block for several years. But instead of giving up, he returned stronger than ever, composing his celebrated Prelude in C sharp minor. Through every challenge and triumph, in sickness and health, music has always been my unwavering constant.

Born Into Music (Literally)

Born on Christmas Day, I entered the world to a live musical performance. No joke. As my family prepared for the biggest musical celebration of the year, little were they aware that the baby still in the womb would be the most enthusiastic audience member, kicking along to the beat.

Music was simply part of everyday life. My mom played Christmas carols on her violin, my dad sang in a gospel quartet, and our home was filled with the sound of *White Christmas,* and *I'll Be Home for Christmas* long before I took my first breath. But there was one song, *The Christmas Song* (Chestnuts Roasting on an Open Fire), that they played on repeat. Every. Single. Day. I was basically marinating in Nat King Cole's velvety voice for months. And let me tell you, to this day, whenever I hear that song, my heart melts. The power of music-memory connection is real.

My Grand Entrance Right on Cue

On that special Christmas Day, my family was busy preparing for the Christmas church service, musical performances, and dinner. Clearly, I didn't want to miss any of it. Christmas morning, my mom went into labor. My dad quickly took her to the hospital, and I arrived later that day at 6:20 p.m. My mother joyfully proclaimed, "Glory to God the child is born." And just like that, I had my name Glory. I was born into music.

My musical journey didn't start after birth, it began in the womb, where I was already absorbing the tonality, rhythm, and emotion of music. Science confirms that in the last trimester babies can hear and remember melodies played before birth. Perhaps that's why I start playing Christmas music in October. (Okay, September. Don't judge.)

Learning music requires commitment, perseverance, and willingness to develop skillsets. Despite frustrating hours of practice, immense discipline, and challenges along the way, I persevered, becoming a piano teacher at sixteen. Young and naïve, I didn't realize how much I had yet to learn about teaching. Now, as a professional educator, I recognize those early mistakes. However, those early experiences provided my students with a starting point in their musical journeys, just as my journey began with the symbol of the Treble Clef.

The Treble Clef's evolution dates back to the 9th century when Gregorian Chant used "neumes", simple dashes or dots to indicate pitch. Today's Treble Clef descends from the G Clef used in plainchant notation. The Treble Clef symbolized much more than music notation, for me it was the universal language connecting written music to sound, profoundly impacting relationships in life.

As an educator, my relationship with music extended to relationships with my students. I've witnessed students struggling with family, friendships, and themselves, often turning to music as their most reliable companion and escape. Iconic musicians like Billy Joel and jazz guitar genius Lenny Breau demonstrate music's power as a lifeline amidst life's challenges.

I recall a Korean student arriving with her music books, marveling that I "spoke Korean" when I effortlessly played her music. Although I didn't speak Korean, I spoke the universal language of music. Her music became the bridge that connected us.

Our musical relationships are treasures we cherish deeply.

Can you imagine a world without music? IMPOSSIBLE

I grew up in a musical family. My dad was a multi-instrumentalist playing guitar, piano, stand-up bass, organ, harmonica, banjo, you name it, he played it. Music lessons in our home were like brushing your teeth, yes you do it every day and more than once.

My mother played the violin and at the age of 65 began accordion lessons. Why? Because my mother Rosabel loved music. She also knew that learning music makes you smarter. Many scientific studies have been conducted researching how the consistent practice of music increases cognitive function in specific neurological areas.

And my mother told me that teaching music *makes you better looking*, apparently another fun fact from my mother, yet to undergo scientific research. When my mother was diagnosed with breast cancer, she could no longer play her accordion and so it remained in the case, which I still have to this day. I remember thinking about the musical sound an ambulance plays on its hurried way to save a life. A sound that scares you and gives you hope all at the same time. When my mother lay in the hospital bed for the last four days of her life, I stayed in the room with her, along with my daughter Sherry, son David and husband Ray. She asked me to play some recordings of the music that she loved so dearly, so she could hear uplifting songs that brought back memories of times when she played with "her orchestra" called the *Pembina Players.*

She asked me to turn up the music louder so she could close her eyes and truly immerse herself in the memory of performing on stage with her beloved musicians. The nurse came in and quietly said, "your mother is dying, turn down the music". I said, "my mother is the one who told me to turn it up." "Ah" was her reply as she left quickly, knowing the end for my mother would soon be here.

My mother brought me into this world of music the day I was born, and when she passed away and took her last breath, she left with the sound of music to be with my dad, who passed away years earlier. Now, my mother's Stradivarius violin and my dad's Hummingbird guitar are my greatest treasures.

I felt alone but not lonely. The music seemed different. But the relationship of music that we shared, as I reflected on years gone by, as one often does at the time of a loved one passing, I remembered the lessons my mother taught me.

As I felt not good enough as a music teacher, she would simply smile and say, just watch as your students learn to fly and soar higher than you ever imagined. Memories are brought back through music.

This symbol, the Treble Clef or G Clef (and now you know that stands for the Glory Clef), is a symbol of new beginnings. Each piece of music begins with a clef, just as each day begins with a sunrise. Each piece of music ends up leaving you with a memory, just as each day ends with a sunset.

I recognized that my fixed mindset persona of "Nervous Nellie" thinking I was not good enough could be altered to my growth mindset persona of "Glory the Gladiator".

Thinking I could improve my skills with effort and practice led me to accept each new challenge just as I accepted each piece of music that begins with a clef.

Now, it's time to pause and reflect on your mindset for transformation.

⌢ *Fermata* (Pause to Ponder): Three Steps to a Mindset Transformation

Did you choose to become a music teacher, or did music choose you to impact the lives of others?

Do you believe in the power of music to change lives?

Do you have the mindset and confidence to become an elite educator, the thought-leadership skills to help others achieve their goals while being open to your professional development?

Your success begins with your mindset - your attitude towards what's possible. Take "think time" to see the big picture of where you want to go and what's possible for you.

Step #1 Name your fixed mindset persona.

Take "think time" to identify how your fixed mindset is impacting your outcomes. Name your fixed mindset persona something that really defines this persona. It could be a silly name, anything that symbolizes your fixed mindset.

What's one shift you can make to acknowledge your fixed mindset and alter results?

_____

_____

What self-talk beliefs do you have that limit your ability to change your thinking?

_____

_____

What relationships will change when you are open to listening to your inner voice?

_____

_____

Step #2 Write down three things about your fixed mindset persona.

Be aware of your fixed mindset triggers that shift your mindset away from thinking that your abilities can be improved to thinking that your abilities are fixed, or make you think you are not good at something and that you never will be.

What does your fixed mindset persona make you think about your teaching abilities?

_____

_____

How does your fixed mindset persona make you feel about your teaching business?

_____

_____

What does your fixed mindset persona make you do and why?

_____

_____

Step #3 Name your growth mindset persona.

Invite your persona to join you on your journey as you learn more about how you can develop a growth mindset and help others develop one, too. Name your growth mindset persona to reflect the challenges you can overcome.

What does your growth mindset persona make you think about the path to mastery?

_____

_____

How does your growth mindset persona make you feel about clear goal setting?

_____

_____

What does your growth mindset persona make you do to embrace learning?

_____

_____

"Happiness depends on your mindset and attitude."

~ Roy T. Bennett

The totality that you use with your inner voice - your fixed mindset and your growth mindset - will have a powerful effect on the outside results of your life.

Inside Thoughts Create Outside Results

My student Connor Derraugh had to focus on listening to the positive *tonality* of his growth mindset to overcome massive obstacles in his life. Each challenge presented new opportunities to learn and grow both personally and professionally.

My client Heather Revell also implemented her growth mindset training as a young child, musician, and educator using her mindset to heal from each obstacle she had to overcome to continue her passion to live a joyful and productive life.

Now, you have a choice which mindset you will be open to listening to, learning from and embracing to be your guide in helping you achieve your goals and therefore helping others achieve theirs as well.

May your relationship with music uplift you when you need to climb, heal you when you need to cry, and give you strength when you need to persevere, and ultimately bring you joy as you celebrate your life through the magic of musical relationships.

♪ Your Coda Notes ♪

The 12 Key Strategies include online
Ultimate Music Teachers Bonus Resources.

TEACH MUSIC CHANGE LIVES
What You Think, You Create

Dive deeper into **KEY STRATEGY #2** – get your
Ultimate Music Teachers
FREE Bonus Workbook to tune into the tonality of your
teaching journey.

Go To: UltimateMusicTeachers.com/guide

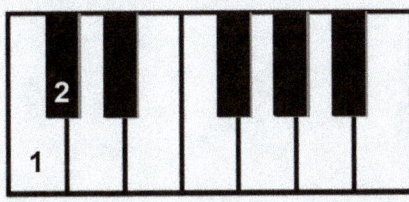

Key Strategy #3
BEING SEEN, HEARD AND UNDERSTOOD
Articulation

"Education requires concise articulation with clarity, creativity and critical thinking to stimulate curiosity in the thought process of learning."

~ Glory St. Germain

Have you ever felt like you were speaking a completely different language even though you were technically speaking English? Because let me tell you, there is nothing more frustrating than saying something clearly (or so you think) and being met with blank stares, confused nods, or my personal favorite, enthusiastic agreement followed by the student doing the opposite of what you just explained.

It didn't take long for me to realize that teaching isn't just about what you say, it's about how you articulate it. Our *articulation* determines how we are received as clear, engaging, inspiring or confusing, overwhelming, and (gulp) forgettable. I remember one particularly humbling moment as a teacher. I had just finished explaining a seemingly simple music theory concept. I was so sure I had nailed it. The example? On point. My explanation? Flawless. My enthusiasm? Unmatched. And then one brave student raised his hand and asked: "So what does that mean?" Oof. Cue the ego-deflating like a sad, out-of-tune tuba. That was the day I truly understood that being knowledgeable isn't enough; we must be understandable. It's not about how much we know. It's about how well we articulate it. And once I embraced that lesson, everything changed.

When we learn to articulate with clarity, we don't just teach, we inspire. We don't just talk, we connect. And we don't just give instructions, we empower transformation. As music teachers, we must master the art of *articulation* not just in music, but in how we communicate, educate, and elevate our students. Because when we are seen, heard, and understood, that's when real learning happens.

In music, the word *articulation* means the fundamental technique used to express the sound of musical notes through touch that determines the sound (*staccato, legato, marcato, tenuto, accent, fermata*). As musicians, it is essential that we understand the elements of *articulation* to communicate the music's intended meaning.

In teaching, the word *articulate* means the ability to communicate instructions fluently and coherently, connecting segments of ideas, repetition for complete comprehension and problem-solving feedback to effectively enhance learning.

ARTICULATE WITH CLARITY

One of the essential skills every music teacher needs is the knowledge of how to teach music theory concepts with a simple step-by-step system through joyful creativity. The "special sauce" of clear *articulation* when explaining concepts for complete comprehension is what leads to mastery of musicianship skills. To stand out as a music teacher, you must know what *your* special sauce is. If you refine your methods and you infuse your teaching system with joyful creativity, you will stand out.

In other words, to be a successful business owner as a music teacher, you need to improve your pedagogy. Music Pedagogy refers to teaching methods and instruction focused on enhancing ability, building knowledge, developing experience, understanding music theory and interpretation in all areas of music education. You need to refine the language you use with your students to implement success in your music teaching methods.

This will determine the success of your music teaching business. And that's how you get the multiplier effect. By changing the way you teach, you can amplify the passion of your students by conquering the challenges of music education.

One glimmer of hope is all I was looking for. A simple flicker to let me know I was headed in the right direction. Learning music theory is one thing, but knowing how to teach music theory effectively is another thing. I know, because I learned the hard way.

I continued my education to become a Neuro-Linguistic Practitioner. Neuro-Linguistic Programming (NLP): Neuro is how we think, Linguistic is how we communicate, and Programming is how we get the results that we get.

Years later, I now see the value in implementing NLP into my teaching system to develop rapport building skills at all levels of communication.

One of the most powerful relationships we have is our magical relationship with music.

You may think I'm referring to the music itself as the relationship between Major keys and their relative minor keys, or dominant chords and their relationship to the Tonic. However, the real meaning of a musical relationship is in fact our relationship to the power of music and its influence upon us and how it makes us feel.

As a professional educator, I have seen many music students struggling in relationships with their parents, their friends, their siblings and most importantly the inner relationship that they have with their thoughts both positive and negative. Often frustrated, depressed, afraid and even suicidal, they turn to music, to the one relationship they could count on to pour their heart out, to play their music as an escape where no one could come between them and ultimately to heal their mind, body and soul.

In fact, Billy Joel's song "You're Only Human (Second Wind)" deals with teenage depression and suicide. Many have said this upbeat song saved them.

Now more than ever is the time for strategic planning, discussion of specific issues and challenges in our teaching industry.

- **Problem Solving in Articulating Education – using the right words, the words that connect with your students. The right words matter – connecting with positivity in your teaching is essential for comprehension. Play "you be the teacher" so your students can articulate the lesson they learned for complete mastery.**

- **Developing Goals in Analyzing Outcomes – set up measurement tools for each step of learning with incremental goals of achievement. Celebrate the milestones of accomplishments and discover what works and what doesn't work to motivate your students' learning drive.**

- **Implementation Steps in Achieving Success – for all learning styles and abilities. One of the keys to successful teaching and learning is to implement performance analytics.**

Measuring these analytics can help you decide if it's time to teach content in different ways for visual, auditory or kinesthetic learners.

Performance analysis is not just for an actual performance or examination result, but rather the weekly performance progress of learning retention, motivation and goal attainment. With performance analysis you can track and visualize key performance indicators and help students improve their performance levels with actionable insight.

Because without performance analysis, we're all just guessing and hoping the practice fairy did her job this week. Have you ever tried to decode the mystery of a student's comment: "I practiced, I promise." Really? And, if motivation could be measured in snack bribes and sticker charts, we'd all be running Fortune 500 music studios.

Three Steps to Articulate, Analyze and Achieve Success in your teaching:

Step #1—Articulate and define what goals and systems to assess that will drive all aspects of improvement for both you and your students. Identify the processes to improve your teaching and your students' learning. Remember to appreciate the effort.

Step #2 — Analyze and determine what factors or behaviors affect the outcomes of your teaching processes. Use a journal, or vision board to map out goals and discover what motivates students 'towards' or 'away from' goals. Remember to praise the process.

Step #3 — Achieve and decide what metrics to measure. You may want to measure commitment of practice time, creativity of performance, composition of originality, etc. to identify the process improvements. Remember to celebrate the accomplishment.

Use Performance Analytics to track and visualize key performance indicators customized for your teaching system for each unique student to reach their full potential.

Remember Connor's story, and how his performance analytics shifted through various stages of his learning, re-learning and continuous learning stages in his life. Being flexible, being open to change and being "teachable" is the key to success.

Empower yourself and empower your students to take action steps with measurable results. Customize your performance analytics to meet the needs of your music teaching business. Display actionable processes that tell the story of your teaching business process.

Display the information so you can see your own progress in how you want to grow your music teaching business and help your students elevate their musicianship skills. Explore simple systems to help you track your data, customize it for your teaching business and review it monthly. Empower your students to take ownership of their goals and provide them with actionable steps to improve their skillset.

Implementing Performance Analytics into your business and understanding how the information flows through your teaching platform, will ultimately result in your ability to visualize process improvements.

Music Teachers Educate Students To Succeed - One Note At A Time

Reflecting on my dream, I never realized how challenging teaching music theory could be. My students viewed it as boring and, frankly, I didn't blame them. I struggled to understand it myself. This lack of clarity deeply affected my confidence. Something had to change, and it started with me.

The Worst of Times: Not Being Heard And Understood

Teaching music theory wasn't fun for my students or for me. It felt complex and overwhelming, yet I knew it was essential for musicianship. The real issue? I didn't fully understand music theory myself, which crushed my confidence as a teacher.

I blamed myself, stuck in a fixed mindset that whispered, "You're not good enough." Finally, I realized that to effectively teach, I first had to shift my own attitude. I needed a Positive Mental Attitude. It was time to silence the self-doubt and start believing in my own ability to make a difference.

AN ATTITUDE ADJUSTMENT

My mindset was simple: *"I'm the teacher you should pay attention."* (Spoiler alert, I was wrong.)

I vividly remember teaching a tall, skinny teenage boy who carried himself as if he knew far more than I did. His resistance was clear: eye rolls, slouching shoulders, and a general disregard for my suggestions. As a passionate educator, I found his attitude incredibly frustrating and even hurtful. It made me question my own abilities. Perhaps you've had students like this too, the ones who test your patience and teaching skills in equal measure.

We were preparing for his Level 8 piano exam, just weeks away. Yet, despite his talent, his pieces were unmemorized and unprepared. When I insisted that he memorize his pieces by next week, his body language shouted, "Not happening."

That day, my usual cheerful encouragement dissolved into exhaustion. Part of me wanted to quit right there or send him to another teacher. But instead, I changed tactics. Rather than offering positivity, I challenged him directly.

"I bet you can't memorize your pieces in a week. I bet you can't express those melodies the way the composer intended. And I bet you won't be ready by next week's mock exam."

Little did I know this shift in my approach would teach me a powerful lesson about motivation and attitude.

My *articulation* was completely different than what it normally was with many exclamation points at the end of each sentence. I simply stated the facts as I saw them in a firm authoritative voice (not my normal smiley "you got this" teaching voice). The truth is, I was done. I felt like there was something missing in my teaching, that I was not being a good teacher, communicator or music cheerleader to help take my student successfully across the finish line.

The following week, I realized it was my attitude that needed adjusting first, to understand the attitude of my students. Although we had set goals together, what I discovered was the best way to achieve a goal is to create a big why behind the desired goal. There are two powerful emotions that drive us in goal setting success.

1. **Towards Pleasure – Achieving a Goal to seek pride and accomplishment.**

2. **Away From – Achieving our Goal to avoid pain and embarrassment.**

A Surprising Transformation

The following week, my "know-it-all" student walked in proudly, handed me his music books, and calmly sat at the piano, signaling that he was ready to perform from memory. I proceeded with our mock exam, astonished as he delivered each piece beautifully with emotion, expression, and perfect articulation.

As I watched from my desk, I was completely stunned. What inspired this dramatic shift? Even his posture had changed; he sat taller, clearly proud of his achievement.

After the exam, I acknowledged his outstanding performance and asked what had motivated him to put in such dedicated practice. With a mischievous grin, he spun around on the piano bench, looked me straight in the eyes, and declared:

"Miss Glory, I just wanted to prove you wrong."

Discovering Real Motivation

His entire motivation was to prove me wrong. What? That moment taught me something important: he was motivated by avoiding pain (embarrassment), while I was driven by seeking pleasure (pride and accomplishment).

Understanding this "Away From" versus "Towards Pleasure" framework helped me realize that everyone is motivated differently and understanding each student's "why" makes all the difference.

I reflected on my own experience running a marathon. Initially, my goal was set as an "Away From" goal. I wanted to escape the pain of an overweight, unhealthy body.

Eventually, it evolved into a "Towards Pleasure" goal. I imagined the joy and pride of crossing the finish line, proudly wearing my marathon medal. (And yes, I wore that medal for a full week. I still cherish it in my jewelry box.)

That day transformed my teaching. Now, whenever I am setting goals with students, I ask these three key questions:

1. **What must change for you to achieve this goal? (Mindful practicing, consistent dedication, clear scheduling.)**

2. **What pain will you experience if you don't achieve this goal? (Missed opportunities, frustration, feelings of failure.)**

3. **What pleasure will you experience by taking action? (Pride, sense of accomplishment, personal growth.)**

Attitude shapes thinking, behavior, and results.

Replace the hesitant statement "I should" with the decisive "I must", focusing on your desired outcome:

- **I must practice mindfully, dedicating focused time regularly.**

- **I must remain motivated and seize this opportunity to succeed.**

Change your attitude, change your results.

ATTITUDE IS THE KEY TO EVERYTHING

Teaching becomes challenging when students have the attitude that "this is boring," "not interesting," or "too confusing."

Remember my doll students and how that same disinterest showed up in my real human students? If you haven't encountered this yet, you just haven't been teaching long enough. If you have, congratulations. You're officially in the Real Teachers of the World club.

How do we turn it around? It starts with us.

Teachers must first embrace a Positive Mental Attitude and become effective communicators. Elite educators clearly and simply articulate their teaching because they have mastered PMA.

Developing PMA involves:

- **Practicing positive self-talk.**

- **Expressing daily gratitude.**

- **Surrounding yourself with positive influences.**

- **Embracing humor and joy in your teaching.**

Be intentional with your words both internally and externally. A helpful practice is to add "and that's just the way I want it" to the end of your statements. This transforms your language into a declaration of intention rather than mere observation.

For example, saying, "I can't find students to fill my classes, and that's just the way I want it," is clearly not something you would desire. Instead, carefully choose words that reflect your true intentions and goals.

Internally, you might affirm:
"I am a confident, engaging, and knowledgeable teacher who students love to learn from, and that's just the way I want it."

Externally, you could declare your business goal:
"I am successfully running my freedom lifestyle teaching business four days a week, generating $7,500 per month, and that's just the way I want it."

Ultimately, the best measure of your attitude and clarity in teaching is seen in the positive results and lasting impact you have on your students.

In my TEDx Talk "3 Secrets to Unlock Your Students' Success", I opened up about my personal struggles with self-doubt, limiting beliefs, and the painful temptation to quit. I shared three powerful lessons, anchors, that helped me overcome adversity, deepen my purpose as a teacher, and create transformational learning experiences for my students.

I QUIT.

What compels us to say those words, even when our desire to succeed still burns inside us? I said, "I quit" because I doubted my own worth. Despite the smiles and hugs from students who loved me, one day a curly-haired young boy looked me in the eye and said, "I quit. I don't want to learn music anymore. Time signatures and counting it's too hard." His words shook me to the core.

I stood there, devastated, wondering if I had failed him. Could I have done more? The truth is, I could have. I could have helped him feel the music, not just play it.

Then another student came. A young girl in a pretty purple dress who walked up to me and said, "Miss Glory, if you can teach me the next level of music, I'll be happy to learn from you." She believed in me. But at that moment, I wasn't yet qualified to teach her the next level. Still, her faith in me became my turning point. I made the decision to upgrade my training, earn my teacher's diploma, and never miss another opportunity to empower a student.

The first magical lesson I learned was symbolized by a Clock, a reminder that we do have time. Time to learn. Time to teach. Time to change our story. I realized that success doesn't come from waiting. It comes from showing up with focus, purpose, and consistency. I stopped saying "I don't have time" and started making time.

The second magical lesson came from a Rubik's Cube. Without a system to solve a Rubik's Cube, it's frustrating, and you may even say, "I quit". But when you have a step-by-step method to easily implement, you succeed. Music students are no different. Most students quit, not because they can't succeed, but because they don't have a system, a clear path to follow. I realized I hadn't given the curly-haired boy a system. But I did give one to the girl in the pretty purple dress and that's why she excelled.

The third magical lesson was an Iceberg. Relationships are like an iceberg. What's visible above the surface is only a fraction of what matters. With the boy, I failed to look deeper, below the surface, into the relationship between him, his learning needs, and his parents. But with the girl, I listened. I understood. I looked below the surface and built a deeper connection and that created harmony.

I never got a second chance with the boy. But the girl became an award-winning musician and a successful music teacher, running her own studio. And I'll always be grateful for what they both taught me.

These three anchors now live at the heart of my teaching philosophy:

- **A Clock** represents the importance of intentionally dedicating time for personal and professional growth.

- **A Rubik's Cube** symbolizes the value of teaching with an organized, systematic approach.

- **An Iceberg** illustrates the significance of building deep and meaningful relationships beneath the surface of every interaction.

Whenever you feel like quitting because of challenges, self-doubt, or uncertainty, remember these anchors. They aren't just tools. They are transformational truths. And they have the power to change everything, starting with you.

One Glimmer of Hope Became the Ultimate Success Story

When my son David was ten, I watched him receive guitar lessons from the talented Denis Hammerstedt (my husband Ray's lead guitarist). Denis's approach to teaching music theory was empowering, clear, and motivating. David loved his music lessons.

But it was a very different experience when my daughter Sherry, at age eight, received a music theory scholarship for a gifted youth program at the University of Manitoba. Initially excited, I soon felt disheartened by the teacher's abrupt tone and rigid teaching style. The students sat silently like little statues, attentively memorizing terms and analyses but disconnected from the joy and meaning of the music itself.

I struggled to stay quiet. Though it wasn't my place to intervene, I deeply wished the lessons could connect theory to the sound and feeling of music. Why wasn't there any listening, discussion, or enjoyment? This was not how music theory should be taught and not the way I wanted to teach it.

Music theory is too often taught in a manner that drains away excitement, leaving students bored and disengaged. Both students and teachers deserve a better approach that enhances the joy we all feel in music itself.

This experience sparked my passion to create something different. When my incredible writing partner, Shelagh, and I developed the *Ultimate Music Theory Supplemental Series,* we intentionally designed materials to make music theory relatable, memorable, and yes, fun. We created engaging characters to help students connect and enjoy learning.

At UMT, our mission is to support teachers and students by providing the most effective, enjoyable, and engaging music theory materials on the planet so learning theory becomes a joyful part of experiencing music itself.

Meet So-La and Ti-Do. The Ultimate Music Theory Teaching Aids that help students learn in a fun and engaging way.

So-La   Ti-Do

So-La loves to sing and dance. She is expressive, creative and loves to tell stories through music. So-La feels music in her heart. She loves to teach, compose and perform. So-La Sparkles are musical terms and signs that add *"sparkles"* to music, such as dynamics, tempo, changes in tempo and *articulation*.

Ti-Do loves to count and march. He is rhythmic, consistent and loves the rules of music theory. Ti-Do feels music in his hands and feet. He loves to analyze, share tips and conduct. Ti-Do Taps are the rules of rhythm and rests that add *"pulse"* to the music, indicating where the rhythmic emphasis falls in the Time Signature.

Together, So-La and Ti-Do blend the elements of music into style, performance and overall enjoyment as they guide students through mastering music theory. Students of all ages can relate to these two musical guides in the journey of learning throughout the Ultimate Music Theory Program. Embrace both So-La and Ti-Do characteristics to develop to your full musicianship potential.

I remember one of my advanced students preparing for a Level 9 Piano Exam. It was a few weeks before her exam and as we reviewed her performance it was evident she was a Ti-Do. Rhythmically solid and consistent. All that was missing in her performance were the "So-La Sparkles", the sparkles that make a performance memorable.

So-La and Ti-Do were both sitting on the piano (yes, we have So-La and Ti-Do Stuffies), and I simply asked her, "how would So-La perform this piece"? I immediately saw a shift in her posture, as she sat a little taller, and with more exaggeration in bringing her dynamics and articulation into the music with heartfelt passion, her performance elevated to the next level. As I encouraged her to "play like So-La" on her exam (and she did), she received a mark of 90% on a Level 9 Piano Exam. Wow. Helping students connect the elements of music theory to the practical application of their instrument/voice, is the way to score success.

That's why I became a teacher and a course creator. My passion is helping teachers learn how to teach music theory with systems and strategies that can have a powerful impact on musicians of all ages so educators can teach music theory with confidence, purpose and, ultimately, joy.

I did not want to see the reflection of what I observed in my daughter Sherry's theory class. I wanted to take this glimmer of hope, this faintly shining star, and let it sparkle, glisten and shimmer like Beethoven's

Moonlight Sonata. It was time to take all these twinkling lights and create the Ultimate Music Theory Certification Course for teachers.

I remember the day like it was yesterday. I was attending a teachers' workshop with approximately 30 teachers. As I was sitting in the audience listening to the speaker, the topic of music theory came up and no one was excited about discussing it. Then the light bulb went on in my head. I had a bright idea. What if I could help these teachers become passionate about teaching music theory?

I quickly grabbed a blank piece of paper and announced that I was creating the Ultimate Music Theory Certification Course for teachers and if anyone was interested, please write your name, phone number, and email on the page and it will start in 90 days.

The Ultimate Transformation – Educator to Course Creator

When I first presented the idea for a music theory certification course, I hadn't written a single word of content. Perhaps my brilliant idea wasn't so brilliant after all. Yet, my passion was clear: to help teachers break free from boring music theory lessons and embrace theory as a joyful, essential element of music education. Teaching music theory could elevate their teaching, enhance their students' learning experiences, and offer additional income, an attractive proposition for any music educator aiming for business growth and personal fulfillment.

Initially, my goal was modest, hoping just five or six teachers would enroll from a workshop of thirty educators. To my amazement, fourteen teachers enthusiastically signed up. That overwhelming response revealed something powerful: traditional approaches to teaching music theory often drain the joy out of music itself. It didn't need to be that way.

This became my "aha" moment, a deep recognition of an unmet need among music teachers who sought fresh, effective ways to engage students and enhance their own professional growth. Remarkably, all fourteen teachers who enrolled completed the course and became certified, confirming the demand for this new approach.

That moment launched the Ultimate Music Theory Certification Course. It was clear that educators needed a comprehensive program to transform their teaching and empower their business growth. Supported by my talented editor and co-author, Shelagh McKibbon-U'Ren, we developed a course designed to provide the practical tools, strategies, and inspiration that teachers craved.

Our vision rapidly expanded. Shelagh and I traveled across Canada and the U.S., presenting live teacher-training events that were enthusiastically received. But something essential was still missing, and that was global access. Music teachers everywhere needed this training, without having to travel.

So, during our annual writing retreat, Shelagh and I asked ourselves: why not create an online version? It was a massive undertaking: scripting, filming, editing, exams, certificates, worksheets, and countless details behind the scenes. But that small glimmer of hope blossomed into a powerful reality and launched the international online Ultimate Music Theory Certification Course.

Today, that vision continues to grow through our UMTC Elite Educator Program and the vibrant UMT Teachers Membership, featuring weekly coaching calls, insightful articles, engaging worksheets by Shelagh, and creative educational games and activities by UMT Certified Teacher Joanne Barker, our Creative Design Specialist.

When you sense that small spark of possibility within you, whether it's creating a course, transforming your teaching, or making a meaningful difference, embrace it. Let your vision shine. As I like to say, "Sparkle like a So-La," and see how your passion can enrich lives through music education, one note at a time. As I began writing my *Ultimate Music Theory Workbooks*, two key insights quickly emerged.

First, music theory concepts must be taught clearly and simply, accommodating all learning styles, ages, and abilities. Effective teaching means serving your clients at the highest level ensuring they truly understand, enjoy, and remain motivated to learn.

Successful students become repeat clients, vital for the long-term health of your music teaching business. They not only stay but also enthusiastically refer others to your program because they appreciate how you teach, facilitate learning, and help them achieve their goals. Connection equals currency: your business thrives when students deeply understand and resonate with your approach.

Second, concepts must be presented creatively to maximize comprehension and engagement. Imagine attending an art class where you're only allowed to paint with one color, pink. You might try at first, but you'd quickly become bored and lose interest. The same applies to teaching music. If you don't open the creative "crayon box," providing endless opportunities for exploration and expression, lessons become monotonous. Students will lose motivation, stop practicing, or leave altogether.

Connection equals creativity. Your music teaching business flourishes when you inspire students to explore, express, and experiment, developing lifelong musicians who passionately share their gift with the world.

Teaching becomes effortless with the right tools and resources, but what happens when adversity strikes? Whether physical, mental, or emotional, every challenge offers valuable lessons. Will you discover the silver lining in each cloud, transforming obstacles into opportunities?

"Always seek out the seed of triumph in every adversity."

~ Og Mandino

Case Study:
UMT Certified Teacher Joanne Barker

"You have breast cancer." Four words no woman ever wants to hear.

In August 2012, Joanne Barker was on top of the world. She had just become an Ultimate Music Theory Certified Teacher, earning first-class honors with distinction. She was celebrating, mapping out her future as an elite educator, and feeling unstoppable.

Then, one week later, everything changed. A life-altering diagnosis, breast cancer. The whirlwind of emotions was overwhelming. Fear. Uncertainty. The unknown road ahead. But Joanne refused to let cancer define her. Just six days after surgery, she was back to teaching.

As chemotherapy treatments began, she continued showing up for her students, determined to be seen as a leader, heard as a passionate educator, and understood as a resilient force of inspiration. She wouldn't be seen as simply a cancer victim losing her hair. She wouldn't let fear silence her voice. And she wouldn't allow the brain fog from treatment to diminish her purpose.

Instead, she chose to rise, to be seen as strong, to be heard with confidence, and to be understood as a woman determined to live with joy and make a difference in the world. She took a deep breath, rose up, and took charge of her life. Not only did Joanne continue teaching piano throughout her treatment, but she also used her journey as fuel to create something extraordinary. She developed her own group piano curriculum, transforming the way students experience music education. Her determination, creativity, and resilience didn't go unnoticed.

Her passion led me to invite her to join the UMT Dream Team, where she became an essential part of the UMT Creative Design Team as a specialist and coach. But Joanne's impact didn't stop there.

A Voice of Inspiration

Joanne became more than a music educator, she became an inspirational spokesperson for breast cancer awareness, using her platform to empower others with her story of strength and perseverance. She went on to become a five-time international best-selling author in *The Power of WHY Musicians* Book Series, sharing her journey of triumph over adversity. Her ability to articulate her story with clarity and conviction has touched countless lives proving that when you are seen, heard, and understood, you create a legacy far beyond the piano bench.

Joanne continues to share her passion for teaching UMT Club Classes through her innovative Combo Lesson System Course, creating engaging resources for the Ultimate Music Teachers Membership and inspiring educators worldwide. Joanne's creative brilliance makes her an invaluable member of our UMT Dream Team in her role as Creative Design Specialist and Coach, consistently elevating our community through imaginative design, heartfelt dedication, and empowering mentorship.

She is living proof that no matter what challenges life throws your way; you always have the power to rewrite the melody of your story.

Read Joanne 's inspiring story in *The Power of WHY Musicians 5 Book Series.*

You have a choice, to live your life on your terms. Dream Big and keep moving forward. What is your heart's desire to make a difference in the world of music education? Now you can teach music theory concepts through creativity with "discovery learning" inside the UMT Workbook Program, Games and our Online Ultimate Music Theory Teachers Membership. When you teach concepts with simplicity, a clear purpose, and intent for your students, then learning becomes more enjoyable and positive.

When you teach with creativity and add themes, composing, games and challenges for your students, then learning fosters a sense of accomplishment and achievement. Teaching concepts through creativity develops important musical skills and builds confidence in learning through gamification.

Musical Gamification is a set of activities and processes to solve problems by using or applying the characteristics of game elements. As educators, we need to be seen, heard and understood to create effective learning strategies for successful teaching and for growing our music teaching business.

⌢ *Fermata* (Pause to Ponder): Three Steps to Being Seen, Heard and Understood

What is your preferred method of teaching? Do you teach online or in person, private or groups? Whatever your preferred teaching method is, they all require effective communication skills and clear articulation in providing your students with the highest level of professional education. Your success depends on how your students relate to your messaging.

Step #1
Start being seen as an Elite Educator.

Your elite brand as a music educator is determined by how you are seen in the music community as a professional teacher. How you show up with integrity and showcase your own interest in your students' success will determine how your clients see you.

How can you showcase leadership qualities to be seen as an industry professional?

_____

_____

What image and messaging can you share to be seen as a purpose driven educator?

_____

_____

What organizations can you contribute to, so you are seen as an expert in your field?

_____

_____

Step #2
Write down 3 strategies you can implement to be heard.

The key to being an effective educator is being heard. It's empowering to know that our messaging is being valued. An important aspect of teaching is often counter-intuitive, in that we need to listen more - listen to understand, not just listen to reply.

What can you do to be fully present when wanting to be heard and keeping it short?

_____

_____

How do you hold space for active listening with non-judgment so you can serve better?

_____

_____

When you serve better, you are being heard better.

_____

_____

How do you embrace confidence in the skills of being heard with value and respect?

_____

_____

Step #3 Commit to being understood.

Silence your inner critic, your feelings of self-doubt, in not being an effect communicator. If you want to be understood, focus on the messaging of communication to build rapport with clear articulation in understanding your teaching message.

How can you create understanding as a goal, not to persuade, but to be understood?

_____

_____

How will understanding your message bring greater willingness for students to learn?

_____

_____

How does your appreciation for listening and acknowledging lead to being understood?

_____

_____

"Tell me and I'll forget; show me and I may remember; involve me and I'll understand."

~ Chinese Proverb

The key to being heard and understood is adopting a positive attitude in your own professional development of learning and teaching. As you articulate clearly the concepts you are teaching, not only will you achieve massive success as an educator, but your students will achieve success in lifelong learning with positivity as well.

If you truly want to understand... TEACH.

♪ Your Coda Notes ♪

_____

_____

The 12 Key Strategies include online
Ultimate Music Teachers Bonus Resources.

TEACH MUSIC CHANGE LIVES
Being Seen, Heard and Understood

Dive deeper into **KEY STRATEGY #3** - get your
Ultimate Music Teachers
FREE Bonus Workbook to articulate your value with
clarity and confidence.

Go To: UltimateMusicTeachers.com/guide

Key Strategy #4
YOUR PASSION-BASED TEACHING FORMULA
Dynamics

"Passion arises from the dynamics of energy that propel you to succeed in accomplishing the goals you focus on."

~ Glory St. Germain

Do you ever feel your teaching enthusiasm is set to *fortissimo*, while your students seem stuck at *pianissimo*? Ever leave a lesson wondering if your energy inspired or overwhelmed? Like any great piece of music, the magic is more than loud or soft, it's knowing when to crescendo and when to gently whisper.

My husband Ray jokingly labeled me "annoyingly happy." Was that a compliment or subtle hint to lower my volume? Possibly both. Sometimes he sought peace while I celebrated loudly. Honestly, my kids and some of my students might have agreed. Passion is wonderful, but how we express it, our dynamics, determines whether others feel inspired or overwhelmed. I didn't need less passion, just better control of my "dynamic volume."

Imagine music played at *fortissimo* all the time. Or every conversation at maximum volume. (You know who you are, enthusiastic coffee lovers and toddlers.) That gets annoying quickly. I soon realized my teaching style needed dynamic adjustments. So, I experimented, starting softly (*pianissimo*), building gradually (*mezzo-forte*), and observing student responses.

Guess what? It worked beautifully.

As Ray would remind me, enthusiasm wasn't the issue, my constantly loud approach simply needed a balanced touch of *mezzo-piano*. Lesson learned.

Dynamics in music, symbols or terms like *fortissimo, mezzo-piano, crescendo, decrescendo,* indicate volume to convey emotion and meaning. *Dynamics* create moods, highlight melodies and harmonies, and enhance expressive intention.

Think of Beethoven's Fifth Symphony: without dynamic contrast it would lose its drama, excitement, and emotional power. *Dynamics* add interest, humor, surprise, and emotion, turning music into an inspiring, captivating experience.

Just as music needs dynamic variety, so does teaching. *Dynamics* in teaching connect personality and relationships. Understanding the dynamics of your personality, disposition, beliefs, and communication style determines your teaching outcomes.

Imagine a teacher delivering every lesson in monotone, with no dynamic variation. Without contrast, lessons become dull, the message unclear.

Effective teaching involves using dynamics intentionally and shifting from quiet intensity to enthusiastic energy to capture attention, deepen understanding, and foster connection.

Dynamics in teaching also means adapting to each student's personality, being curious, optimistic, and spontaneous. Sometimes the best teaching moments happen when you toss aside the lesson plan and address what's relevant in the moment, creating unforgettable learning experiences.

Your Dynamic Formula for Passionate Teaching

- **Use dynamic variety:** Shift your teaching from *pianissimo* reflection to *fortissimo* excitement as needed.

- **Adapt to personalities:** Match your energy to students' needs to build rapport and engagement.

- **Stay spontaneous and open:** Embrace curiosity, optimism, and spontaneity to keep lessons fresh and meaningful.

How will you use dynamics in music, personality, and relationships to ignite your passion-based teaching formula to inspire your students and enrich your teaching business?

PASSION-BASED TEACHING FORMULA

Passion-Based Teaching leads to Passion-Based Learning, it's a simple yet powerful formula; focus on your students' passions to ignite their desire and enthusiasm for learning music.

Passion-based teaching creates engaging and dynamic lessons by tapping into what excites your students. Whether teaching in-person or online, your enthusiasm for music is contagious. Your passion ignites their interest, making learning easy and enjoyable.

Ask meaningful questions:

- What style of music excites your students?

- Which musicianship skills are they most curious about, composing, improvising, or performing?

- How can you align their musical interests with your curriculum?

When you genuinely connect your teaching to their interests, whether it's classical, jazz, contemporary, or their own creative compositions, you create a vibrant, effective learning environment.

Let your students share their passions openly and honor every passion equally. Because when your passion meets your students, learning truly becomes magical.

"What a teacher writes down on the blackboard of life can never be erased."

~ John Cotto

Case Study:
UMT Certified Teacher Janet Olsen

What truly defines a great music teacher? Is it formal training and prestigious certifications? Or is it something deeper, a belief in the transformative power of music, compassion, and the ability to ignite a student's passion?

Janet Olsen's journey proves that the greatest teachers are those who inspire, uplift, and see potential where others might overlook it. Janet's first music teacher wasn't formally trained, she was her own mother, whose only qualifications were a deep passion for music and unstoppable determination. Having lost her family at just sixteen and tasked with raising her younger sister alone, Janet's mother found refuge in singing. With no formal experience, she courageously auditioned for the National Choir, performing the only song she knew, *Silent Night*. Despite her lack of musical theory, the committee recognized her undeniable talent, accepting her into the choir and setting the foundation for Janet's own musical journey.

But not every teacher saw Janet's potential.

The Teacher Who Almost Stole Her Dream

Janet dreamed of attending the prestigious music arts school in her city and turned to her middle school music teacher, Mr. R, for guidance. Despite her enthusiasm and dedication, Mr. R ignored and dismissed her. One painful day, Janet overheard him telling classmates, "She's wasting her time. There's no way she will ever get in."

Heartbroken yet determined, Janet decided she would prove him wrong. Without a mentor, she researched tirelessly, practiced relentlessly, and prepared herself thoroughly for the rigorous audition process. Hundreds auditioned; many were eliminated, but Janet's passion and resilience carried her through every round.

When the acceptance letter arrived, Janet read it repeatedly in disbelief. She had done it. She had proved that one teacher's doubt could never define her destiny. From that day forward, Janet chose to surround herself only with mentors who believed in possibility, rather than limitations.

The Legacy of Belief

Today, as a UMT Certified Teacher and respected music educator, Janet welcomes students from diverse backgrounds, embracing each student's unique journey and potential. Her experiences have taught her that while talent matters, it is resilience, belief, and determination that truly shape success.

Each morning, before beginning her lessons, Janet pauses to look at her diplomas and certifications. She doesn't just see her name, she sees every mentor, teacher, and friend who supported her journey.

As a State Board Member of the Utah Music Teachers Association, a Royal Conservatory of Music Representative, and an Ultimate Music Theory Certified Elite Educator, she carries their legacy forward, empowering the next generation of musicians to believe they, too, can achieve greatness.

Read Janet's inspiring story in *The Power of WHY Musicians 5 Book Series.*

Janet's story is a powerful reminder that our impact as teachers extends far beyond the lessons we give, it shapes the confidence, resilience, and future success of our students. When we teach with passion, we ignite possibility.

And for me, that passion has always been infused with something a little extra, a reason to celebrate. Because when you infuse passion into everything you do, life becomes more than just a journey, it becomes a party.

The Party Queen Becomes the Teaching Queen

My passion for celebration began with the magic of a smile on the snowy Christmas Day I was born. My mother described how tears of joy filled her eyes as I opened my blue eyes for the first time and saw her smiling back at me, a smile that would profoundly shape my life.

My Christmas birthdays became legendary celebrations. My mother even named me "Glory the PARTY Queen." Born into the festive spirit of Christmas, I arrived with plenty of white-blonde hair, resembling, according to my proud mom, a little Christmas angel. Born in the small town of Winkler, Manitoba, word traveled fast about the Christmas baby, turning the hospital into a joyful celebration with doctors dressed as Santa and nurses wearing reindeer antlers.

Every year, I eagerly planned my birthday parties, loving the creative anticipation that built excitement leading up to each event. My early passion for organizing parties, giving gifts, and celebrating became as deep as my passion for learning music. Through it all, my mother Rosabel's simple smile became my guiding star, reflecting joys of celebration and helping me through life's challenges.

By age sixteen, I was already an entrepreneur, proudly opening my own piano teaching studio in the family room of my parents' basement. It was a simple space: white walls with brown wooden accents, a bookshelf filled with music books and stickers, a record player, a small glass desk (which I still have today), a comfy white leather office chair (perfect for teenage spinning), and my beloved shiny walnut piano.

To me, this wasn't just a basement, it was "Glory's Piano Studio," my gateway to entrepreneurship. Having been a YMCA Camp Counselor from age thirteen, my passion for teaching and connecting with kids naturally extended into music lessons. Inspired by my entrepreneurial mother, who told me if I wanted designer clothes and makeup, I'd need to earn the money myself, I set out to generate real "cash flow."

Babysitting wasn't going to fund my big dreams, so it was time to scale my income. My father, a business accountant and hobby musician, always talked finances around the family dinner table, and for my sixteenth birthday, he gifted me my very first 14-column coil-bound green accounting workbook. I still vividly remember that moment as I was officially in business as a music teacher. (That was my favorite birthday gift.)

Over the next five years, my passion for music and business flourished, but doubts crept in: Was I good enough, smart enough? Would anyone truly want to learn from me? Once again, my mother's heartfelt smile and encouraging words lifted me up:

"Glory, you are the Party Queen, you can do anything. Your smile brightens every room. Remember how much you love organizing celebrations and creating systems to ensure success? Use those strategies in your teaching, and you'll become the Teaching Queen."

Her words have sung in my heart ever since, continually reminding me that "I can do anything." And now, you can do anything too, as you discover the one powerful word my mother taught me through five incredible life lessons: "party".

P. A. R. T. Y. FIVE POWERFUL LESSONS

P. Process Plan to Success

A process plan is your step-by-step guide to achieving goals. My mother taught me this early, carefully planning each Christmas-Birthday Party with color, music, surprises, and joy. I brought this same magic to my teaching creating engaging, creative lessons, themed recitals, and joyful celebrations of milestones.

Action Steps:

- Design engaging lesson plans with creative activities.

- Plan recitals with themes to surprise and delight listeners.

- Involve students in the process and remember to smile, it's free.

A. Attitude to Positivity

Attitude is everything. My mother showed me how positivity transforms challenges like cleaning rooms, practicing piano, and washing dishes into joyful, shared experiences.

Rather than demanding, she always inspired by emphasizing positive outcomes we would celebrate together.

Positive Mental Attitude attracts growth, success, and powerful opportunities. I've witnessed it firsthand and implemented it as an educator and a parent.

Action Steps:

- **Practice gratitude daily.**
- **Surround yourself with positivity.**
- **Use empowering language in your self-talk.**

R. Relationships to Impact

Relationships are life's greatest gift with family, friends, clients, and yourself. My mother kept motivational notes on her mirror, always reminding herself (and me) to smile and radiate positivity.

She'd say, "Smile till others smile back at you".

When my mother faced breast cancer at age eighty, her smile remained, encouraging me to continue building my music business. Her supportive relationships impacted my teaching profoundly.

Action Steps:

- **Cultivate positive self-talk.**
- **Foster meaningful relationships through kindness.**
- **Smile freely and generously; it's contagious.**

T. Transformation to Mindset

Transformation begins in your mindset. Throughout my life, I've faced transformations in confidence, business growth, and personal resilience, each deepening my growth mindset.

During my mother's illness, I recognized her as my first and greatest coach. She encouraged me to continue writing, growing, and serving others, even in her final days.

Realizing the power of coaching, I now coach music educators to achieve massive success, just as my mother coached me.

Action Steps:

- **Adopt a growth mindset, open to continuous learning.**
- **Seek coaching to accelerate your transformation.**
- **Reflect daily on what you've learned and how you can help others.**

Y. You and Your Why

You choose how to live your life and pursue Your Why. My mother, despite only completing grade 8 and facing challenging farm life, chose joy.

She became a passionate learner, entrepreneur, and successful businesswoman, owning a dress shop where I learned valuable life and business lessons.

Even during sadness, her joyful spirit prevailed. In her final days, our family surrounded her with music, stories, and laughter. She passed peacefully, smiling as she always did, leaving a legacy of joy and purpose.

Your Why gives life meaning, fulfillment, and deep gratitude. Celebrate opportunities before you. Live joyfully because my mother smiled and said so.

Action Steps:

- **Clearly define your why, your purpose.**

- **Create a vision board reflecting your dreams and goals.**

- **Celebrate each step toward your goals with passion and acknowledge your progress.**

Now it's your turn. Embrace the P.A.R.T.Y. philosophy to elevate your teaching, enrich your relationships, and enhance your life.

The Magic of a Smile and my mother's 5 Powerful PARTY Lessons are my gift to you.

P—What Process Plan will you create to successfully achieve your goals?

A—What Attitude adjustments will help you develop a positive mental attitude?

R—What Relationships will you nurture to positively impact those you serve?

T—What Transformation will empower you to embrace gratitude and a growth mindset?

Y—What's Your Why, the inspiration behind creating the greatest PARTY ever?

Passion and Music: From Elvis to Pizza

My husband Ray's passion was simple; he wanted to be Elvis. He sang like Elvis, moved like Elvis, and even looked like Elvis. Known affectionately as Winnipeg's Elvis, Ray St. Germain had it all including me. His hit song "She's a Square" captivated me as a young fan, dancing and singing along, long before I ever met him. The song, a rockabilly chart-topper, sparked my curiosity about songwriting and composing, setting me on a lifelong path toward understanding the magic behind memorable music.

Years later, fate intervened. As Ray performed at the Miss Manitoba Pageant, (I was one of the ten finalists, modeling and showcasing my piano skills), our paths crossed on stage as he sang *The Girl From Ipanema*. His voice once again captured my heart. To my surprise, he invited me, the "square girl", out for pizza. Shortly thereafter, I married the man, my own personal Elvis, legendary musician Ray St. Germain.

Throughout our life together, we traveled the world, and I proudly watched Ray's career flourish with countless standing ovations, award-winning TV shows, and memorable albums. Our children joined the musical journey too, performing alongside him and eventually producing his music. Yet, among the many milestones, one stands out as particularly special.

Christmas in July: The Family Album

One July, Ray needed to record a Christmas album, complete with three original songs. But how do you summon holiday spirit in the heat of summer? Determined to help, I decorated the house, prepared a festive Christmas dinner, and soon Ray invited me to co-write the songs with him. My childhood dreams of composing music came true as we created three heartfelt songs: "I Lost One Reindeer", "Christmases of Long Ago", and "I'm Missing You This Christmas". Our children David and Sherry produced the album, featuring all five of our children, and two of our grandchildren, Jeff and Catie, sang backup vocals. It was truly the best Christmas-Birthday gift ever. This passion-based collaboration was a joyful celebration of our family's shared love of music, culminating in the unforgettable Ray St. Germain Family Christmas Show on my 60th birthday. Watching my husband, our children, and grandchildren perform together, I felt my parents' spirits smiling down. It was more than music, it was legacy.

The Art of Composing and Teaching

Composing is a gift, a creative process that allows musicians to share emotions and tell stories through sound. As a music teacher and author, I've always believed strongly in connecting theory with practical composition. When developing the *Ultimate Music Theory Workbooks*, I focused on crafting original compositions to clearly demonstrate theory concepts, making them easy and enjoyable for students to learn and perform.

In the *UMT Supplemental Workbook Series* co-authored with Shelagh McKibbon-U'Ren, we developed the ICE (Imagine, Compose, Explore) program, guiding students from beginner levels through advanced, nurturing their composing skills at every step. Why emphasize composition in teaching? Because music isn't just theory, it's personal. Composing helps students express themselves creatively and deeply connect with music. Many of my students, including Connor Derraugh (whose remarkable story you read earlier), have gone on to become accomplished composers themselves.

Ray's Legacy and My Musical Journey

Ray's profound impact as a musician and composer extended far beyond his awards and accolades. His powerful song "The Métis" celebrated his Indigenous heritage and earned him numerous honors, including induction into the Canadian Country Music Hall of Fame and receiving the Aboriginal Order of Canada. Ray created a musical legacy most performers only dream of. My legacy? It began with a simple composition humorously titled "No More Pizza", a nod to Ray's loving gesture of ordering dinner (always pizza) while I spent endless hours writing. This modest piece symbolized the supportive partnership we shared and marked the beginning of my deeper journey into composition and teaching music theory.

The Struggle and Turning Point

Early in my teaching career, I found music theory incredibly challenging. My students were frustrated, and so was I. Although passionate about teaching, I lacked confidence and struggled with imposter syndrome, feeling like "just a music teacher". I didn't realize that the real issue was my limited understanding of different learning styles.

My breakthrough came unexpectedly when Ray fell seriously ill, landing in the hospital and causing our family's income to plummet. I was forced to confront my teaching and financial realities head-on. How could I make more money without adding more hours?

Suddenly, it clicked. I could teach group music theory classes. Teaching groups transformed my life. My income skyrocketed from $50 per hour to $270 per hour, providing financial security when we needed it most. With newfound clarity, I invested in professional development, hired a coach, and dedicated myself to mastering group teaching strategies. I went from maxed-out credit cards to building a thriving, six-figure music teaching business.

Your Passion-Based Legacy

Music teachers hold a profound responsibility. Through passion-based teaching, we nurture lifelong musicians, composers, and learners. You have the power to inspire your students, ignite their creativity, and empower them to carry forward your musical legacy.

As you explore your passion for teaching, ask yourself:

- **What legacy do I wish to create through music education?**

- **How can I inspire creativity and lifelong learning in my students?**

- **How will my passion impact future generations?**

Teach Music. Change Lives. One beautiful note at a time. As we reflect on the legacy we leave through teaching, let's pause to explore how we can intentionally create a greater impact through passion-based teaching.

⌒ *Fermata* (Pause to Ponder): Three Steps to Passion-Based Teaching

I believe there are two teaching legacies that must be shared in living our best life. First, your passion as a teacher. Your passion enables you to combine the knowledge of your professional development with educating students to develop lifelong musicianship skills in Passion-Based Learning. What are you most passionate about in your teaching business?

Second, Your dynamics as a teacher. Your personality dynamics and how you develop major elements, alterations and processes will ultimately be your legacy as a music educator. Your legacy is determined by what your students do, who they become and how you empower them to learn music. How will you use your teaching passion and dynamic personality to help others learn and leave your legacy?

Step #1 Start with Dynamics in Teaching.

Your dynamic personality can be infectious in connecting to a meaningful relationship with your students. Adjusting the dynamics of the lesson can transform your teaching results, just as altering the dynamics within the music can enhance its impact.

How can you alter the dynamics of your personality to be a more effective educator?

What dynamic techniques can you implement for greater connection in communication?

How can you encourage students to explore greater contrasts in expressing dynamics?

Step #2 Write down 3 ways you can introduce passion-based learning.

The role of passion-based learning requires a significant need for high quality passion-based teaching.

You can make a difference through your desire and enthusiasm for music education by creating an effective learning environment that enhances your students' understanding.

_____

_____

What can you do to introduce passion-based learning to your students with creativity?

_____

_____

How do you commit to listening to students who are passionate about sharing ideas?

_____

_____

How can you build passion-based relationships to enhance learning systems?

_____

_____

Step #3 Commit to passion-based teaching.

Passionate teachers can make a difference in their students' lives and in their music education achievements.

Passionate teachers are focused on commitment to their students' learning through their own beliefs, attitudes and professional development.

How can you commit to being in the forefront of your professional development?

_____

_____

How will you implement your passion-based teaching to elevate comprehension?

_____

_____

What can you do to impact technical skills, knowledge and empathy with students?

_____

_____

"Go with your strengths and develop your passions to discover your purpose."

~ Barbara Bray

Passion fuels motivation, driving high-quality teaching and enthusiastic learning. Discover your Passion-Based Teaching and Teach with Passion.

♪ Your Coda Notes ♪

_____

_____

The 12 Key Strategies include online Ultimate Music Teachers Bonus Resources.

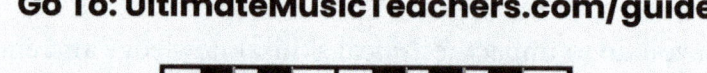

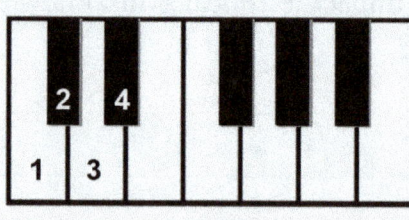

TEACH MUSIC CHANGE LIVES

Your Passion-Based Teaching Formula
Dive deeper into **KEY STRATEGY #4** - get your Ultimate Music Teachers
FREE Bonus Workbook to embrace the dynamics of bold, expressive teaching.
Go To: UltimateMusicTeachers.com/guide

PART 2
TEACHING HOLISTICALLY TO DISCOVER YOUR PURPOSE

Key Strategy #5
SIMPLE STEPS TO COMPOUND CONNECTION
Rhythm

"Move to the rhythm of life, embrace change in rhythmic diversity."

~ Glory St. Germain

What are you doing to create a lifestyle you truly love? As musicians, parents, and teachers, we often think of rhythm in musical terms, but rhythm also pulses through every part of our lives. Our daily habits, how we breathe, move, sleep, eat, work, and play create a personal tempo that either moves us forward or drags us down like a sluggish ritardando. (And yes, I've had plenty of adagio days.)

In my life's symphony, rhythm wasn't just a musical concept, it was a survival skill. With five children (Chrystal, Cathy, Ray Jr., David, and Sherry) and my grandson Jeff, who is my stepdaughter Chrystal's firstborn and the same age as my son David, our home was a joyful jam session of melody and chaos.

Some days felt like a waltz, others like a free jazz improv with no time signature in sight. David, Sherry, and Jeff even toured together as pro musicians. To keep from losing my rhythm (or my mind), I had to find balance emotionally, physically, and financially, like a finely tuned metronome. Because when life is out of sync, everything feels offbeat. And it doesn't just affect us, it ripples outward.

In music education, our personal rhythm impacts our students, too. Teachers often feel disconnected from their students, and vice versa, simply because their internal tempos are misaligned. So, what's the solution? It starts with us.

When we take care of our own rhythm, we build stronger connections with our students, our families, and ourselves.

The Three Rhythmic Beats for Transformation

- **Beat 1 is the Rhythm in Your Life. How you show up matters. When you're in sync with your personal rhythm, your well-being elevates everything around you.**

- **Beat 2 is the Rhythm in Your Relationships. The energy you bring to your studio sets the tone. A balanced rhythm creates a space where students feel safe, inspired, and connected.**

- **Beat 3 is the Rhythm in Your Business. Like music, your business thrives on a steady beat. Knowing your financial rhythm, income flow and growth patterns are the key to sustainability.**

These beats intertwine to create a holistic rhythm for your life as a music educator. Like simple rhythms evolving into rich, compound patterns, your consistent efforts build momentum personally, professionally, and financially. Think of it like compound interest: the more aligned your rhythm, the more impact you create over time.

Every decision is a rhythmic transaction, a note in your life's composition. And remember, you are the "who" for your students. But you also need a "who" to help you grow your business and elevate your journey as an entrepreneur. By aligning the rhythms of your life, relationships, and business, you are conducting transformation.

Embracing a holistic teaching approach is like conducting an orchestra where every instrument and every element matters. Just as harmony in music arises from the blend of melody, rhythm, and dynamics, holistic teaching aligns the physical, emotional, and intellectual aspects of learning.

Each student has a unique composition. By tuning into their individual rhythms, their passions, challenges, and learning styles, we create lessons that resonate on a deeper level. Holistic teaching doesn't just develop musical skills; it empowers students to discover their inner rhythm and compose their life's symphony with confidence and purpose.

When I made a rhythmic shift in my own life, building habits and patterns that supported my health, my business, and my family, I began to experience rapid growth. I committed to early morning writing, scheduled workouts, and protected my time with my husband and loved ones. I discovered that life, like music, isn't about rushing through endless eighth notes, it's about balancing movement with rests, momentum with reflection.

As I became more aware of my own rhythm, I became more productive. I learned when to work *on* my business and when to work *in* it. I recognized which tasks were profit-producing and which ones were draining my energy without a return.

Rhythm isn't always easy to maintain, it's not a sprint, it's a marathon. And like every marathoner, I had to train for mine. I had to learn the rhythm of breathing and pacing.

Just like athletes, we as teachers, musicians and business owners need to find our internal rhythm because the rhythm in our lives fuels the vitality of our business.

Three Rhythmic Shifts for Energizing Growth

The First Rhythmic Shift is Rhythmic Balance, learning to pause.

Just as music blends rapid sixteenth notes with well-placed rests, our lives need a similar ebb and flow. Rhythmic balance is about knowing when to move fast and when to pause.

When I built pauses into my daily rhythm, especially for writing, I created space for growth. That balance led me to write the *Ultimate Music Theory Series* and grow my business as an author.

The lesson? Productivity isn't just about speed; it's about structure and intentional timing.

The Second Rhythmic Shift is Rhythmic Diversity, mixing up your teaching tools.

In music and in life, sameness dulls the spark. Rhythmic diversity is about infusing new energy into your routines and teaching tools. When I added variety to my teaching, explored new presentation formats, and shifted my daily patterns, my business expanded internationally. Connecting with retailers, hosting workshops, and introducing UMT Workbooks created momentum and excitement. That rhythmic shift brought growth, not just for me, but for teachers worldwide.

The Third Rhythmic Shift is Rhythmic Creativity, thinking outside the box.

To stand out in business you need to dance to your own beat. Rhythmic creativity is about stepping beyond the ordinary and embracing your uniqueness. I didn't fit the mold. I was building a business to help teachers teach music theory and succeed financially. That meant becoming the unicorn: building a brand, innovating my content, and believing in the vision no one else had yet seen.

The result? Growth, impact, and a business that sings to its own rhythm.

Six Ways to Set Your Unique Business Rhythm

1. Take Time for Creative Visioning. Step back and dream big. Think beyond your day-to-day to envision what your music teaching business *could* be, whether that's integrating technology, launching new programs, or redefining how you teach. Inspiration thrives when you give it room to breathe.

2. Offer New Educational Programs. Stay current and expand your reach by creating new offerings: online classes, niche music genres, theory camps, or group sessions. This keeps students engaged and excited while attracting new students looking for something fresh.

3. Seek New Revenue Streams. Grow beyond traditional lessons by selling your own teaching tools, offering paid workshops, or partnering with music stores. Multiple income streams help build a profitable, sustainable business that supports your freedom lifestyle.

4. Get Out of the Box. Innovation is the heartbeat of growth. When Joanne, a traditional piano teacher, added group lessons with interactive games and flipped learning, everything changed. Her students were engaged, her studio filled up, and her creativity soared. All it took was the courage to break the mold and it paid off, establishing her as a forward-thinking educator and attracting a wave of new students.

5. Get a Coach. A great coach can help you clarify your goals, create smarter systems, and achieve more with less stress. I know, because I've been that teacher. With the help of business and life coaches, I scaled my studio, built group programs, and designed a flexible schedule that supported both my income and my well-being. That's why I now coach others inside the UMT Teachers Membership, to pass on what's possible.

6. Choose Your Collaborators Wisely. Success doesn't happen solo. Surround yourself with mentors, coaches, and peers who uplift and challenge you. Inside our UMTC Elite Educators community, we share strategies, support, and celebrate wins. The right team becomes your rhythm section, keeping you steady, inspired, and moving forward.

When you align your life and business with a rhythm that's uniquely yours, you create momentum that transforms everything: your teaching, your income, your confidence, and your joy. My rhythmic creativity opened doors I never imagined, leading to my role as a coach, course creator, and CEO. Now, I lead a team, speak on international stages, and help teachers build thriving businesses.

Changing your rhythm can change your life. So, what's your next rhythmic shift?

Rhythm of Life

The rhythm of life and the business I'm proud to have built began with one crucial step: awareness. When I started my music teaching journey, I noticed that without intention, negative thought patterns crept in and threw my life out of sync. External pressures and people sometimes knocked me off course. The only way forward was to take full responsibility for my rhythm and my results.

Stress had its grip; anxiety, procrastination, and overwhelm took center stage. But then I discovered a powerful key: consistency. I didn't overhaul everything overnight; it was more like learning to run a marathon than sprinting to success. But with each small, intentional step, I began to recalibrate the tempo of my life.

What changed?

- **My sleep schedule**
- **Healthier food choices**
- **Regular movement and exercise**
- **Dedicated time for learning and implementation**
- **GSD energy (get stuff done)**
- **A balance between working *on* and *in* my business**
- **Writing in my gratitude journal daily**

These shifts weren't just habit changes; they became the foundation of a new rhythm for my life and my purpose.

Rhythm is more than a tempo; it's the pulse of your purpose. When you align your energy with your vision, you begin to move through life with clarity, confidence, and calm. Rhythm isn't one-size-fits-all. It can be simple or compound, fluid or firm, structured or spontaneous.

The important part? That it's yours.

Just like in music, rhythm is what keeps us alive physically, emotionally, and spiritually. It guides how we think, speak, move, create, and connect. And when you find the rhythm that resonates with your soul, everything changes.

Rhythmic Harmony with Your Students

The rhythm of your life directly influences your connection with students. When you're in sync with yourself, you can create powerful rhythmic harmony in your relationships by listening with intention, playing music together, and engaging in conversations that truly resonate. Not just to respond but to understand.

In music theory, harmonic rhythm gives structure to compositions, with patterns shifting between melody and harmony. Whether between vocalists and accompanists or among instruments in an orchestra, these rhythmic shifts deepen the dimension of musical conversation.

As rhythm shapes music, it also shapes your business. Without rhythm, there's no flow. When the rhythm of your daily life at home, at work or with family or friends is out of sync, everything feels off. We all slip into patterns that either drain us or push us too fast. Awareness becomes your metronome.

By recognizing where you're out of time with your goals, you can reset your pace and realign with purpose.

And just like a skilled musician who listens deeply to stay in time with the ensemble, we must listen inwardly to realign with the rhythm of our own lives.

The more aware you are of your internal rhythm, the more open you become to receiving the gifts life has to offer. Gratitude flows in harmony with growth and when you're aligned, your business and your relationships become a symphony of success.

OPERATING RHYTHMS + SPECIFIC SYSTEMS = SUCCESS

In the day-to-day rhythm of running your music teaching business, Operating Rhythms are essential. These are your consistent, repeatable systems including scheduling, invoicing, lesson planning, and reporting that keep everything running smoothly.

When these rhythms fall out of sync, even small issues can spiral into overwhelm, leaving you scattered and unable to fully show up for your students.

I understand that pressure firsthand. Whether it's scrambling to send invoices or managing a schedule that doesn't flow, these disruptions create ripple effects that impact your energy, your presence, and your ability to lead with confidence.

A flawed operating rhythm is often the root cause of many business frustrations. Without intentional systems, stress builds up and teaching begins to feel more like surviving than thriving. But here's the shift: when you implement solid operating rhythms and pair them with specific systems, you reclaim your focus, confidence, and clarity.

Let's break it down:

- **Planned Communication includes your scheduling, studio management, income tracking, and admin duties.**

- **Creative Communication is your time spent inspiring students, designing engaging lessons, and building real connection with the true heart of your teaching practice.**

When you master your operating rhythms, you free up your energy to invest in creative communication. That's where transformation happens for you *and* your students.

Here's what a strong operating rhythm can give you:

- **Efficiency in studio systems, marketing, and lesson delivery.**

- **Effectiveness in preparing for performances, exams, and student progress.**

- **Productivity and profitability in your teaching business.**

Now imagine your business as a well-rehearsed orchestra:

- **You know which projects are in motion.**

- **You've got a strategic plan with performance indicators.**

- **You refine what's not working and eliminate what no longer serves your growth.**

A key takeaway? Spend 70–80% of your time on income-producing activities such as teaching, mentoring, creating content, etc., while minimizing the 20–30% spent on tasks that can be automated or delegated. Ask yourself:

- **Are you spending too much time on things someone else could do better?**

- **What systems are missing that could save you hours every week?**

- **Are you making space for creativity and connection or just crossing things off a list?**

When you refine your rhythm, your business becomes more aligned. You become more present. And you create a business model that not only works but sings.

Your Rhythm of Life Strategy: How to Make Your Business Flourish

To build true rhythmic harmony with your students, you first need to explore your own rhythm and theirs. What gets your students excited to learn?

When you develop rapport, their desire to explore music blossoms right before your eyes. I use rapport-building techniques not just in teaching, but in every part of life, it's how we connect.

Reignite Your Passion for Teaching

Think back to when you first began music lessons. Were they exciting and engaging, or dull and repetitive? Did you fall in love with music because of the subject or because your teacher lit a spark in you?

Now look at your own students. Are their faces lighting up when they see you or are they dragging their bags in with excuses about not practicing (don't worry, we've all heard *that* one.). Students look to you for inspiration, motivation, and meaningful connection.

So, ask yourself: What can I implement right now to innovate and invigorate my students' lessons? Parents and students don't want "just music lessons", they want a "transformational learning experience" that is profoundly impactful.

Reflect on Your Flow

What were your biggest wins last week? Last month? Last year? If your answer is a shrug, you're not alone.

That's a sign it's time to create a Time and Scheduling Flow, a rhythm that helps you shift smoothly between the different areas of your business without overwhelm.

Whether it's planning, teaching, marketing, or professional development, managing your flow means:

- **Prioritizing tasks that move the needle,**
- **Teaching more effectively, and**
- **Still making space for *you time*.**

When your life rhythm is aligned, your business thrives and so do you. What are you cultivating to grow your business to its full capacity?

Maximize Your Capacity with Three Rhythmic Strategies

Your capacity to grow your business comes from how well you learn, implement, and adapt these rhythmic strategies:

1. **Student Rapport Rhythm. Build trust and connection through consistency and presence.**

2. **Creative Teaching Rhythm. Stay innovative and passionate by keeping your lessons fresh.**

3. **Business Flow Rhythm. Run your day with seamless transitions that boost productivity.**

Your results reflect how well your rhythms support your goals and how deeply your students are learning and thriving.

Rhythm of Life + Rhythm of Business = Teaching Success

These two rhythms, your personal rhythm and your business rhythm, intertwine to create a thriving teaching studio. They're the heartbeat that drives your purpose.

Student/Teacher Rapport: The rhythm you establish in your daily interactions fosters trust, energy, and a positive learning environment. When your personal rhythm aligns with your teaching, magic happens.

Innovative Teaching: A well-balanced rhythm fuels creativity. It keeps you energized, inspired, and excited about each lesson which translates to deeper student engagement and lasting impact.

Time and Workflow: The Rhythm of Business is your flow between planning, teaching, marketing, and admin. A structured rhythm keeps your day moving with clarity and ease, reducing stress and increasing impact.

Self-Management and Capacity: Your Rhythm of Life nurtures your personal growth and vision. With time for rest, reflection, and learning, you lead with clarity and show up at your best consistently and confidently.

When you master these rhythms, you are composing a lifestyle of purpose, profitability, and personal fulfillment.

Now, let's keep the tempo moving forward as we dive into your next strategy: *The Rhythmic Conversation Game.*

PLAY THE RHYTHMIC CONVERSATION GAME

When teaching rhythm, one engaging exercise is to have a Simple Rhythmic Conversation. This is an engaging and fun exercise that engages in understanding rhythmic patterns, time signatures, basic beat, pulse and creativity while maintaining a harmonic rhythmic connection with nonverbal conversations between you and your student.

Nonverbal refers to the way you convey information without speaking, by simply expressing yourself through creative rhythmic patterns and facial expressions (eye contact and body movements, etc). This is one activity your students will love.

It's a great party idea too. Here's how it works:

Step 1: Choose a Time Signature, for example 4/4. Then determine the tempo and set the conversation for two rhythmic measures of 4/4 time for each person to communicate their idea, statement, question or answer.

Step 2: Grab a couple of chopsticks or rhythm sticks, tap 4 beats to determine the pulse and person 1 begins with only a rhythmic pattern (two measures of 4/4 time) and facial expression, body movement, etc. The key here is the importance of listening to the rhythmic pattern, preparing your rhythmic answer while observing the visual nonverbal communication to determine the message being conveyed.

Step 3: Maintaining a steady tempo without missing a beat as person 2 replies with only nonverbal expressions and rhythmic patterns (two measures of 4/4 time). Continue the nonverbal rhythmic conversation as each person communicates for 2 measures. This is developing the art of listening and the creativity of response.

See how long you can keep the rhythmic conversation going while staying in time. For even more fun, try adding an accelerando to speed up the conversation or variations in tempo. Change the Time Signature to make it more challenging. This is one way of having a creative nonverbal conversation with rhythmic elements only.

To add another layer of creativity, use your chopsticks to tap on various objects such as: the table, a glass, wood, drums, etc. to incorporate another element of sound variation. Just as in speaking, your tonality alters depending on the conversation you are having and how you want to express yourself.

I remember presenting this exercise at one of our live Ultimate Music Teachers training events and it was followed by much laughter. It can be challenging to express yourself only through rhythm and nonverbal communication (smiling is highly recommended).

This exercise opens the holistic pathway for discussion and analysis on the rhythmic elements chosen by composers in communicating their ideas through music. Embracing a holistic pathway in curriculum design is fundamentally about nurturing connections.

It involves crafting lessons that transcend traditional boundaries, allowing for a rich interplay among various facets of music. This includes performance, composition, cultural and historical relevance, as well as critical analysis and response.

Moreover, it acknowledges music as a vibrant form of human expression that intersects numerous disciplines like art, literature, and history. This activity deepens communication connection and is an innovative way to teach students about the elements of rhythm.

When I implemented these techniques in my own teaching, I learned the value of feeling the rhythm in communication through nonverbal conversations as well as the importance of listening and understanding the rhythmic expression students explored to effectively communicate their message.

Rhythm Note and Rest Names

Rhythm is one of the most challenging concepts to teach, and even more challenging when there are variations in the terms used to describe the note or rest names.

Musical note and rest symbols may be called different names even though the value itself remains the same within the rhythm and Time Signature of the music.

For example: In American English, the music note symbol ♪ representing one eighth of the duration of a whole note value is called an eighth note.

In British English the same music note symbol ♪ representing the same note value is called a quaver (eighth note) - one eighth of the duration of a semibreve (whole note) value.

American English - eighth note = ⅛ value of a whole note; quarter note = ¼ value of a whole note; and a half note = ½ value of a whole note.

British English - quaver = ⅛ value of a semibreve; crotchet = ¼ value of a semibreve; and a minim = ½ value of a semibreve.

In today's world with so many musicians collaborating with fellow musicians and educators around the world, it is important for us to understand the vocabulary of music theory notation as found inside your Ultimate Music Teachers Theory Guide for Rhythm (yes, another present for you at the end of this chapter).

Rhythm in Time Signatures

Rhythm in music is divided into measures based on the Time Signature. The top number of the Time Signature indicates how many beats are in each measure. The bottom number indicates the type of note that receives one beat. Together, the top and bottom numbers establish the Time Signature and define the pulse, whether it's an undotted beat, a dotted beat, or a combination that creates strong, weak, or medium pulses and rhythmic patterns.

The first beat of each complete measure is the strong beat, setting the foundation for the rhythmic flow of the piece. When a piece begins with a pickup beat (anacrusis), the rhythm resolves in the final measure, a reminder that balance and structure matter.

Before we dive into beams, dotted notes, and time signatures that could make your head spin faster than a sixteenth note run, take a deep breath. You're about to become a Rhythm Detective. (No magnifying glass needed, just your musical mind. Oh, and spontaneous toe-tapping, head-bobbing, and occasional counting out loud may occur, just sayin').

Simple, Compound, Hybrid or Unmetered Rhythm

Simple Time Signatures have a top number of 2, 3, or 4, showing how many basic beats are in each measure. The bottom number shows which note value equals one beat.

Compound Time Signatures have a top number of 6, 9, or 12, indicating groups of beats that naturally divide into three parts. Again, the bottom number tells you the note value of each beat.

How to Tell the Difference? Look at how the notes are grouped:

- **If six eighth notes are beamed into three groups of two, it's 3/4 (Simple Time).**

- **If six eighth notes are beamed into two sets of three, it's 6/8 (Compound Time).**

Example:

- **3/4: three quarter-note pulses (strong, weak, weak)**

- **6/8: two dotted quarter-note pulses (dotted strong, dotted weak)**

Irregular groupings can show up too, like triplets, where three notes are played in the time of two, marked with a little "3" above or below the beam.

Hybrid (Mixed Meter) Time Signatures mix simple and compound beats within the same measure.

- **The top number may be 5, 7, 9, 10, or 11.**

- **For example, in 5/8 time, you may see one group of three eighth notes (compound feel) and one group of two eighth notes (simple feel), blending different rhythmic patterns into one time signature.**

When teaching time signatures, start with simple and compound time before introducing the exciting world of hybrid time. Music Detective Tip: when in doubt, follow the beams, they'll lead you to the right time signature clue.

The art of teaching music often involves breaking down complex concepts into simple, understandable terms. As educators, our responsibility is to make learning not only accessible but also engaging, memorable, and enjoyable. This approach transforms education into a journey of discovery, steering students away from feelings of dread or frustration and towards those 'aha' moments where everything clicks and learning becomes an adventure, not a challenge.

Six Practical Strategies to Empower Your Teaching

These simple yet powerful strategies not only address common challenges but also enhance your impact as an educator:

1. Understand Student Reluctance: If a student seems disinterested in practicing, dig deeper. Is it boredom with the material? Confusion about the concept? Something else? Explore the "why" behind the behavior to find meaningful solutions instead of surface-level fixes.

2. Develop Empathy: Put yourself in your students' shoes. If they're struggling with a new piece, imagine their frustration. Empathy builds patience and that patience strengthens your ability to guide them effectively.

3. Enhance Communication: When a student doesn't grasp a concept, don't just repeat it, reframe it. Practice explaining ideas in new, simpler ways. Great teachers change the approach to teaching.

4. Master Effective Problem Solving: When you meet resistance, brainstorm creative solutions. Could you integrate a favorite song into the lesson? Add gamification? Adaptability in problem-solving is your 'secret sauce' for keeping students engaged.

5. Prepare for Real-Life Challenges: Think through these scenarios now so you're prepared for real-life teaching moments. Having flexible strategies already in mind keeps you calm, confident, and responsive when challenges arise.

6. Cultivate Creative Teaching Techniques: Every challenge is a chance to innovate. If scales are boring, turn them into a race, a story, or a mini-composition project. The more creatively you teach, the more joy you ignite and the more your students of all learning styles and preferences will thrive.

As we journey through the evolving landscape of music education, it becomes clear that the art of teaching is a dynamic and ongoing process. In my early years as a young music teacher, I quickly realized that mastering the art of teaching music was not a destination, but a continuous journey.

Over time, I learned that developing new techniques and strategies is essential for becoming an Ultimate Music Teacher. It's about embracing the simple rhythms of life and understanding the intricacies of compound rhythm, both in teaching and in business growth.

Exploring the Freedom of Unmetered Rhythm

Just as music finds its beauty in both structured and free rhythms, so too does teaching. The concept of unmetered or free rhythms in music parallels the flexibility and adaptability we need as educators.

A musician exploring freedom within unmetered rhythms learns to listen deeply, to breathe with the phrase, and to move with feeling rather than a rigid framework. Likewise, as teachers, we must sometimes step away from strict structures and learn to navigate the ebb and flow of our students' needs, emotions, and learning styles.

Flexibility allows us to create personalized, impactful educational experiences, helping each student find their own authentic musical voice.

Unmetered or free rhythms occur when music is performed without a strict meter or time signature. Gregorian chant is a famous example where the music flows like sung poetry, free from a regular beat. Instead of strict metric divisions, performers rely on expressions like slowly, freely, or with rubato, offering space for full creative self-expression.

The pulse and power of free meter unlocks layers of musical consciousness whether through laments, healing songs, or improvisations that touch the deepest parts of the soul.

As music educators, embracing free meter in our teaching opens new possibilities for creativity, emotional connection, and healing through music, reminding us that rhythm is not just a set of rules to follow, but a powerful language of the heart.

Before we dive into the vibrant world of percussion, here's your friendly reminder:
Music isn't just played, it's felt, explored, and invented. So, take a deep breath, tap your toes, wiggle your shoulders a little (yes, really), and get ready, because next, we're unleashing the wild, rhythmic playground that lives inside every musician, starting with the joy of percussion.

Our Purpose to Teach Rhythm with Creativity: Percussion Instruments

As a music teacher, our purpose is to teach all the elements of music with creativity, including rhythm. Teaching rhythm with purpose puts you at the top of the elite educator list for students wanting to learn from you and it strengthens retention in your music teaching business. As you evolve as an educator, your students evolve as musicians.

There are hundreds of percussion instruments, yes, way more than just drums. I always loved experimenting with rhythmic changes when practicing my piano pieces (which, technically, is a percussion instrument too, since hammers strike the strings). I'm sure I drove my piano teacher crazy when I changed a 4/4 Time pulse into 6/8 Time or added a cheeky syncopated rhythm. If that wasn't enough, I even dabbled with free rhythm completely altering the composer's intended message. (Oops. Creativity in action.)

My body moved to rhythm naturally, and experimenting became pure joy. Imagine my excitement when, on my fourteenth Christmas birthday, I woke up to a full set of drums under the Christmas tree. (A gift my parents may have second-guessed later, but oh how I treasured it.) That gift sparked a passion for rhythmic creativity that would serve me well as a music teacher for years to come.

Percussion instruments aren't just drums and triangles, they're anything that can be struck, tapped, or shaken. Look around your house. You might find a flyswatter, spoons, a broomstick, a vacuum cleaner pipe, different sizes of glasses, or glasses filled with different amounts of liquid. Percussion is everywhere and yes, some of these "instruments" even have different pitches. Cool, right?

It's time to play the Rhythmic Conversation Game again. When I started teaching at sixteen, I'd play my drum set (now tucked downstairs into my teaching studio), while my students would answer on the piano (my beloved walnut Yamaha upright with a "grand piano" lid. Yes, I dreamed big even back then). Our call-and-response rhythmic conversations were a fun masterclass in learning strong, weak, and medium beats, different time signatures, and free rhythm exploration.

Want to know your secret teaching superpower?

Your superpower is creating connections across ages, abilities, and learning styles. Be open. Be playful. Be innovative. And watch your music teaching business soar.

Teach different things. Teach things differently. Above all, keep the rhythm of joy alive.

No Instrument? No Problem. Body Percussion to the Rescue.

Body percussion is something you've probably used countless times whether you realize it or not. A simple handclap, a rhythmic stomp, or even a playful snap of the fingers becomes an instant instrument of expression.

Imagine the difference between a roaring, standing ovation of rapid applause and a polite, reluctant clap. Two very different messages all through body percussion.

Body percussion includes using the body to create sound: clapping, rubbing hands together, tapping thighs, snapping fingers, stomping feet, or making clicks and pops with the mouth. Around the world, body percussion is a powerful part of rhythm-based dance and cultural storytelling.

How does body percussion fit into your teaching? Your body is the most accessible, versatile instrument you have and it's an incredible teaching tool for students of all ages.

Body Percussion

- **Helps students experience and understand pulse, rhythm, and tempo physically.**

- **Reinforces polyrhythm skills combining multiple rhythms while maintaining a steady beat.**

- **Prepares students for rhythmic sight-reading, improvisation, and performance.**

In group classes, you can start by teaching everyone the same pattern, then split into smaller groups to layer rhythms building complexity while keeping the joy alive.

Diversity in Rhythm

Diversity shines through the heartbeat of music. Different genres, dances, and cultures can often be identified simply by their rhythmic patterns. Body percussion opens a gateway to exploring this rhythmic diversity without the need for traditional instruments, inviting students into a global celebration of sound.

Rhythm, Analysis, and Connection

By teaching rhythm through percussion and body percussion, you help students internalize beat patterns, build musical intuition, and lay the foundation for confident performances. Your greatest responsibility as a music educator is to *decide*:

- **What to teach.**

- **When to teach it.**

- **How to deliver it in a system that meets each student where they are and elevates them to where they can go.**

Rhythm is in the music, the conversations, the connections, and the creativity you share. Which rhythmic element will you implement first? It's time to decide and to dance to the rhythm of your own teaching brilliance. Decisions set your rhythm in motion, one bold choice at a time, your symphony begins.

"Nothing happens until you decide.
Make a decision and watch your life move forward."

~ Oprah Winfrey

Case Study:
UMT Certified Teacher Caroline Joy Quinn

Amazing Annie or Inadequate Irene, who's capturing the lead? We all have those internal voices battling for center stage. One lifts us up, urging us forward, our Amazing Annie. The other whispers doubts, fears, and excuses, Inadequate Irene. And depending on the day, the challenge, or the moment, one of them always seems to take the lead.

For Caroline Joy Quinn, these two voices shaped the rhythm of her life in profound ways. Rhythm is the steady pulse that guides our daily lives.

And for Caroline, her journey has been a dance between hesitation and determination, doubt and confidence, fear and faith.

Many years ago, Caroline took a leap of faith. She boarded a plane alone to pursue her dream of studying music therapy. Anxious, and uncertain, but determined, she knew life would never be the same again.

Three years later, she earned her accreditation and joined the rehab team at the Hugh Macmillan Medical Center in Canada, using the power of music to heal and transform lives.

But dreams don't end when a diploma is earned, growth never stops. So when the opportunity to become an Ultimate Music Theory Certified Teacher presented itself, Caroline embraced the challenge, ready to take her teaching to the next level.

Or at least, that's what Amazing Annie had planned. Because just as quickly, Inadequate Irene swooped in with self-doubt: "What if you fail? What if you can't do it? Maybe you should just stop now before you embarrass yourself."

And suddenly, her once steady rhythm faltered. For two weeks, the momentum stopped. Her study notes disappeared from sight. The final exam loomed, untouched. The rhythm of her life, the energy, the passion, the drive, slowed to an uneasy pause. But then something shifted. Amazing Annie had had enough.

"Are you really going to let all your work go to waste?"

That was the wake-up call Caroline needed. She picked up her books, put in the work, and passed the final exam with first class honors. But more importantly, she had won something even greater; the power to silence doubt, to reclaim the rhythm of her life, and to teach her students to do the same.

As an educator, she now recognizes the offbeat moments in her students, the hesitation before playing a new piece, the frustration of getting a rhythm wrong, the self-doubt that makes them afraid to try.

And she knows exactly how to guide them through. She reminds them, as she reminded herself:

Growth happens when we push past doubt.

Confidence is built through perseverance.

Success is a rhythm, a pulse we create with every step forward.

Of course, struggles don't magically disappear. Life brings heartbreak, setbacks, and challenges that can make even the strongest among us feel like quitting.

But Caroline refuses to let fear disrupt the rhythm of her life. She continues to rise, teaching with a heart full of gratitude, faith, and resilience. And when doubt creeps back in, she turns to the tools that keep her grounded: prayer, music, movement, and rest. Because she knows one undeniable truth: the voice we choose to listen to determines our path, and the rhythm we embrace defines our future. And Caroline? She chooses Amazing Annie every time.

Read Caroline 's inspiring story in *The Power of WHY Musicians 5 Book Series.*

YOUR RHYTHM

Our mind and body have natural rhythm whether we are looking for it or not. If we are not intentional with our rhythmic patterns it can cause stress in our lives and affect the outcome of our goals in both our personal and professional lives. As you turn your attention to the rhythm of your life, you can create a positive rhythm in three areas:

First: Rhythm of Physical Activity

Rhythm of Physical Activity (easier said than done, I know), as we always seem to put other things and other people ahead of ourselves. The balance is to put the rhythm of daily active movement into your schedule, so you are not staying motionless and bored, but also not overstimulating your movement to leave you exhausted and drained, putting things off for yet another day.

Plan your daily movement (walk, stretching, etc.) to create the rhythm of your physical activity. When I implemented the rhythm of physical activity into my life, not only did I feel better physically and mentally, but it led me to run a marathon and learn the rhythm of breathing as my rhythm of running. Just do it.

Second: Rhythm of Routine

Rhythm of Routine (this was a game-changer for me), as we create a rhythm of morning, evening and sleep routine, our body clock adjusts to help us feel more prepared for our daily activities.

Routines can help you find comfort, creativity and productivity in having a daily rhythm of familiarity, including your personal "you time", to relax without guilt, but rather to enjoy the rhythm of life's activities.

When I implemented the rhythm of routine into my life, my productivity in teaching, writing and business was elevated while my enjoyment in personal "me time" became a zone of freedom as my rhythm of routine was working.

Third: Rhythm of Adjustment

Rhythm of Adjustment (understanding free rhythm was my key to overcoming the overwhelm). Life naturally comes with shifts in our plans, responsibilities, and unexpected changes that can throw our rhythm off meter, often leaving us feeling overwhelmed. Recognize that your rhythm of activity and routine may sometimes change.

This is part of embracing a flexible rhythm of creativity, intentionally designed so you can feel guilt-free, fulfilled, and joyful as you live freely with purpose.

When I embraced this flexible approach in my life, I started seeing the bigger picture differently. What mattered most was smoothly integrating rhythms of activity and routine into my daily life, while allowing flexibility to help me achieve my goals successfully with joy, passion, and purpose.

⌒ *Fermata* (Pause to Ponder): Three Steps to Harmonize Your Life Rhythm

The Life Rhythm you choose to live will determine your success in sharing your purpose of music education and leaving your mark in the world. Your decisions will impact not only your life, but the lives of your students - the future of music education and continued exploration of the creativity of music.

Step #1 Start with Rhythm in Teaching.

Connect with your students by exploring the aspects of rhythmic conversations. Play the rhythmic conversation game with creativity and variation.

Open the door of rhythmic diversity to explore simple, compound, hybrid and free rhythm.

How can you use percussion instruments to be a more creative educator?

_____

_____

What rhythmic techniques can you implement for greater connection in communication?

_____

_____

How can you encourage students to explore body percussion in learning rhythm?

_____

_____

Step #2 Write down 3 ways you can introduce rhythmic diversity.

Your role as a purpose driven educator is to ignite curiosity in exploring new music and new elements of rhythmic diversity into your music teaching business.

To keep students engaged, excited about learning from you and entertaining the idea of possibilities, your openness to learning will be contagious in creating lifelong learners in your students too.

What can you do to implement rhythmic diversity into each lesson?

_____

_____

How do you want to create space for body percussion as part of your lessons?

_____

_____

How can you teach rhythm differently and teach different rhythms?

_____

_____

Step #3 Commit to your positive rhythm.

Successful music teachers focus on a commitment to themselves first. Commit to your own positive rhythm for a happy and successful teaching business. Ultimate Music Teachers who decide to implement proven systems and strategies are one step closer to their goal.

How can you commit to your rhythm of physical activity?

_____

_____

How will you implement your rhythm of routine and productivity?

_____

_____

What can you do to accept the rhythm of adjustment and avoid overwhelm?

_____

_____

"The capacity to learn is a gift; the ability to learn is a skill; the willingness to learn is a choice."

~ Brian Herbert

Your rhythm is the key to shining brightly as a music educator. Your dedication to learning, refining your skillset, and embracing new ideas from simple steps to complex connections distinguishes you as a passionate, purpose-driven educator.

Through this rhythm, you'll create harmony between teaching and personal growth, inspiring your students not just in music, but in life's grand composition. As you continue your journey, carry these lessons close to your heart.

Embrace each beat, each challenge, and each triumph and let them guide you toward becoming an Ultimate Music Teacher, one note at a time.

♪ Your Coda Notes ♪

The 12 Key Strategies include online Ultimate Music Teachers Bonus Resources.

TEACH MUSIC CHANGE LIVES
Simple Steps to Compound Connection

Dive deeper into **KEY STRATEGY #5** - get your
Ultimate Music Teachers
FREE Bonus Workbook to find your unique rhythm for
growth and impact.
Go To: UltimateMusicTeachers.com/guide

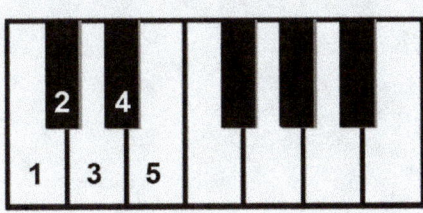

Key Strategy #6
ENGAGE IN THE COOPERATIVE LEARNING THEORY
Tempo

"In the symphony of learning, honor the unique tempo of each student's journey, for in their rhythm lies the melody of progress."

~ Glory St. Germain

Have you ever looked at your to-do list and thought, *what tempo do I need today just to survive this rhythm section of life?* Or taught a lesson where every student moved at their own speed, some racing ahead, others barely finding the beat?

Teaching often feels like conducting an orchestra where half the students are sight-reading, one's still tuning, and someone just discovered the triangle (and is now playing it with the enthusiasm of a rockstar who thinks it's a drum kit).

But here's the truth: the goal isn't getting everyone to match pace. It's learning to honor and harness each student's unique tempo and create a Tempo of Positivity.

My own life tempo? Always set to *presto*. Between raising five children (each with their own tempo), managing my husband's performances, growing my studio, and leading music teacher communities, it often felt like I was improvising through unexpected key changes at lightning speed. Some days were a perfectly timed orchestral masterpiece; others… well, let's call them "jazz."

And yet, I wouldn't have it any other way. Yes, there were times I wished for *adagio* to slow things down or longed for *accelerando* when things felt stuck. But I've learned that the magic lies not in controlling the tempo, but in embracing the one we choose and adjusting when needed. That's where Cooperative Learning Theory comes in. It's about being coachable and staying open to learning new ways of teaching.

THE COOPERATIVE LEARNING THEORY

The Cooperative Learning Theory is a transformative approach to education and especially powerful in music teaching. At its core, it recognizes that learning is not just an individual pursuit, but a collaborative adventure.

When students engage in group activities where each member contributes and learns from others, a sense of belonging and self-esteem is activated. In this community of connections, students feel valued, seen, and empowered and their confidence and motivation soar.

When students collaborate, whether in a group performance or a theory exercise, they're not just learning notes and rhythms. They're learning to listen, respond, adapt, and appreciate diverse perspectives, developing essential musical and interpersonal skills that extend far beyond the classroom.

Incorporating the Cooperative Learning Theory beautifully aligns with the *Tempo of Positivity* philosophy. Group learning environments encourage risk-taking, creativity, and resilience, while providing a safe, supportive space to grow.

Mistakes become opportunities. Progress becomes a shared celebration. And every student contributes a vital note to the grand symphony of learning.

In a music teaching business, this collaborative approach offers profound benefits. It differentiates you from solo-focused studios, enhances student retention, and builds your reputation as a leader in inclusive, joyful education. Parents and students are drawn to environments where education feels holistic, dynamic, and welcoming.

When you combine Cooperative Learning with a Tempo of Positivity, you create a studio culture where learning becomes a communal and enriching journey, and your students thrive in ways that traditional models can't always achieve.

A Brief History

While small-group learning has existed for centuries, the Cooperative Learning Theory was deeply researched in the early 1920s by American philosopher John Dewey and later expanded by social psychologists like David and Roger Johnson of the Cooperative Learning Institute.

Their research showed that students who learn together through collaboration rather than competition develop greater academic, social, and emotional strengths.

Internationally recognized educator Guy Duckworth identified five key dimensions of growth that flourish in a cooperative learning environment:

The 5 Student Benefits of Cooperative Learning

1. Membership - Belonging to a group enhances well-being and motivation. In a UMT Group Theory Club Class, every student, whether they've played for five months or five years, starts on an equal foundation, building theory skills together.

2. Positive Influence - Students learn the power of encouragement, support, and leadership. They grow not only through personal effort, but by inspiring one another, developing communication skills through face-to-face interaction and group problem-solving.

3. Feelings - As students gain confidence, they express themselves more freely. Positive interdependence flourishes: when one student succeeds, everyone celebrates and when one struggles, the group lifts them up.

4. Embracing Differences - In a group setting, differences aren't obstacles, they are strengths. Students recognize and value diverse experiences, perspectives, and skills, building emotional intelligence, respect, and teamwork.

5. Productivity - Learning as a group often accelerates individual progress. Students master material more quickly, complete more work, and develop high-level reasoning and problem-solving strategies that prepare them for performance, examinations, and life-long musicianship.

Why it matters? In 1982, the International Society for Music Education stated:

"Group teaching can create a musical environment where good learning may exceed what is possible in individual instruction. A group supports, motivates, and challenges students through collective decision-making, critical listening, and performing together."

In your UMT Club Class, Cooperative Learning nurtures leadership, collaboration, creativity, and resilience. It builds a musical family, strengthens the spirit of your studio, and empowers every student to reach their full potential.

Teaching in a cooperative environment is a method and a mission. It's how we connect, how we inspire, and how we create the next generation of confident, compassionate musicians.

Today, I implement the cooperative learning theory, choose the tempo of my life and set it with intention. That's the beauty of being a music educator and an entrepreneur. We get to decide when to go slow, when to speed up, and when to pause for breath. At first, we may move at *adagio*, unsure and cautious. But with confidence and clarity, we step into our *allegro*, a tempo that fuels our passion, our purpose, and our growth.

In music, tempo sets the pace from tranquil *lento* to energetic *presto*. It's the heartbeat that guides both musicians and listeners through each phrase and movement. In life and teaching, it's the rhythm with which we move, learn, and grow. And when we apply that tempo to our teaching style, especially through the lens of cooperative learning, we begin to guide our students with greater empathy, energy, and effectiveness.

Elizabeth Pérez-Hickman (affectionately known as Eli), a Venezuelan-American oboist, embodies the transformative power of music education through her remarkable journey. Deeply influenced by her Venezuelan roots and the El Sistema USA® inspired Miami Music Project, Eli's story beautifully illustrates how music programs can profoundly change lives.

Born and raised in Miami, Florida, Elizabeth's early exposure to music began with piano lessons. Financial challenges, however, abruptly ended those initial lessons, but they serendipitously led her family to discover the Miami Music Project, a free program inspired by Venezuela's El Sistema. Here, Elizabeth began playing the violin and spent five enriching years developing her musical foundation. Yet, her true passion ignited when she switched to the oboe, an instrument she connected with deeply.

Programs like the Miami Music Project became pivotal in shaping Elizabeth's future, providing her with opportunities that would have otherwise remained unattainable. With their support, she attended the New World School of the Arts, followed by the prestigious Interlochen Arts Academy, where her tuition was fully covered by scholarships from the Miami Music Project. Her path continued to unfold with a full scholarship to the Peabody Institute in partnership with El Sistema USA®, demonstrating the profound impact these programs had on her life.

Elizabeth's dedication and talent took her to iconic venues such as the Walt Disney Concert Hall and the Hollywood Bowl, experiences she describes as life-changing. She was especially influenced by performing under the baton of Venezuelan conductor Gustavo Dudamel. These moments solidified her conviction that music was indeed her life's calling.

Additionally, winning NPR's Jack Kent Cooke Young Artist Award allowed her to purchase her first professional oboe and essential reed-making tools, affirming her family's faith in her career choice.

Recognizing her role as a Latina woman in the predominantly white male field of classical music, Elizabeth actively champions diversity. She purposefully includes works by underrepresented composers in her performances, ensuring minority voices are amplified. Her commitment extends into teaching through Peabody's Tuned-In and the Do Re Mi Project, programs offering free music education and mentorship to young musicians from diverse backgrounds.

Elizabeth's dream is to inspire future generations, much like Dudamel inspired her, demonstrating that success is possible regardless of background or financial circumstance. She passionately believes music should be accessible to everyone, emphasizing community and collaboration as central to her cultural and musical ethos.

For Elizabeth, music transcends performance, it's about meaningful connection and transforming lives. Experiences performing in rehabilitation centers and homeless shelters profoundly shifted her perspective from perfectionism to gratitude, realizing music's power to offer comfort and healing.

Elizabeth is deeply committed to continuing her dual passions of performing and educating, dedicated to using music as a tool for positive change.

Elizabeth Pérez-Hickman's story is a vibrant testament to the powerful impact music education can have, reminding us that when we teach music, we truly change lives.

To learn more about how the *Teach Music Change Lives* book project supports the El Sistema USA® inspired programs, see the Giving Back with Gratitude section at the back of the book.

Elizabeth's inspiring journey exemplifies exactly how tempo and cooperative learning can beautifully shape lives. Her experience reveals the power of inclusive music education to not only transform individuals but entire communities, instill confidence, passion, and joy.

Elizabeth's dedication reinforces an essential truth I've embraced throughout my career - yes, education is about learning but when that learning is infused with fun and community, it becomes powerful.

That belief is why I became a teacher and later, a course creator. I've seen firsthand that when students are having fun, their minds open and they learn faster, deeper and with greater joy.

Fun is a bridge that transforms traditional methods into dynamic experiences that educate *and* inspire.

This new tempo of teaching shaped everything I now do, from student lessons to training educators worldwide. This sparked a true paradigm shift in how I define success in my teaching business.

Four Paradigm Shifts That Will Change Your Music Business Right Now

Once I understood the possibilities of emphasizing music theory through our UMT Certified Teachers Program, everything changed.

1. Music Theory Isn't the Problem; It's the Key to Unlocking Your Teaching Magic.

When taught with creativity and energy, music theory transforms from intimidating to illuminating. It becomes a language of expression that brings music to life for you and your students. The real magic? It rekindles your love for teaching and ignites your students' passion for learning.

2. Teaching Music Theory Makes You a More Resilient Business Owner.

For entrepreneurial educators, music theory is an academic business builder. By creating Ultimate Music Theory Club Classes, you have introduced an income stream that doesn't add teaching hours but adds value, retention, and revenue. It's a strategic move toward financial growth and flexibility.

3. Music Theory Helps You Stand Out in a Competitive Market.

In a world of talented teachers, theory is your secret edge. It positions you as a well-rounded educator who teaches not only how to play music, but how to understand it. And the best part? Music theory is inclusive of all instruments and voices, so students of all disciplines can learn together in one class, building community and confidence.

4. Music Theory Deepens Your Musical Journey.

More than a teaching tool, theory deepens your personal connection to music. It expands the joy, purpose, and beauty of what we do every day. When we teach music theory, we add to our lessons and elevate the soul of music itself. Becoming an Ultimate Music Teacher means you inspire transformation.

The Tempo of Positivity

Operating from a foundation of service, infusing every endeavor with a tempo of positivity is crucial. Whether it's the early inklings of an ambitious goal, the desire to make a meaningful impact, the vision to develop transformative courses, or the pursuit of enhancing teaching efficacy to elevate your practice, let that energy shine brightly.

Teaching efficacy leads to better student outcomes, more confidence, and creative problem-solving in the music lesson.

Teaching efficacy isn't about being perfect; it's about believing you can make a difference and having the tools to do it with purpose.

It's about harnessing the right mindset, strategies, and tools to not only expand your teaching business but also enrich lives through the power of music education. The tempo at which we teach, conduct our business, and live our lives is instrumental in charting the course to our goals. It's this chosen pace, this deliberate cadence of action and thought, that steers us towards the fulfillment of our aspirations.

What's Possible When Teaching a Student Who Is Blind and Autistic? Two Words: Kodi Lee.

When we first think about the challenges of teaching a student who is blind and autistic, we might wonder, is it even possible? The answer, as the world discovered in 2019, is a resounding *Heck Yeah*. You may recognize the name Kodi Lee, the incredible blind and autistic singer-pianist who captured hearts around the globe with his breathtaking performances on *America's Got Talent*. But behind Kodi's brilliant performances is another star you might not know: his remarkable piano teacher, Yiyi Ku.

Yiyi Ku, a professional pianist and founder of the Yiyi Ku Music Studio in Murrieta, California, has taught students of all ages and levels including prodigies like Kodi Lee.
Starting in 2016, Yiyi nurtured Kodi's extraordinary gift, navigating challenges that would make many teachers shy away. Teaching a musical savant like Kodi, with an astonishing memory and the ability to hear and instantly replicate music, is no small feat. Yet Yiyi rose to the occasion with patience, innovation, and unconditional love.

The Challenges

- **Teaching correct fingering to a student who couldn't rely on sight.**

- **Guiding arm and wrist movement entirely through touch, sound, and trust.**

- **Building flexibility while honoring Kodi's unique learning style.**

Through it all, Yiyi emphasized one thing: connection first. Music was their common language.

The Rewards

- **Kodi won First Prize at the Golden Classical International Music Awards.**

- **Kodi performed at Carnegie Hall.**

- **Kodi captivated the world on the biggest stage at America's Got Talent and reminded us all of music's power to heal, connect, and uplift.**

When I interviewed Yiyi Ku, she shared the Five Foundations of her Teaching Philosophy, principles that helped Kodi soar and can inspire every one of us as music educators.

1.   **Patience: Meet students where they are.**

2.   **Trust: Build a relationship first, technique comes after.**

3.   **Creativity: There is no "one size fits all" method.**

4.   **Commitment: Growth takes consistency and heart.**

5.   **Joy: Celebrate every step, every note, every breakthrough.**

Music is about connection. Yiyi's devotion to her students reminds us that great teaching isn't measured by how fast someone learns, it's measured by how deeply they believe in themselves because you believed in them first.

Yiyi so beautifully said:

"As the world will once again be moved by the power of music, love that is unconditional, and genius that is our one and only Kodi Lee."

One teacher. One student. One moment of belief that changed everything. The power of teaching is the power to change lives. And when you teach music—you change lives.

Teaching, at its highest level, is about passion, patience, and the tempo of positivity we bring into every lesson. Whether we are guiding a musical savant to the world stage or encouraging a shy beginner to play their first scale, the rhythm we set matters.

Teach Music. Change Lives.

Building intellectual, social, and emotional rhythms into your studio enhances your students' experiences and accelerates your Tempo of Positivity. This new rhythm uplifts your spirit, energizes your students, and drives the profitability and sustainability of your music teaching business. It's about harmonizing your passion for teaching with savvy business acumen, turning your love of music into a lasting legacy.

What is Savvy Business Acumen?

Savvy Business Acumen is your secret superpower. It means having perceptive insight into the world of business, combined with the wisdom to make strategic, profitable decisions in your teaching journey.

It's about leadership, vision, and impact.

Here are the **Seven Key Qualities** that make up your teaching business brilliance:

1. **Knowledgeable:**
    You're well-informed about the fundamentals of your business from marketing and finance to strategy and operations. You don't need an MBA, you need a clear map and a willingness to learn.

2. **Strategic Thinking:**
    You don't just plan for today, you look ahead. You anticipate opportunities, prepare for challenges, and make decisions that align with your long-term vision.

3. **Problem-Solving Skills:**
    You spot issues early, pivot fast, and find creative, efficient solutions. When something's not working, you problem-solve with purpose.

4. **Adaptability:**
    Markets change. Students change. Life changes. Your superpower? Adjusting with grace, trying new approaches, and staying relevant without losing your rhythm.

5. **Financial Literacy:**
    You understand your numbers. You know how to budget, price, invest, and make decisions that grow your business and protect your peace.

6. **People Skills:**
    Whether you're leading a team, teaching a group class, or connecting with parents, you communicate with clarity, compassion, and confidence. People don't just learn from you, they trust you.

7. **Understanding and Applying Educational Theories:**
    When you apply models like the Cooperative Learning Theory, you're teaching and leading innovation. You elevate both your pedagogy and your profitability.

Being an **Ultimate Music Teacher** means cultivating these qualities as part of your rhythm.

You are mastering the art of teaching music and conducting a symphony of success in your life and business.

Let your Tempo of Positivity lead the way and watch your music teaching business soar in perfect harmony.

VAK LEARNING STYLES - Visual, Auditory and Kinesthetic

Do you know your own Learning Style? Can you identify each of your students' Learning Styles? That may be a bit of a challenge.

How can you incorporate theory easily into a private lesson or group setting so that students of all Learning Styles get it?

Each student has a unique preference of learning and retaining knowledge. As teachers, we must address the individual and collective needs of each student in our class and understand how each student learns best.

The *Ultimate Music Theory* materials are highly effective because they align with all three learning styles: Visual, Auditory, and Kinesthetic (VAK). Understanding these learning styles allows us to communicate concepts clearly and engage students more successfully by matching their preferred method of receiving information.

Identifying Learning Styles – Visual, Auditory and Kinesthetic

Have you ever noticed how you connect instantly with some students because you just seem to speak the same language, and they simply get everything and with other students you struggle to connect with them?

The reason is that we learn in three different ways.

The Visual Learner learns best through reading, seeing pictures and images. They appreciate well-organized print and visual materials and notice new things. If you are focusing on images and the written words, you just might be a Visual Learner.

The Auditory Learner learns best through listening. They respond to both verbal instructions and musical cues and often repeat what they have just learned. If you are focusing verbally and repeating key words in your head, you just might be an Auditory Learner.

The Kinesthetic Learner learns best by doing through body movement. They are active, often fidgety and always on the move. If you are writing down every word that you have read, while tapping your toes or bouncing a leg and you are already counting down the minutes until the coffee break, there is a good chance that you might be a Kinesthetic Learner.

So how can we best communicate and teach our students more effectively? By Matching their Learning Style.

Match the Visual Learner

Visual Learners prefer to see the information written in a workbook or on a whiteboard. They have a vivid imagination and absorb what they see better than what they hear. Each of the Ultimate Music Theory Workbooks is divided into 12 Lessons with a comprehensive review test at the end of each lesson that is cumulative: it reviews everything from the beginning of the book up to and including that lesson.

How can we match the Visual Learner? Before you even pick up a piece of music, ask "What do you see?" Can they see the Time Signature and identify it?

Visual Learners tend to link words such as Basic Beat with images such as the quarter notes and the scoops representing each beat. Can they see the Basic Beat? In 4/4 Time, can they see the 4 quarter note groups in each measure. Identify them. Use scoops. Before you play a piece of music, students should see the rhythm by looking at the notation, values and patterns of the notes and rests.

Hint: Visual Learners often have difficulty with memorization. Break the learning process into the elements of music by first seeing and then memorizing the rhythm using rhythm sticks. Using rhythm sticks will bring a fun element to the lesson. This will help them memorize the piece as they see the rhythm.

Match the Auditory Learner

Auditory Learners prefer to talk and hear the information. They have a good ear for singing and pay attention to how words sound rather than what they look like. After completion of each music theory lesson, use the exercises for Sight Reading and Ear Training to reinforce the theory concepts learned in each lesson.

How can we match the Auditory Learner? When you communicate with an auditory learner, talk about the piece before playing it.

Hint: Auditory Learners often have difficulty with reading the details such as pitch, rhythm or expression. Break the learning process into the elements of music. Talk about the rhythm. What will they see? Talk about the melody. What will they hear? Help them to see the rhythm and hear the melody before even picking up their instruments.

Match the Kinesthetic Learner

Kinesthetic Learners want to be doing things rather than watching and listening. They learn best by activity. So stand up, have fun and let your student be the teacher and use your large whiteboard with different colored markers to complete rhythm exercises.

How can we match the Kinesthetic Learner? When communicating with kinesthetic learners, engage students through hands-on activities, such as reviewing Note and Rest Values using the Ultimate Music Theory Chart in the UMT Prep 1 Workbook.

Hint: Kinesthetic Learners often have difficulty with sitting still when reading or listening to details during a lesson. Break the learning process into the elements of music by using the whiteboard and the different colored markers. Do whiteboard exercises while standing, your Kinesthetic Learner will learn better. Why? Because they will have their Thinking Feet on. Kinesthetic learners like to immediately play what has been discussed verbally. This will help them see the rhythm, hear the melody and feel the music.

Matching the VAK for focus will help the Visual Learner, Auditory Learner and Kinesthetic Learner stay on track and stay focused. Can you identify your own learning style now? Are you a Visual Learner, Auditory Learner or a Kinesthetic Learner? You may also be a combination of more than one. How can you gain a better assessment of which learning style suits your student best? Discover more about Learning Styles inside the Ultimate Music Teachers Resources.

When teaching group theory club classes, it's important to lay the foundation for successful learning and develop good habits. You can't "make students listen", "make them engage" or "make them want to learn". If you want to change their behavior, and that includes attitude and language patterns, you need to change your own. You need to match their VAK for focus and successful teaching and learning.

In fact, understanding learning styles is so important for elite educators, I included this training in our curriculum inside the Ultimate Music Theory Certification Course for teachers. Your purpose in running a successful music teaching business is to impact the lives of your students by providing them with the best possible music education. As a business owner, it is also important to understand that as a business, you need to know your numbers to maintain your passion-based teaching business.

Set the Tempo of Your Teaching Business

When running a music teaching business, you've got rhythm and options. It all starts with defining what works for you:

- **How many hours do you want to teach?**

- **How many students do you want in your studio?**

- **How many students return year after year?**

- **What are your payment policies?**

Decide on your fees for both private and group lessons. While prices may vary based on your location or market trends, always remember your value. You are a professional music educator. You're committed to your students, to your growth, and to the art of music education and that is worth recognizing (and charging for).

Next comes visibility. Market yourself. Be seen. Be heard. Be known. Whether you're connecting with fellow educators, parent groups, schools, or community programs, find where your ideal students are and show up with confidence. Decide what kind of education you want to offer such as exam prep, camps, recitals, festivals, composition, or auditions and structure your business accordingly. Will you charge by the lesson, or teach groups to boost your revenue without increasing your teaching time?

Here's the harmony: when you prepare materials for one class, you can repurpose them for a second (or third). That's not just teaching smarter, that's scaling your impact and doubling or tripling your income. Group teaching is a powerful rhythm, especially when paired with the Cooperative Learning Theory and a steady beat of SMART goal setting.

SMART Goals + Learning Styles = Business Brilliance

Embracing the Tempo of Positivity in both teaching and business starts with one thing: understanding the individual learning rhythms of your students. Just like a musician adjusts tempo to suit a piece, we can fine-tune our goals and strategies to match the pace of our students' growth. This is where SMART Goals come in.

SMART Goals are:

- **Specific** – What exactly do you want to achieve in your teaching business? (Think: number of students, teaching hours, monthly income)

- **Measurable** – How will you track your success? (Number of paying clients, hitting your income goals, rewarding yourself with a vacation or renovation.)

- **Attainable** – Has anyone done it before? (Find your role models, reach out, learn from their strategies, and replicate with rhythm)

- **Relevant** – Why does this goal matter? (How will it impact your life, your family, your students, and your legacy?)

- **Time-Bound** – What's your deadline? (How will you celebrate when you succeed and what happens if you don't follow through?)

Teaching with Intention = Results with Impact

At times, it may feel like you're carrying the weight of your students' struggles, unsure how to "fix" everything. But remember, progress starts with one step, and it begins with you. Understanding learning styles, emotional needs, and motivations is the first note. Implementing SMART Goals, both personally and professionally, is the chorus. When you model goal setting for yourself, you empower your students to set (and achieve) their own.

And here's the magic: When your students rise to the next level, so does your business.

YOUR ULTIMATE INVESTMENT IN YOURSELF

One of the most powerful investments a music teacher can make is the one they make in themselves. Why? Because when you grow, your students grow. When you engage in meaningful learning, you create meaningful teaching.

From the very beginning of my teaching journey, my mother instilled in me the value of NEPD. That mantra has become the cornerstone of my work. I've made it my mission to invest in my own growth so I can support music educators globally through our Ultimate Music Theory Certification Elite Educator Program.

There Are Two Key Elements That Impact The Success of Your Teaching

1.   Your Investment in Your Own Education

Investing in yourself keeps your skills sharp, your confidence high, and your creativity flowing. Whether it's learning a new strategy, exploring updated resources, or diving deeper into learning styles, it all begins with you.

NEPD is a celebration of your commitment to teach at the highest level. Each step you take to expand your knowledge elevates your studio, enriches your students, and amplifies your impact.

2.   Your Engagement with Your Students

Teaching is about creating connection through understanding your students' learning styles, identifying their goals, meeting them where they are, and guiding them in the way they learn best.

When you bring intention to your teaching and engagement to your lessons, learning becomes a transformation. Let this be your guiding rhythm and invest in your own education to elevate others.

"If a child can't learn the way we teach,
maybe we should teach the way they learn.

~ Ignacio Estrada

Case Study:
UMTC Elite Educator Thulane Akinjide-Obonyo

The words still echoed in his mind. "You can't count. You should just give up." At twelve years old, Thulane Akinjide-Obonyo found himself crying on a basketball court during Music Camp at Peterhouse School in Zimbabwe. Despite being the best recorder player in the country, it didn't matter. Not here. Not against "real" musicians.

Ridiculed and dismissed, Thulane felt like an outsider. But then, amidst the chatter and chaos, something shifted. He heard it, the deep, resonant groove of a contrabass saxophone. The sound was electrifying, commanding, unlike anything he had ever heard before. It awakened something within him.

From that moment, Thulane knew: he had to play the saxophone.

His father, however, had other plans. "Play the French Horn," he insisted. But Thulane didn't give up easily. He spent two years begging before his father finally relented. At fourteen, he picked up his first saxophone and the struggle began.

In high school, musicians weren't exactly respected. They were the punchlines of jokes, dismissed and underestimated. But Thulane didn't let that stop him. He practiced three times a day, pushing himself toward his goal: passing the Grade 8 ABRSM (Associated Board of the Royal Schools of Music) Examination.

Then, disaster struck.

His saxophone was stolen. Not just any saxophone. This was his saxophone, the one he had meticulously customized with the best mouthpieces, ligatures, and reeds. The one housed in a custom case from France, imported by his father.

And as if fate wasn't already testing him enough, Zimbabwe's land reform crisis escalated. ABRSM examiners stopped coming to the country. His dream of passing his Grade 8 exam? Impossible. Or was it?

How do you keep going when it feels like the world is against you? For Thulane, the answer was simple: you find your WHY, your tempo of positivity. He refused to let obstacles define his future. He kept pushing forward, reinventing himself, and expanding his skills.

When Thulane enrolled in our UMTC Elite Educator Program he said this: "Glory is constantly encouraging me to go forward and challenge myself to make things happen. The Ultimate Music Teachers Coaching Calls are the heartbeat of the program."

Today, Thulane Akinjide-Obonyo is a professional saxophonist, course creator, and saxophone coach living in Zimbabwe. He teaches students how to play the saxophone, unlocking the soul of jazz and traditional folk music so musicians can express themselves in the most authentic way possible.

Are you curious about what happened with his Grade 8 ABRSM examination?

Read Thulane's inspiring story in *The Power of WHY Musicians 5 Book Series*.

⌢ *Fermata* (Pause to Ponder): Three Steps to Elevate the Tempo of Positivity

By embracing a holistic approach to teaching and weaving the principles of the Cooperative Learning Theory into the core of your educational philosophy, you naturally elevate the Tempo of Positivity in both your students' experiences and your own life as a teacher.

Step #1 Start with Tempo in Attitude.

Your attitude shapes your perspective and sets the tempo for every action and decision in your life. In teaching, just like in music, the tempo can vary. Sometimes a quick decision is necessary, while at other times, a more measured, thoughtful approach is beneficial.

No matter the speed, creating a sense of Membership and belonging for every student elevates the atmosphere of learning and joy. When students feel they are a valued part of the group, their motivation, engagement, and musical progress naturally accelerate.

How can you shift your attitude to create a stronger sense of belonging and support in your studio?

_____

_____

What specific cooperative learning strategies can you introduce to foster a positive and inclusive environment?

_____

_____

In what ways can you inspire your students to feel seen, heard, and connected, enriching the tempo and spirit of their learning journey?

_____

_____

Step #2 Write down 3 Ways to Integrate the Cooperative Learning Theory of Positivity.

As an Ultimate Music Teacher, your role transcends teaching notes and celebrating performances. It's about building a space where Positive Influence and Embracing Differences flourish and where collaboration, creativity, and resilience are daily practices.

We are instructors and leaders of possibility, turning challenges into opportunities and cultivating musical communities where every voice matters.

What specific strategies can you implement to encourage student collaboration, leadership, and creativity in your lessons?

_____

_____

How can you transform challenging or negative situations into opportunities for deeper group connection and shared success?

_____

_____

In what ways can you adjust the learning environment to better celebrate individual strengths while promoting teamwork and group achievements?

_____

_____

Step #3 Communicate with Clarity of Purpose.

As purpose-driven educators, mastering the art of clear, heartfelt communication is essential. When instructions are confusing or overly complex, students can become disengaged or frustrated, slowing down the learning tempo.

Clear communication, grounded in a spirit of productivity and encouragement, ensures students stay motivated, focused, and excited to keep progressing toward their musical goals.

What strategies can you use to ensure your communication is clear, supportive, and action-driven for every learning style?

How will you express encouragement and clarity when students face challenges, guiding them with confidence and understanding?

In what ways can you inspire trust and open dialogue, helping students become active, motivated participants in their own learning journey?

"To play a wrong note is insignificant; to play without passion is inexcusable."

~ Ludwig van Beethoven

Communicating with Clarity of Purpose underscores the vital role of connection. Clear instructions enhance student understanding and engagement, directly influencing retention and business profitability.

This step emphasizes the need for educators to convey concepts concisely and empathetically, ensuring students are inspired, involved, and capable of following through with their learning tasks and transforming musical minds to play with passion.

Embrace this step as your call to action, transforming every lesson into an opportunity to profoundly impact your students' musical journey. Teach music. Change lives.

♪ Your Coda Notes ♪

The 12 Key Strategies include online Ultimate Music Teachers Bonus Resources.

TEACH MUSIC CHANGE LIVES

Engage in the Cooperative Learning Theory

Dive deeper into **KEY STRATEGY #6** - get your Ultimate Music Teachers
FREE Bonus Workbook to set the tempo for collaborative growth in your studio.

Go To: UltimateMusicTeachers.com/guide

 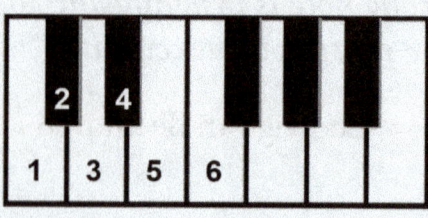 

Key Strategy #7
L-E-A-R-N TECHNIQUES FOR TEACHING MASTERY
Harmony

"Just as in music, the harmony in our lives can produce tension or foster a holistic resolution, leading to inner peace and a sense of purpose."

~ Glory St. Germain

Has music ever made you laugh? You might be thinking, "Glory, that's a weird question... music is supposed to be serious." Oh really? Then tell me why Looney Tunes and Tom & Jerry made us howl with laughter, thanks to the sheer brilliance of musical timing.

Imagine watching a comedy movie with no music. Awkward silence. No suspense before the punchline. No dramatic orchestral crash when someone trips over a banana peel. Not funny at all. But add the right music? Instant comedic genius.

- **The old-school drum roll dump-ti-dump-dump.**

- **The exaggerated "Wah-Wah-Waaaah" when something goes hilariously wrong.**

- **Or my personal favorite, those ridiculously over-the-top Disney villain harmonies that just scream "dramatic meltdown coming."**

It's the same with our work. I've been writing this book for three years (yes three years!). What's kept me consistently focused? Music. Specifically, "Focus Music" playing non-stop as I write. Today alone, over eleven hours straight, fueled by chocolate, coffee, and jazz hands. (Even Bach, composer of the famous *Coffee Cantata*, would suggest I take a coffee break right about now.)

Here's the real takeaway: harmony paired with humor unlocks engagement. Without them, teaching can feel as dry as a metronome stuck at 40 bpm. Add rhythm, laughter, and a few "fall-off-the-piano-bench" moments, and suddenly, your students are energized, engaged, and truly retain what you teach.

Now, it's your turn. What's one piece of music that's made you laugh? Maybe a clever musical with hilarious lyrics or a student-composed masterpiece about their dog eating their homework performed in a minor key for maximum dramatic effect (10/10 for creativity). Music isn't always serious; it's about expression, joy, and creating moments that make you laugh so hard you almost need a new chair.

As we L-E-A-R-N with harmony and humor, we master the art of teaching in ways that are delightfully unforgettable. In music, harmony is the art of combining different notes to create something richer, fuller, and more alive.

In life and teaching, it's the same, blending structure with spontaneity, tension with resolution, and personality with purpose.

Teaching Mastery draws a beautiful parallel. Just as harmony shapes music, harmony shapes our relationships and inner peace. It influences our leadership, our classroom dynamics, and ultimately our success.

Harmony Has Two Elements

Dissonant Harmonies Think of this as a family road trip gone wrong. Minor seconds, tritones clashing, messy, unresolved. It's like trying to harmonize with someone singing half a step off key. (Or two kids fighting over the last juice box.) But dissonance, uncomfortable as it is, often leads to growth. It forces change. It paves the way for the most powerful breakthroughs.

Consonant Harmonies Major thirds, perfect fifths, the cozy Sunday morning of music. Everything just clicks. These relationships are where collaboration feels natural, create flow, peace, and pure synergy.

Moral of the story? Life, like music, is about balancing tension and release. And if all else fails throw in a Picardy third for a happy ending.

In the symphony of life:

- **Dissonance reflects the challenges that grow us.**
- **Consonance reflects the connections that ground us.**

Both are essential to crafting your masterpiece. As I created the Ultimate Music Theory Program, I encountered both kinds of harmony. In music and in the relationships, struggles, and triumphs that came with building a thriving business.

One of the fundamental truths of both teaching and entrepreneurship is that harmony supports the melody. It's what gives depth to our leadership, richness to our lessons, and momentum to learn new things.

Through my musical journey, life taught me 5 harmonic techniques to **L-E-A-R-N.**

The first technique to LEARN is L – Listen.

Listen to your inner voice. What makes your heart sing? What sets you apart as a teacher? Teaching music is about sharing your passion. When that inner nudge whispers, "How can I be a better teacher and communicator?" listen. What happens when your student doesn't practice or do their theory homework? Or shows up without any books or even worse, doesn't show up at all and eventually quits?

Now flip the perspective. Listen to your student. Really listen. What makes their heart sing? What kind of music are they passionate about? What lights them up musically? Students don't want what you teach, they want to connect to why you teach. That's where true engagement begins. Listen to your inner voice and listen to your student. Remember, we are inspiring musicians in the making, and we want real results.

Listen to music and compose music. Why should you express your story through music? Why teach students to compose? You understand that your creative abilities can be developed through effort and education. With the right mindset, your voice grows stronger and so does your artistry.

Your mindset shapes your music, your message, and your life. Shift the "I can't" to "I can." Will your composition be a masterpiece right away? Maybe not. But with openness to listen and learn, you will succeed.

The second technique to LEARN is E – Engage.

Engage your students with imagination, activities, and storytelling that captivate their curiosity. Because the brain doesn't pay attention to boring things. Over 50% of students quit music lessons within the first two years. Why? The number one reason: lack of interest. We only learn when we're interested, motivated, or bribed with snacks or dollar bills. (True story: My dad once paid me $1/hour to practice piano. Years later, when I earned my music degree, he asked if he could get his money back. I took him out for a father/daughter dinner instead.)

Teach intervals by connecting them to familiar melodies. Then let students imagine harmonic intervals beneath the melody. Engage them through creativity using ICE: Imagine, Compose and Explore.

Imagine your idea starting with a title, a melody, a lyric, or a single chord progression waiting to come alive.

Compose by capturing your idea while you play, sing, record, or notate it, whatever works for you.

Explore new ways to express your ideas, collaborate with others, stretch your creativity and share your music with the world.

Compose different things and compose things differently.

The third technique to LEARN is A – Articulate.

Articulate clearly the meaning and message of your communication. To create harmony in your relationships with students, one of the most important skills you can develop is the ability to articulate with clarity, creativity, and confidence. In communication, the meaning of the message is the response it elicits.

Clarity isn't just about what you say, it's about how it lands. In music, articulation gives notes their personality such as legato, staccato, accented, or smooth.

Imagine listening to the *Moonlight Sonata* played entirely staccato. (Yes, I felt your eyebrows rise.) The experience would be jarring and completely different from the mood Beethoven intended to convey. That's the power of articulation. It shapes perception and creates an emotional connection.

So how effective is your articulation in communicating with your students? When we teach, it's easy to feel overwhelmed. There's so much content to deliver, so many skills to build.

Sometimes it feels like we don't even know where to start. But here's the truth: it's not only about *what* we teach, it's about *how* we articulate it.

Music is a language, and every composer must decide what emotion, story, or message am I trying to convey? The articulation of your ideas through phrasing, dynamics, harmony, and form becomes the voice of your message. Are you composing just for yourself, or to connect with others?

The most impactful music connects first with the composer, then with the listener. That's how it's received, remembered, and felt.

The fourth technique to LEARN is R – Relate.

Relate knowledge to real-world relevance. When I first learned theory, I didn't retain it. Why? Because I didn't relate to it. What's the point of identifying a dominant 7th chord if you don't know what it does? Whether you're preparing for exams or simply teaching musicianship, students need to relate theory to application to hear it, feel it, and use it.

And how do we help them retain that knowledge? Mistakes. Real learning and retention come from making mistakes, and mistakes come from implementation. That's how you retain 90% of what you learn. Teach it.

In teaching, the only thing that really matters is results. Specifically, how well students relate to the content, retain the knowledge, and apply it to their musicianship.

Relate your musical ideas to the elements of composing expressed through melody, harmony, rhythm, and texture. Why does this matter? Because creativity never ends. And thank goodness; can you imagine if it did? (Yawn. Who's with me?)

One powerful tool to relate ideas meaningfully is storytelling. Storytelling allows you to connect with listeners through shared emotion and memorable experiences. It gives your music life.

Storytelling is learning.
Storytelling is expression.
Storytelling is your voice, made audible.

When listeners relate to your music, they'll hear the message, feel the emotion, and dance, cry, reflect, or rejoice, just as you intended.

This final technique can transform how you communicate and how you understand the harmony of teaching and learning.

The fifth technique to LEARN is N – NLP Neuro Linguistic Programming.

NLP Neuro Linguistic Programming is Neuro meaning how we think, Linguistic meaning how we communicate, and Programming meaning how we achieve results.

How can you become more than you are, a better musician, composer, educator, human? How can you help others reach their full potential? Goal setting isn't enough. In teaching and in life, we must help people focus not on what they don't want, but on what they do want. With Neuro Linguistic Programming you can help students build confidence, motivation, and long-lasting transformation. Inside the Ultimate Music Teachers Academy, you'll learn how to build rapport, match physiology, and work with the powerful mental filters that shape learning and behavior.

"It's not what you get, it's what you become."

~Jim Rohn

NLP techniques have transformed the harmony in my life and in my teaching. I remember attending a week-long NLP training in Chicago and hearing Dr. Wyatt Woodsmall, co-founder of the International NLP Trainers Association, speak on "learning how to learn." Fueled by coffee, diet coke, bananas, peanut butter, and chocolate (of course), I didn't want to sleep, I just wanted to learn. I could hardly contain my excitement as I discovered new ways to communicate, think, and connect more effectively.

As I continued my training and became a certified NLP Practitioner, specializing in teaching and communication, I began to see real change in my students. When I "spoke their language" honoring their learning styles, adjusting my approach, and teaching with intention, they began to shine brightly.

Let me share a personal story. My husband had Parkinson's disease and often spent his days in his recliner watching TV. When I asked, "How are you feeling?" he'd often say, "I'm tired" or "I didn't sleep well."

But one day, instead of asking how he felt, I asked, "What was your favorite part of our trip to Disney World with the kids?" His eyes lit up. He told stories about the rides, the beach, and the matching Disney outfits. Just by changing the question, I changed his emotional state. That's the power of NLP.

Ask different questions and ask questions differently. It can shift everything. NLP is a holistic methodology that helps you become a masterful, intentional communicator. It teaches you how to set SMART goals and how to coach students through them successfully. In this fast-paced, ever-changing world of technology, one thing hasn't changed; the need for real human connection. For communication that's clear, authentic, and effective.

Our students are the future generation of musicians and teachers. It's our job to help them not just learn music, but learn *how to learn*, and how to connect.

In communication:

- **WORDS = 7%**
- **TONALITY = 38%**
- **PHYSIOLOGY = 55%**

It's not *what* you teach. It's *how* you teach that creates the magic to **L-E-A-R-N.**

Listen to your inner voice and your students. Be harmonious. (Unless your inner voice is telling you to break into an operatic solo mid-lesson, then maybe rethink that one.)

Engage in exciting ways to educate. Be aware. (Because if your students start blinking in Morse code for help, your lesson might need a tempo change.)

Articulate in a clear, creative, and concise way. Be fun. (If your explanation requires a flowchart, a PowerPoint, and a decoder ring, it's time to simplify.)

Relate and retain music theory knowledge with practical application. Be bold. (Yes, even if that means explaining modes using pizza slices. Whatever works, right?)

NLP techniques help you communicate effectively. Be inspiring. (Because if your student's learning style is "hands-on," but you're lecturing for an hour, you've just narrated a very long, very silent movie.)

Music Business Mastery and The Power of Mnemonics

You are an inspirational leader. You are the one students believe in. You are the educator who helps them feel better about their place in the world. And you have the superpower to change the harmony of relationships and help your students take significant steps toward their purpose-driven dreams.

To thrive in your music teaching business, you must create harmony in both your teaching techniques and your business strategies. One of the powerful teaching tools we use inside the Ultimate Music Theory Workbook Program is Mnemonics; clever memory devices that help learners recall and retain information with ease. These techniques can be applied in both educational and business settings to boost memory, create connections, and build a memorable brand.

Here are the 9 Types of Mnemonics for Better Memory:

1. Image Mnemonics

In Teaching, image mnemonics use visual representations to help students remember information more effectively, especially visual learners. In music theory, we use these to make concepts more interactive and memorable.

Take intervals, for example:

A harmonic interval is written with one note above the other, played together to create harmony. Picture the letter H as two vertical lines with a horizontal bar between them. The image mnemonic for "Harmonic Intervals." H = Harmonic Interval (notes stacked, played together).

A melodic interval is written with one note beside the other, played one note after the other to create a melody. Now, picture the letter M, with two points side by side. The image mnemonic for "Melodic Intervals." M = Melodic Interval (notes side by side, played one after the other). These simple visuals make complex ideas click. Image mnemonics turn abstract theory into something students can see and remember.

In Business, the same concept applies to your studio branding. A consistent image like a keyboard, logo, mascot, or icon creates a visual hook for your audience. It becomes a mnemonic device for your brand identity. Use memorable visuals across your website, print materials, and social media.

Whether it's a stylized music note, a piano bench with flair, or a fun logo your students can point to and say, "That's MY studio". Visuals anchor your brand in your audience's mind.

The Result? When you use image mnemonics in both your teaching and marketing, you're not just helping students remember music theory, you're helping clients remember you. That's brand retention, teaching effectiveness, and music business mastery all in one.

2. Connection Mnemonics

In Teaching, connection mnemonics help students link new information to something they already know, making learning more relatable and easier to remember.

For example, in music theory, you might compare a rhythm pattern to something familiar, like the ticking of a clock or the beat of a favorite song. By creating associations with daily experiences, students connect the concept more deeply.

Inside the Ultimate Music Theory Games, we use Connection Mnemonics all the time. Playful memory devices like Harmony Hotel (one room above the other), and Melody Motel (one room beside the other), make learning intervals fun and sticky:

- **Harmony Hotel = Harmonic Intervals (two notes written one above the other, played together).**

- **Melody Motel = Melodic Intervals (two notes beside each other, played one after the other).**

These mini metaphors connect the music term to a vivid mental image, making it far more memorable than just definitions on a page.

In Business, connection mnemonics also work wonders in branding. When you connect your studio's message to something familiar like community, family, or fun, your audience remembers it.

Use brand associations intentionally: Your studio may remind people of a cozy coffee shop vibe or a high-energy concert stage. Create marketing cues that spark familiarity, like signature phrases, metaphors, or themes that reinforce your studio's identity.

The Result? Connection mnemonics turn your lessons and your business into something people feel connected to. And when they connect, they stay. That's music education magic in action.

3.   Name Mnemonics

In Teaching, name mnemonics use letters of a word to represent a list or sequence, making complex information easier to remember. In music theory, we use this method when teaching the Circle of Fifths. For example, the word BEAD helps students remember the order of the first four flats: Bb, Eb, Ab, Db. These are the first four major keys with flats, as introduced in the Ultimate Music Theory Basic Rudiments Workbook. By linking each flat to a letter in a familiar word, students are more likely to retain the pattern. Simple. Effective. Memorable.

In Business, you can also create name mnemonics to represent your brand's mission. Example: M.U.S.I.C. means Melodic Universe of Students and Instructors in Concert.

It suggests a beautiful blend of harmony between students and teachers, each playing their part in the symphony of learning. This name encapsulates unity, collaboration, and the magic of music education. In the universe of music, *everyone* has a role whether they're learning a new scale or guiding the next generation of performers.

The Result? A name mnemonic like M.U.S.I.C. resonates not just with the ears, but with the heart. It reminds us that our work as music educators is about creating a lasting impact through shared growth and inspiration. Now that's a name that sings.

4. Expression Mnemonics

In Teaching, expression mnemonics use fun, memorable phrases to help students recall important sequences, like the order of sharps and flats in music theory. Inside the Intermediate Rudiments Workbook, we teach students to remember the seven sharps using this sentence:

> Father Charles Goes Down And Ends Battle.
> And when reversed, it becomes the order of flats:
> Battle Ends And Down Goes Charles Father.

This clever wordplay helps students recall key signatures as they appear on the staff and in the Circle of Fifths. It's simple, rhythmic, and it works.

In Business, expression mnemonics aren't just for students, they're an amazing tool for teachers, too. You can use them to make your mission, values, and goals *stick* in people's minds. Here's an example of a music teaching business statement:

"Our mission is to empower musicians with innovative tools and comprehensive education, fostering a community where every note counts and every student resonates success."

Now turn that into a mnemonic:

N.O.T.E.S. Nurture. Outreach. Tools. Education. Success.

Nurture: Support the growth and confidence of every music student.
Outreach: Extend your impact into your greater community.
Tools: Provide the resources that simplify and amplify learning.
Education: Deliver meaningful, engaging, results-driven instruction.
Success: Celebrate student progress and parent satisfaction every step
of the way.

The Result? This expression mnemonic doesn't just summarize your
business; it sings your purpose. It becomes a guiding principle, a
marketing message, and a memory anchor for your mission to enrich
lives through music education.

5.   Spelling Mnemonics

In Teaching, spelling mnemonics use word structure to reinforce
memory. This is particularly helpful when learning new theory terms.
In the Ultimate Music Theory Intermediate Rudiments level, students
are introduced to the concept of diminished intervals, which are one
semitone (or half step) smaller than a minor or perfect interval.

Here's where the spelling trick comes in:

Break the word into chunks, dim-in-ished. This helps anchor
the word in the brain and connect it to its musical meaning.
A diminished interval is abbreviated as dim, and in Advanced
Rudiments, students learn about diminished triads, which use the
diminished symbol: °. Now add a visual cue: imagine using the
symbol ° as the dot over the "i" in the word *diminished*. This clever
pairing of spelling and image mnemonics reinforces the concept, the
abbreviation, and the symbol all in one memorable trick.

In Business, spelling mnemonics can also enhance your brand
messaging and course clarity. By breaking down business terms
or program names into digestible parts, you create strong memory
anchors for your audience.

For example, when naming your studio packages or lesson
programs, you can spell out a meaningful word (like G.R.O.W.) and
align each letter with a benefit your students receive. This creates
clarity, adds emotional value, and makes your brand stand out. You
can also simplify technical language in your marketing by spelling

it out in everyday terms helping clients understand, connect, and say "yes" faster.

The Result? Students are learning a term, seeing it, spelling it, and understanding it from multiple angles. And in your business, spelling mnemonics help you communicate with clarity and creativity, making your offers easier to remember and your brand easier to love. It's clever and connection-building. And that's what great teaching and business is all about.

6.   Model Mnemonics

In Teaching, model mnemonics use visual representations like diagrams, shapes, or symbols to help students understand and remember key concepts. In the Ultimate Music Theory Intermediate Rudiments Workbook, we use the crescendo sign (<) as a model mnemonic to represent how intervals increase in size. Just like a crescendo increases volume, intervals can expand by half steps.

Inside the crescendo model, students learn the relationships between:

- **dim → Per → Aug for intervals 1, 4, 5, and 8**

- **dim → min → Maj → Aug for intervals 2, 3, 6, and 7**

For example, a diminished 5th increases by one semitone to become a perfect 5th, then grows again to become an augmented 5th. Likewise, a diminished 3rd grows to a minor 3rd, then to a major 3rd, and finally to an augmented 3rd.

It's all visual, musical, and sequential, making it easier for students to recall at test time and apply in real-life playing. So-La Says: Diminished grows into augmented, just like a crescendo, building step by step.

In Business, model mnemonics can also be used to map out growth in your music business. By visually representing your client's journey, sales funnel, or teaching process, step by step, you help prospective clients see the transformation they'll experience.

Think of your business roadmap as a crescendo:
Start with a simple inquiry, build with consistent communication,

lead to enrollment, grow into long-term engagement. You can also model your own professional growth this way, tracking your progress from passion to profit, one intentional step at a time.

The Result? Model mnemonics connect abstract theory to concrete visuals helping students see the relationships, feel the progression, and remember with clarity. In business, they allow you to present your process or value visually, making it easier for clients to trust the journey and say yes to the experience you offer. Because when you make your message visible, you make your impact inevitable.

7.   Music Mnemonics

In Teaching, how do you remember the words to your favorite song? That's a music mnemonic in action and the same method can work wonders in music theory. One of the most classic examples? The ABC Song. You probably learned your alphabet by singing it and guess what? You can use the same trick to memorize the musical alphabet too.

Here's the Musical ABC Song: Sing the seven letters of the musical alphabet forwards and backwards, three times in a row, using the melody from the familiar alphabet song.

$$\text{♪ A B C D E F G, G F E D C B A, A B C D E F G, G F E D C B A,}$$
$$\text{(deep breath),}$$
$$\text{A B C D E F G, G F E D C B A ♪}$$

It's rhythmic, it's repetitive, and it works.

So-La Says: Sing the Musical Alphabet Song. Start moderato and sing with an accelerando all the way to prestissimo.

In Business, music mnemonics are also brilliant branding tools. By incorporating catchy musical phrases or jingles into your marketing (like a branded studio song or themed tagline), you create a memorable and emotional connection with your audience. You could even use a simple melody in your videos, welcome email, or group class intro to help students and parents instantly recognize your brand and hum it later. When your business has its own "theme song" (even if it's just a clever jingle or musical phrase), it elevates your brand from ordinary to unforgettable.

The Result? This fun little tune helps students quickly identify ledger line notes above and below the staff and builds their confidence in reading notation faster than you can say G-clef. And in your business, music mnemonics become memorable hooks that engage students, connect emotionally with clients, and set your studio apart in a noisy world. Because when your brand sounds like you, people remember it.

8.　Rhyme Mnemonics

In Teaching, one of the fastest ways to help students retain information is by putting it into a rhyme. That's the power of rhyme mnemonics, they turn facts into fun little poems that stick. You've likely heard the classic: "In 1492, Columbus sailed the ocean blue." A catchy rhyme, and boom you've memorized a date.

In music theory, we do something similar. To identify the space notes in the Treble Clef, we use: F A C E because it literally spells FACE. But let's be honest, learning the Bass Clef isn't always as intuitive.

BONUS. Joanne Barker, a graduate of the Ultimate Music Theory Certification Course and creator of UMT Games, took it one step further. She combined this rhyme mnemonic with a music mnemonic. FACE in the SPACE below the BASS.

It's catchy. It's clear. And it connects visual learning with verbal rhythm.

When teaching the space note names in the Bass Clef, beginning with the space below the bass staff, she paired the letter pattern with a melody from the *William Tell Overture*.

♪ F A C E G B D, F A C E G B D, F A C E G B D, F A C E G B D ♪

It's fun, fast, and wildly effective for helping students learn note names, especially those ledger lines that tend to trip people up.

In Business, rhyme mnemonics are also a secret weapon in your brand communication. Using playful phrases or alliteration in your studio name, course titles, or marketing slogans can make your business sound more approachable and much more memorable.

Here are three examples of rhyming business phrases:

- **"Teach it, Reach it, Repeat it."**
  Perfect for promoting mastery-based learning and student success.

- **"From Keys to Confidence."**
  A powerful phrase that highlights personal growth through music education.

- **"Make Music. Make Progress. Make Memories."**
  A heartfelt call to connection, celebration, and transformation.

Whether it's a tagline or a signature phrase rhyming language adds rhythm and personality to your messaging. And guess what? Clients remember clever. That's the magic of rhyme.

The Result? When you pair rhyme with rhythm, student retention soars and so does brand recall. It's a lyrical learning experience. And in your business, rhyme mnemonics create a friendly, fun identity that students and parents will remember long after the lesson ends. Because when your words have rhythm and rhyme, your message has staying power.

9. Note Organization Mnemonics

In Teaching, the way we organize information can either confuse students or unlock their memory. That's where Note Organization Mnemonics comes in.

At Ultimate Music Theory, we use visual tools like: Flashcards, Memory Notes, Square Boxes, and a Step-by-Step System. These aren't just design elements, they're memory devices.

Flashcards help learners to visually connect terms and definitions, and practice recall in preparation for exams. When students consistently see musical terms, notes, and rhythms formatted in clear, bite-sized chunks, the information sticks.

Square Boxes featured throughout the UMT Series are used to highlight key concepts, separate main ideas from supporting details, and visually organize steps in a process.

Each Rudiments Workbook includes 80 Music Theory Flashcards, offering structured repetition that transforms cramming into confident comprehension.

In Business, note organization mnemonics are just as powerful behind the scenes. Clear organization from lesson plans to marketing materials streamlines communication, boosts productivity, and builds client trust. Use simple visuals like icons, checklists, and summaries to make your resources easy to navigate. Organized information helps clients feel confident and connected and an organized workflow keeps your studio running smoothly and sustainably.

The Result? When notes are organized clearly, learning becomes easier and retention becomes natural. Structure becomes the silent partner in student success. And in your business, well-organized communication builds trust, clarity, and confidence. Because in music, and in entrepreneurship; it's what you present and how you present it that creates lasting harmony.

Mnemonic Devices Increase Recall

Research on the effectiveness of mnemonic devices, including a study published by Gerald R. Miller in 1967 at the University of Texas at El Paso, showed that using mnemonics can significantly boost memory retention and increase recall by up to 77%.

In music education, the power of mnemonics is especially profound. When students use memory tools consistently, their comprehension, confidence, and test results improve dramatically. For example, students who used structured mnemonics alongside their Ultimate Music Theory Exam and Answer Books (Set #1 and Set #2) achieved an average score of 92%.

Organized tools enhance results even further. The Ultimate Music Theory Flashcard System (powered by Brainscape) offers over 11,000 interactive flashcards aligned with every lesson across all UMT Workbook levels, from Beginner A, B, C, Prep 1, Prep 2, Basic, Intermediate through to Advanced Rudiments, Music History, and Music Trivia. Each flashcard reinforces learning through visual, auditory, and kinesthetic engagement, providing a seamless experience whether accessed on a computer, iPhone, iPad or any device. When students study with structured resources and powerful mnemonic strategies, mastery isn't just possible, it's inevitable.

Why implement Mnemonics and L-E-A-R-N the greatest lessons ever? So you can:

Listen to your heart. Compose with purpose to shift from confusion to clarity.

Educate yourself. Apply the ICE method to move from frustrating to flourishing.

Articulate clearly. Shift your mindset from scared to strategically savvy.

Relate to listeners. Connect to transform lives from overwhelm to opportunity.

NLP. Communicate with compassion to shift from conflict to connection.

"The life of inner peace, being harmonious and without stress, is the easiest type of existence."

~ Norman Vincent Peale

Case Study:
UMT Certified Teacher Kamara Hennessey

How much can a tiny hamster leave a lasting impact on a life? It turns out quite a lot, especially when that hamster is Skippy Rascal, a pint-sized ball of fur with an Olympic-level dedication to his exercise wheel. Every night, like clockwork, Skippy ran his noisy marathon, the steady squeak-squeak-squeak filling the room. But to six-year-old Marty, it wasn't noise, it was a lullaby. A rhythmic, comforting sound that signaled all was right in her little world.

When Kamara Hennessey, one of our Ultimate Music Theory Certified Teachers, finally gave in to her daughter's unrelenting pleas to get a pet hamster, she had no idea just how much this tiny creature would mean to her daughter or how Skippy Rascal would forever change Kamara's own musical journey.

Skippy lived in Marty's bedroom, where his nightly marathons on the squeaky exercise wheel became a comforting lullaby to her ears. She slept soundly, soothed by the rhythmic, familiar sound. For two years, Marty adored caring for her beloved pet.

One morning, however, everything changed. Marty woke up to find Skippy lying still in his cage. He had passed away in his sleep. Heartbroken and inconsolable, Marty was devastated. The next day, in an effort to ease her daughter's grief, Kamara suggested they write a song together as a tribute to Skippy. Sitting at the piano, they picked out a melody, note by note, as Marty hummed what she heard in her heart. Kamara wrote down the notes on manuscript paper, making a few small changes until Marty found exactly what she wanted.

The melody was playful and full of energy, eight measures long with upbeats in every two-measure phrase. Marty chose the perfect title: "My Skittish Hamster." Kamara added harmony, and together, they played back the song. Marty beamed, wiping away her tears.

She turned to her mother and said, "Thanks, Mom. I feel better." With a warm hug and a kiss, the melody of healing had begun. That song, born from the grief of a tiny loss, would take on an even deeper meaning just three years later, when Kamara experienced the unimaginable. Marty passed away at a young age, leaving behind a silence that no music could ever truly fill.

Among the keepsakes Kamara treasures is Marty's original handwritten composition, signed in her little daughter's handwriting, a forever melody in the pages of her Memory Album. A year after her daughter's passing, Kamara returned to teaching, leaning on the transformative power of music. That moment of composing together with Marty became the catalyst that redirected her energy as she began composing more, using music, poetry, and art as therapeutic outlets for her grief and healing.

Read Kamara's full story in *The Power of WHY Musicians 5 Book Series*.

Today, Kamara's compositions are often inspired by poetry, personal artwork, or the celebration of life's moments, both big and small. She is a Registered Music Teacher, Composer, UMT Certified Teacher, and Elite Educator, sharing her passion with students and guiding them to discover their own musical voices.

Become a Master Musician and Compose with Purpose

The fact that you're here, reading this book, shows that you are committed to growth, learning, and serving others through your teaching. That speaks volumes about you, your mindset, and your dedication to the power of music education.

We all have a unique journey, just like Kamara. Some days, our teaching feels like a perfectly harmonized sonata, other days, it's more of a free-form jazz session with no sheet music in sight. (Can I get an 'Amen' from my fellow music teachers?)

But here's the beautiful thing: just like in composition, the best teachers know how to blend structure with creativity, technique with heart, and discipline with joy.

The Power of WHY Musicians Book Series provides the precise process and techniques that successful music educators have used to turn their goals into thriving, profitable teaching businesses.

Now is the time to put your knowledge into action. Use what you've learned to elevate your teaching, inspire your students, and create a lasting legacy through music. Because in the symphony of life, teaching is more than instruction, it's about creating harmony, nurturing passion, and composing a future filled with possibilities.

Just as a well-composed piece of music balances tension with harmonious resolutions, so too does the art of teaching. It's a delicate dance of knowledge and empathy, where each note played resonates with the unique frequencies of our students' needs and aspirations.

When orchestrated with intention, this harmony not only cultivates a deep sense of inner peace but also elevates our teaching journey into something profoundly fulfilling. Harmony in music is an abstract concept and a practical guide. It teaches us how to resolve tension, create balance, and inspire transformation.

When we apply these same principles to teaching, we unlock a more holistic resolution, impactful growth, and rewarding experience for ourselves and for our students. The following action steps are your keys to unlocking this harmony, helping you create music and a legacy of learning and inspiration.

⌒ *Fermata* (Pause to Ponder): Three Steps to Create Harmony and Teaching Mastery

Mastery isn't merely a result of talent; it's cultivated through dedicated time, intense focus, and the application of knowledge. By implementing the L-E-A-R-N Techniques, and NLP you can transform these elements into tangible success in your business.

Step #1 Start with L-E-A-R-N Techniques in Your Teaching.

Discover how the L-E-A-R-N techniques can transform your teaching approach. By applying these techniques, you'll be able to teach more holistically and communicate with greater empathy, compassion, and understanding. Watch your teaching success soar.

How can you integrate the L-E-A-R-N techniques to enhance your holistic approach to education?

_____

_____

What harmonic systems can you implement to seamlessly blend elements and emotions in your music teaching?

_____

_____

What is your purpose in learning and teaching music, and how does this journey shape your identity as an Elite Educator?

_____

_____

Step #2 Write down 3 ways you can implement NLP and create holistic harmony.

As Ultimate Music Teachers, our goal is to cultivate a strong inner guiding system and a high level of self-awareness. By understanding learning styles and applying NLP, we unlock the potential to excel in unique ways. Mastery and uniqueness are integral to teaching excellence.

In what ways can you expand your vision and think through NLP to elevate your teaching for greater impact?

_____

_____

What beliefs or practices might you need to release (let go of), to fully embrace your mission in holistic teaching?

_____

_____

Envision the lasting impact of your teaching: How do you want your students to perceive you as a musical maestro and educator?

_____

_____

Step #3 Blend the harmony of composition, mnemonics and creativity in your music teaching business.

As an Ultimate Music Teacher, your unique ability lies in your irreplaceable approach to teaching. Your strategies and inspired creativity stem from your evolution as a purpose-driven educator.

In what ways can you utilize composition to enhance your students' self-expression and deepen their understanding of musical analysis and repertoire?

How can you employ creative mnemonics to simplify complex music theory concepts, making learning both easier and more memorable?

What innovative techniques or creative elements can you adopt as an Elite Educator to stay informed about the latest trends in music education?

"Music is a more potent instrument than any other for education, because rhythm and harmony find their way into the inward places of the soul."

~ Plato

As we reflect on the transformative journey of purpose-driven pedagogy, through the careful integration of the principles we've explored, from the harmonious blending of composition and mnemonics to the innovative use of NLP, we've laid the foundation for a resonant and balanced teaching experience.

This approach fosters mastery within us and our students, and nurtures deep, enduring connections that will echo through generations in the world of music education.

Remember, each note we teach and each concept we share contributes to a larger symphony of knowledge and passion.

As Ultimate Music Teachers, we're not only shaping the present but also composing a legacy that will resonate far into the future, creating ripples of inspiration and excellence in the ever-evolving tapestry of music education.

♪ Your Coda Notes ♪

The 12 Key Strategies include online Ultimate Music Teachers Bonus Resources.

TEACH MUSIC CHANGE LIVES

L-E-A-R-N Techniques for Teaching Mastery

Dive deeper into **KEY STRATEGY #7** - get your
Ultimate Music Teachers
FREE Bonus Workbook to create harmony in every
lesson with clarity and ease.

Go To: UltimateMusicTeachers.com/guide

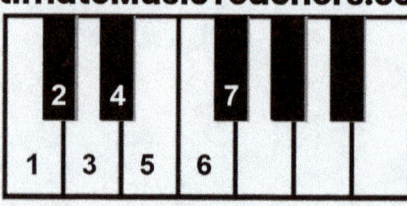

Key Strategy #8
YOUR PURPOSE-DRIVEN TEACHER, COACH & MENTOR TRIAD
Structure

"Music Teachers are like the conductor of the orchestra, creating a vision with clarity, structure and a strategic plan."

~ Glory St. Germain

Who helped Elvis become a legend? Who mentored Beyoncé beyond the music? Who coached Susan Boyle to surprise the world with her voice? Behind every iconic artist, visionary entrepreneur, or world-changing leader - there was a teacher, a coach, or a mentor who shaped their path. No one rises to greatness alone, every success story begins with someone who saw the potential, nurtured the purpose, and helped shape the dream into reality. And let's face it, sometimes that mentor is standing in front of the class with coffee in one hand, sheet music in the other, and a "let's wing it with wisdom" vibe that somehow still changes lives.

My life had a structure, a harmonious triad of wife, mother and teacher. Juggling those three roles felt like an overwhelming opportunity (yes, that's exactly how I'm phrasing it).

Overwhelming because, well, have you ever tried balancing a household, raising kids, and running a music studio all at once? It's like conducting an orchestra where every instrument is playing in a different key, at a different tempo with one kid banging on the cymbals just for fun. Opportunity because those moments of chaos were also the moments that deepened my relationships with my family, my students, and myself.

As a wife, I was basically a coach to my husband, his booking agent, personal shopper, assistant, and occasional human sticky note reminding him to take out the garbage on Tuesdays. (Oh, and let's not forget: the love of his life. That's an important title.)

As a mother, I stepped into my mentor role, guiding my children with love and wisdom whether they wanted it or not. Let's be real; sometimes my mentoring advice was met with eyerolls and the classic "Moooom, I got this" response. But hey, I'm still proud of every piece of wisdom I sprinkled into their lives, whether they knew it or not. And God bless them all for loving me through my life lessons and celebrations.

And then, there was my teacher side, which extended beyond the music studio:

- I taught my mother music theory so she could learn to play the accordion.

- I taught my friends how to Zumba dance (with varying degrees of success).

- I taught my children to embrace learning to play instruments and to perform.

And I taught my husband how to take care of our horses, because, fun fact, we lived on a farm while he filmed his award-winning national television show, Big Sky Country. Yes, you read that right. We were the "Green Acres" couple on the mile road, simple city folks pretending to be farm experts. Spoiler: we had zero clue what we were doing. But with help from our neighbors (and some comical trial and error), we figured it out. We rode horses, tended the land, and my husband sang alongside his guests, Nashville's finest, while filming his TV show. What a time we had.

And then it hit me.

This triad of Coach, Mentor, and Teacher wasn't just a personal thing, it was a professional framework for my life as a music educator. The training (if we can call it that) I had in my personal life had unknowingly prepared me for my role as an entrepreneur and educator. The best part? Once I fully embraced this Purpose-Driven Triad, everything in my business changed.

Developing Your Personal and Professional Triad

Music has a structure that guides us through a journey of emotions and expressions, where every note and rest plays a significant role. Similarly, in education, teaching lays the foundation of knowledge and skill. Performance builds on this transcending technique to capture expression, stage presence, and emotional connection.

In music, a triad creates harmony. In education, the Purpose-Driven Teacher, Coach, and Mentor Triad creates life-changing impact.

Emily was a promising pianist whose technical skills were strong, but whose performances lacked emotional depth. It wasn't until she encountered the Teacher, Coach, and Mentor Triad that her potential blossomed.

- **Her Teacher provided the solid technical foundation, scales, chords, and rhythm.**

- **Her Coach brought the music to life, teaching her to embrace expressive dynamics.**

- **Her Mentor offered emotional support, helping her navigate self-doubt and performance anxiety.**

Together, they shaped Emily into not just a pianist, but a true artist. Each role brought out a different strength: learning, expressing, and believing.

TEACHER:

The Teacher strikes the major chords of knowledge, introducing concepts with clarity and structure. They create the groundwork for skill development through well-structured lessons.

When I teach music educators, I focus on simplification and breaking complex concepts into practical steps. By practicing teaching exercises aligned with student learning styles, educators build confidence for real-world teaching.

COACH:

The Coach moves from theory to application. Coaching fine-tunes performance, adapting strategies to each student's challenges and goals.

When I coach music educators to grow their businesses, I show them how to work smarter, not harder by teaching group classes and using strategic marketing to double or triple their income.

Coaching is about helping students adjust, refine, and succeed in real-world scenarios.

MENTOR:

The Mentor goes deeper, guiding future aspirations and emotional resilience. A true mentorship is built on trust, vision, and vulnerability.

When mentoring UMTC Elite Educators, I focus on helping them envision their future, embrace their values, and believe in their potential. It's not just about achieving business goals; it's about becoming the person they are meant to be.

The stories of Elite Educators who have become international authors and entrepreneurs stand as proof of what's possible when mentoring is purposeful and empowering.

The Triad of Teacher, Coach, and Mentor isn't a one-time destination, it's a continuous journey of growth, evaluation, and action. As you embrace professional development and dream bigger, remember:

a little fear means you're growing. A lot of heart means you're unstoppable.

Teaching Styles in Music Education

Music education worldwide is in the hands of passionate teachers like you. The style you choose, your method of delivering knowledge and skills, greatly impacts your students' engagement, understanding, and overall musical experience. Let's explore the five primary teaching styles in music education and how they influence learning, especially in group settings:

The Authority Teaching Style

Traditionally lecture-based, this style works well when introducing complex music theory or new repertoire. While less interactive, it provides clear, structured instruction essential for consistency and understanding.

By understanding and effectively applying the Authority Teaching Style, you can deliver focused, foundational knowledge that students can build on.

The Facilitator Teaching Style

This approach emphasizes guiding students to discover knowledge through critical thinking, creativity, and collaboration. It's especially powerful for fostering independence and deeper musical understanding in group lessons, where active participation transforms learning into a vibrant, shared experience.

By embracing the Facilitator Teaching Style, you can create a dynamic, student-centered environment where creativity and collaboration thrive.

The Demonstrator Teaching Style

Modeling skills and concepts, then allowing students to replicate them, is the hallmark of the Demonstrator Style. In music education, it's ideal for technical skills, performance techniques, and theory application. By demonstrating, you make abstract concepts tangible providing students a clear path to mastery.

By utilizing the Demonstrator Teaching Style, you can bring clarity and hands-on learning into your students' musical journeys.

The Delegator Teaching Style

Here, students take more responsibility for their learning, with the teacher as a supportive guide.

This style encourages creativity, collaboration, and leadership, perfect for group settings where peer learning accelerates musical growth and confidence.

By applying the Delegator Teaching Style, you can foster independence, creativity, and strong peer-to-peer learning opportunities.

The Hybrid Teaching Style

Also called the Blended Style, it combines elements of all approaches, adapting to the needs of diverse learners.

In your theory club classes, the Hybrid Style lets you create a dynamic, personalized environment where every student feels seen, supported, and inspired.

By implementing the Hybrid Teaching Style, you can meet the unique needs of every learner and cultivate a rich, engaging classroom experience.

Mastering these teaching styles empowers you to harmonize structure with spontaneity, giving your students not just skills, but a deeper love of music.

Each teaching style brings its own harmony to the classroom.

Here's a quick overview of their strengths, challenges, and the best ways to apply them in your music education journey.

Teaching Style	Pros	Cons	Best Applications in Music Education
Authority Teaching Style	- Clear, structured guidance - Efficient for introducing complex concepts - Ensures consistency and discipline	- Less interactive and engaging - Can limit student creativity - May not address individual learning style	- Teaching music theory in groups - Introducing new repertoire - Consistency and clarity in instruction
Facilitator Teaching Style	- Encourages creativity and independence - Fosters understanding and collaboration - Develops critical thinking, active learning	- Can be time-consuming - Requires strong class management - Less effective for very large groups	- Group settings focused on creativity - Fostering independence - Building problem-solving skills
Demonstrator Teaching Style	- Highly effective for technical development - Learn by observation and replicating practice - Combines theory with practical application	- May become too reliant on modeling - Less emphasis on student innovation - May not suit self-directed learners	- Teach performance techniques - Teach music theory through application - Group settings with hands-on activities
Delegator Teaching Style	- Promotes self-directed learning - Encourages creativity and collaboration - Builds ownership and leadership skills	- Challenging for less motivated students - Requires high levels of responsibility - May lead to inconsistent outcomes	- Group projects and ensemble work - Collaborative and creative projects - Advanced or independent learners
Hybrid Teaching Style	- Combines strengths of various teaching styles - Flexible and adapt-able to diverse learners - Supports personalized learning pathways	- Can be challenging to balance approaches - Requires planning of multiple methods - Potential for inconsistency	- Teaching diverse group classes - Adapting lessons for mixed learning - Embrace teaching to all learning styles

How effective is your teaching style?

Understanding how to engage students is crucial for developing a thriving music studio. To meet the diverse needs of your students, it's essential to explore, experiment, and refine different teaching styles.

By challenging yourself to adapt your approach, you create a dynamic, inclusive learning environment where every student can thrive.

Teaching Style Snapshots:

- **Authority:** Delivers structured lessons to build a strong foundation.

- **Facilitator:** Encourages critical thinking, collaboration, and creativity.

- **Demonstrator:** Models skills and techniques for hands-on learning.

- **Delegator:** Promotes self-directed learning and leadership.

- **Hybrid:** Blends multiple approaches for personalized instruction.

Scenario: Teaching a New Piece of Music

Authority Approach: The teacher provides structured direction, demonstrating the piece and setting clear expectations.

Example: "Play measures 1-8 at half speed, focusing on dynamics and exact fingering."
Pros: Clear, efficient instruction for beginners.
Cons: May limit creativity.

Facilitator Approach: The teacher invites student exploration and critical thinking.

Example: "What do you notice about the key changes? How might you shape the phrasing?"

Pros: Builds independence and artistry.
Cons: Takes more time; less suited for beginners needing direct guidance.

Demonstrator Approach: The teacher models technique and interpretation.

Example: "Notice how lifting the wrist brings out the phrase. Try it this way."
Pros: Highly effective for visual and kinesthetic learners.
Cons: Students may become too reliant on demonstration.

Delegator Approach: The teacher fosters independence through student-led analysis and planning.

Example: "Identify the most challenging sections and create a practice plan."
Pros: Promotes self-reliance and critical thinking.
Cons: Requires motivated, self-aware students.

Hybrid Approach: The teacher adapts flexibly, combining directive teaching, modeling, reflection, and independent learning.

Example: "Let's start by listening to a demonstration; next, practice measures 1–4 slowly, then reflect on which dynamics were most expressive to you."
Pros: Personalized, holistic learning.
Cons: Requires ongoing awareness and adjustment.

Scenario: Teaching Through Performance Anxiety

Facing performance anxiety is a pivotal moment for many students. Here's how different teaching styles can address it:

Authority: Set clear, structured goals to reduce overwhelm. "Focus on measures 12–20 at half speed, adding dynamics."

Facilitator: Guide reflection. "Which part feels the most challenging? How can we simplify it?"

Demonstrator: Model calm, expressive performance. "Watch how I breathe and stay relaxed—now you try."

Delegator: Assign independent action. "Create a three-step prep plan before the concert."

Hybrid: Blend structure, discussion, modeling, and independence to meet the student's evolving needs. "Let's practice your most challenging section together slowly, then discuss strategies to stay calm on stage, and finally, you'll develop your own pre-performance routine."

When you flex your teaching style to match the moment, you give students the technical strategies, and the inner tools to manage future challenges, and that's where true transformation happens.

Why Developing a Personal Teaching Style Matters

Understanding and evolving your teaching style allows you to meet students exactly where they are. Each group is different, and flexibility enables you to create lessons that are accessible, engaging, and effective. When your teaching style is intentional, student engagement increases and so does learning success.

A well-developed teaching style:

- **Builds student trust and connection.**

- **Reflects current best practices.**

- **Boosts your professional growth as an educator.**

- **Supports lifelong learning and musicianship.**

Ultimately, the purpose of teaching music is to facilitate both the educational process and the creative journey. The principles of effective teaching guide students not just in technique, but in nurturing a love of learning, critical thinking, and musical artistry.

As music educators, we have the extraordinary privilege of shaping musicians and enriching lives. When we teach with purpose, we deliver lessons and build legacies through music.

The Dynamic Triad of Teacher, Coach, and Mentor in Music Education

In guiding students, educators wear many hats, but mastering the roles of Teacher, Coach, and Mentor creates a holistic, impactful learning experience.

Each role demands a distinct style of engagement, reflecting unique ways we contribute to a student's musical and personal growth.

As **Teachers**, we lay the foundation, imparting knowledge and providing students with the essential tools to understand theory, perform, and succeed. A strong, structured environment invites students to learn through practice, embracing mistakes as part of the process.

As **Coaches**, we elevate students beyond the basics, helping them apply skills in real-world scenarios like live performances or overcoming exam challenges. Coaches act as strategic partners, offering personalized feedback that refines technique and builds confidence under pressure.

As **Mentors**, we journey deeper, guiding students and peers beyond immediate goals toward their long-term dreams. Mentors provide emotional support, broaden visions, and help students step into futures as performers, educators, and creative entrepreneurs.

Ultimate Music Teachers fluidly embody all three roles. I call this the **SEV Path**:

- **Show (Teacher):** Demonstrate skills and provide essential knowledge.

- **Empower (Coach):** Encourage growth, confidence, and real-world application.

- **Vision (Mentor):** Inspire a bigger vision of what's possible, fueling dreams and passion.

The **SEV Path** is the journey of growth and transformation where teachers show the way, coaches empower resilience, and mentors ignite visions of greatness. Together, they provide the personal and educational development needed for students to thrive.

When educators embrace all three roles, we nurture musical proficiency, resilience, creativity, and lifelong passion. The Triad of Teacher, Coach, and Mentor becomes a continuous cycle of mutual growth elevating both educator and student into new realms of success.

By embracing this dynamic triad, you become the leader who inspires students to dream bigger, stretch farther, and realize the extraordinary potential within themselves.

Remember: if your dreams don't scare you a little, they're not big enough.

I believe there are two essential strategies for living your best life:

1. **Your Purpose:**
    Your purpose as a music teacher carries both a profound responsibility and a powerful opportunity to make a difference in the world. What's your vision for your teaching business and your legacy?

2. **Your Principles:**
    Your principles are the blueprint for creativity, connection, and accountability. They shape how you teach, how you lead, and how you impact the future of music education. What principles will you embody to make a global difference?

EDUCATION WITH A DIFFERENT CHRISTMAS

You might wonder how education and Christmas came together as a powerful learning experience for me. Let me take you back to 1983.

Christmas has always been a time of celebration with family and friends. Every year, my parents would share Bible stories of the birthplace of Jesus in Bethlehem, a tradition that filled me with tears of joy as we played music together. Born into a musical family, my dream was simple yet profound: to one day travel from Canada to Bethlehem and experience God's Blessed Land for myself.

Little did I know this dream would also involve thousands of people, one lost magician, and a broken guitar. (Sounds like the start of a great country song, doesn't it?)

At 19, I was a piano teacher and very much in love with Ray St. Germain, a nationally recognized television star, recording artist, and legendary entertainer. (Two years later, he proposed to me with the sweetest words: "I don't want to spend another Christmas without you. Will you marry me?" Spoiler alert: I said yes.)

Marrying into the entertainment world meant my role expanded fast. I became Ray's booking agent, TV show assistant, stage show producer, wardrobe designer, radio promotions hustler and occasional wrangler of chaos.

One of my biggest opportunities came when I decided to lead the effort to book an overseas tour entertaining the Canadian Armed Forces in Germany, Israel, and Cyprus. Producing a show with 24 entertainers including a big band, Vegas-style dancers, magicians, singers, and a French-Canadian MC, all under our company Ray St. Germain Productions, was no small feat.

After months of preparing a meticulously packaged proposal, I was crushed when the first letter arrived: "We regret to inform you that your proposal has not been accepted."

I cried out loud. I stared at the globe on my desk, spinning it slowly, wondering if my dream was truly out of reach.

But I refused to give up. I submitted again the following year mailing in a 25-page proposal (this was BC - Before Computers) and I prayed.

Weeks later, the phone rang. It was The Major. "Hi Glory. Congratulations. You are the first music producer in Manitoba to successfully submit an Entertainment Package proposal to perform for the Canadian Troops overseas."

Tears of joy streamed down my face. I screamed. I hugged Ray. We were going on an international tour. Calling each performer to share the news was pure magic. Rehearsals began. Plans took flight. And this producer was ecstatic.

Christmas 1983 would be a very different one

Our two toddlers, David and Sherry, stayed behind with my parents, while our daughter Catherine traveled with us performing with her band, The Rage. My parents, true to tradition, read the Christmas Bible stories at home, while I prepared to step onto stages across Germany, Israel, Cyprus, and France.

The adventures began immediately.

In Germany, I somehow "misplaced" our world-class magician, Brian Glow. (He still tells this story gleefully.) After a bank stop during a bus transfer, everyone piled back onboard except Brian, who was deep in conversation inside the manager's office. I forgot to count heads. (Yes, only 23 performers got back on the bus.) Several hours later, Brian miraculously appeared at the reception, having talked his way through a military checkpoint with a little magic, of course.

Lesson learned: Always count heads. Twice.

Later, as we landed in Tel Aviv, Israel, unloading the Hercules aircraft revealed another heartbreak: Ray's beloved Ovation guitar engraved with his name and gifted by me for the tour had a crack down the middle. It was now unplayable. It would later be enshrined in the Canadian Country Music Hall of Fame, but at that moment, it was another reminder: things break, but dreams endure.

On Christmas Day, all the entertainers performed for the troops.

As I stood backstage, the music rising all around me, I felt overwhelming gratitude for the dream, the journey, and the chance to bring a different kind of Christmas joy to men and women far from home.

Later, visiting Bethlehem, I stood quietly at the birthplace of Jesus, tears streaming down my face. My lifelong dream realized. My heart was full beyond words.

Today, a plaque hangs in my office:

"Presented by The Royal Canadian Regiment to Ray St. Germain Productions—Glory St. Germain, Producer. January 3, 1984."

Ray, inspired by our journey, went on to write and record a gospel album *Show Me The Way To Jerusalem* because some experiences change you forever.

Why set goals that seem impossible? Why not?

Today, as a Music Teachers Business Coach and Course Creator, my mission is to help you turn those "impossible" dreams into your greatest reality. If you're ready to take the next step, connect with me and let's make your dreams come true.

"The meaning of life is to find your gift. The purpose of life is to give it away."

~ Pablo Picasso

Case Study:
UMT Certified Teacher Suzanne Greer

What if your first introduction to music left you uninspired and ready to quit? That's what happened to Suzanne Greer, a pianist, artist, teacher at the MacPhail Center for Music, Nationally Certified Teacher of Music, and Ultimate Music Theory Certified Teacher.

Suzanne's early experiences with piano and violin lessons were discouraging with uninspiring materials, a lack of connection, and ultimately, a decision to quit both instruments. Yet the music never truly left her heart.

She continued playing by ear, seeking an outlet for her passion, until she found her way back to formal lessons, this time with an Ultimate Music Teacher who embraced the triad of Teacher, Coach, and Mentor. With the gentle but demanding guidance of her teacher and mentor, MaryAnn Swallum, Suzanne rediscovered her love for music. MaryAnn's passion for excellence and heartfelt mentoring helped Suzanne not only develop technical mastery but also find her voice and confidence on the piano, and in life.

Suzanne's journey wasn't easy. Even after earning her Bachelor of Music degree in piano performance, she battled fear, anxiety, and self-doubt. Yet she persevered, fueled by her calling to teach and serve others through music.

Today, Suzanne is a respected educator and leader in her community. She credits her growth to the support of inspiring mentors and to her decision to never stop learning. Through her participation in the Ultimate Music Teachers Coaching Program, Suzanne embraced a positive mindset, conquered limiting beliefs, and proudly stands as an Elite Educator believing in herself, leading others, and inspiring the next generation of musicians.

Suzanne's story reminds us that teaching music is a noble profession. We are more than instructors, we are First Responders to the human condition, guiding our students through triumphs, struggles, and moments of discovery. Leading others through music helps us discover our own humanity and that is the ultimate gift.

Read Suzanne's inspiring story in *The Power of WHY Musicians 5 Book Series*.

Purpose-Driven Teaching: Your Final Reflection

As you explore your Purpose and Principles, think about how you can fast-track your business and quickly achieve next-level learning to become an Ultimate Music Teacher and discover the possibilities waiting for you.

As music educators, we are the conductors of our own educational orchestra, guiding each student through the harmonious journey of learning, growth, and self-discovery. Like a conductor, we must create a vision with clarity, establish structure, and craft a strategic plan that guides our students to success.

By embracing the dynamic triad of Teacher, Coach, and Mentor, we not only teach technical skills but also cultivate creativity, resilience, and passion in our students. Each role of Teacher, Coach, and Mentor uniquely shapes the student's musical and personal development.

Together, they create a learning environment rich with purpose, growth, and the promise of excellence. In the end, a purpose-driven approach transforms not just our students but also ourselves as we continuously evolve, adapt, and lead with both heart and mind.

Let this triad be your blueprint for creating a lasting impact as a music educator that empowers your students to become the musicians and individuals they are destined to be. As you reflect on your role as an educator, ask yourself: How are you integrating teaching, coaching, and mentoring into your students' musical journeys?

⌒ *Fermata* (Pause to Ponder): Three Steps to Purpose-Driven Teaching

Purpose-driven teaching begins with embracing our multiple roles of Teacher, Coach, and Mentor. Each role plays a unique part in shaping a student's journey, from foundational learning to lifelong mentorship. A teacher gives skills and knowledge. A coach gives strategy and support. A mentor holds a vision beyond what the student believes is possible.

> A teacher gives skills and knowledge.
> A coach gives strategy and support.
> A mentor holds a vision beyond what the
> student believes is possible.

Step #1: Start by Aligning Structure in Your Roles

Your ability to flow seamlessly between the roles of Teacher, Coach, and Mentor will greatly impact your students' holistic development.

How can you refine your approach to teaching, coaching, and mentoring to create a more cohesive learning experience?

_____

_____

What adjustments can you make in your communication style to fit each role appropriately?

_____

_____

How can you align these roles to ensure your students' growth not just as musicians, but as confident individuals?

_____

_____

Step #2: Write Down 3 Ways to Apply Coaching Strategies to Your Teaching.

Effective coaching goes beyond instruction; it's about offering real-time feedback, encouragement, and strategies that guide students through their challenges.

How can you adapt your current teaching methods to include more coaching moments during lessons?

_____

_____

What opportunities do you have to provide individualized feedback that builds both skill and confidence?

_____

_____

How can you use coaching techniques to foster resilience, growth mindset, and leadership in your students?

_____

_____

Step #3: Commit to Purpose-Driven Mentoring Beyond Student's Goals.

Mentorship focuses on long-term vision and lasting transformation.

How will you introduce mentorship moments into your lessons to nurture your students' dreams and aspirations?

_____

_____

What specific strategies (like Vision Boards, Goal Reflections, or Celebration Milestones) can you implement to help students envision their future?

_____

_____

How can you build deep trust and connection, encouraging your students to seek your mentorship beyond just musical skills?

"A great teacher doesn't just prepare students for the next performance; they prepare them for life."

~ Unknown

As music educators, it's our responsibility to nurture the whole student not only by teaching them to play or understand music but by coaching them through their challenges and mentoring them toward their future.

The triad of Teacher, Coach, and Mentor is a dynamic process that allows us to leave a lasting legacy in the lives of our students, shaping them as musicians and as people.

Embrace Purpose-Driven Teaching and teach with purpose, guide with intention, and mentor with heart so your students can thrive both in and beyond the music studio. When you teach with purpose, you empower your students to discover theirs.

♪ Your Coda Notes ♪

_____

_____

The 12 Key Strategies include online Ultimate Music Teachers Bonus Resources.

TEACH MUSIC CHANGE LIVES

Your Purpose-Driven Teacher, Coach & Mentor Triad

Dive deeper into KEY STRATEGY #8 - get your
Ultimate Music Teachers
FREE Bonus Workbook to design a structure that
empowers your leadership growth.

Go To: UltimateMusicTeachers.com/guide

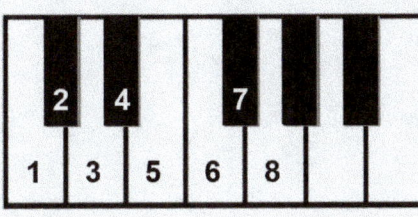

PART 3
GROWING YOUR BUSINESS TO UNLOCK STRATEGIC PROFITABILITY

Key Strategy #9
FINANCIAL PLANNING TO CREATE YOUR FREEDOM LIFESTYLE
Pitch

"The pitch of your financial success rises with focus, planning and perseverance, as you compose the notes of your freedom lifestyle masterpiece."

~ Glory St. Germain

In 1955, Colonel Tom Parker saw a young Elvis Presley perform and made a pitch that would change music history forever. While others saw a local act with swagger and sideburns, Parker saw potential. But more than that, he had a vision. He told Elvis: "You can be the greatest entertainer in the world if you let me guide you." That wasn't just a compliment, it was a pitch. A bold, strategic offer with a clear path, a promise of results, and a whole lot of faith in the dream. And the rest? Well, let's just say Elvis didn't become *The King* by accident.

Because when your pitch is clear, your purpose is strong, and your plan is profitable, the spotlight finds you.

So, what's your pitch?

What are you offering the world?

And are you ready to turn your passion into your freedom lifestyle with focus, planning, and profitability?

I'm proud to say I mastered the art of perfect pitch. No, not in singing (trust me, that's definitely *not* my strong suit). I'm talking about the essential skill of making a perfect pitch in life and business, that moment when you present a solution so compelling that it's a win-win for everyone involved. The truth is that every major success in my life has started with a well-crafted pitch; a clear problem, a creative solution, and the confidence to go for it.

The Grad Dress Pitch

The problem? I needed a stunning grad dress, but the designer gowns were costly.
The connection? My mom, a talented professional seamstress.
The solution? I pitched that she could create a one-of-a-kind gown we'd both love.

She said yes, and that dress remains one of my favorite memories.

The Free Cruise Pitch

The problem? I dreamed of going on a cruise with my husband, but it wasn't affordable.
The connection? A travel agent booking entertainment cruises.
The solution? I pitched that my husband could entertain onboard while we hosted.

They said yes, and we ended up hosting four cruises and traveled for free.

The Family Reunion Pitch

The problem? I wanted a family reunion for a celebration, but travel costs were steep.
The connection? A booking agent at a local casino in Winnipeg, Manitoba.
The solution? I pitched The Ray St. Germain Family Show, a unique performance.

They said yes, covered all travel expenses, paid performers for two sold-out shows.

The Secret to a Perfect Pitch

- **Clearly define the problem.**

- **Know your audience.**

- **Present a compelling solution.**

- **Make it a win-win with proof that it works.**

Whether it's a dream dress, a dream trip, or a dream business, when you believe in your value and deliver it with heart, doors open. Just ask Elvis. That pitch wasn't just about music, it was about possibility. It launched not just a career, but a legacy.

What is Pitch?

In music, pitch is the quality of sound that defines the highness or lowness of a tone, demanding precision, focus, and practice.

In business, your Ultimate Business Pitch is the offer you present when enrolling students. Without a clear, strategic pitch, you don't have a business you have a hobby. A great pitch in business requires the same elements as music: preparation, precision, and passion.

From Uncertain to Unstoppable

At first, one of my clients relied on passion alone, posting signs in neighboring communities and hoping students would come. But without a clear strategy or business pitch, his studio growth stalled.

After joining the UMTC Elite Educator Program, everything shifted. He built a focused marketing plan, structured his financial systems, and gained the confidence to pitch his value clearly.

The result? He transformed his teaching into a thriving, fully booked business proving that with a focused pitch and plan, passion is preserved and multiplied into lasting success.

The Business Booster Formula: Avoiding Common Pitfalls

The Business Booster Formula is designed to help you avoid the common mistakes many entrepreneurs face when growing a teaching business.

The first mistake is not having a clear vision. Many teachers think their goals are specific to "I want more students" or "I want more income" but these are too vague. Without clarity on how many students you need or what type of students you want to teach, it's like setting out on a journey without a map. Progress feels random, and growth stalls.

The second mistake is not having an executable plan. Dreaming about social media posts or hoping for referrals isn't enough. Without a step-by-step strategy, energy is wasted on scattered efforts that don't yield consistent results, like trying to host a recital with no schedule or set list.

The third mistake is not using systems that work. Many passionate teachers rely on manual scheduling, outdated marketing, or mismatched lesson plans. Broken systems create bottlenecks that drain your energy. Streamlined, automated systems free up your time so you can focus on what matters most: teaching and growing your business.

The fourth mistake is not having a coach for confidence. Without a mentor, self-doubt creeps in, procrastination takes hold, and progress slows. A coach provides feedback, perspective, and encouragement helping you move faster and work smarter toward your goals. It's like trying to learn a complex musical piece without any feedback: you miss key opportunities for growth.

When you address these four areas of vision, planning, systems, and mentorship you'll grow your studio and build it with clarity, strategy, and unstoppable confidence.

Focus and Finances - Your Keys to Success

I know firsthand the importance of focus and finances in creating success. There are two essential elements to turning challenges into success-building opportunities: focus and finances.

First, focus determines outcomes.

When I started writing the Ultimate Music Theory Workbook Series, I focused intensely on every step; research, writing, testing with students and teachers, learning design, typesetting, publishing, and crafting my business pitch. I stayed laser-focused on achieving each goal before moving to the next.

The result? Helping musicians worldwide, traveling to present showcases, and living a life of purpose through music education. What you focus on grows. What you consistently channel your energy toward becomes your reality. So, ask yourself: Where is your focus right now and is it moving you toward your dreams?

Second, finances are your responsibility.

When I moved into publishing and created the Gloryland Publishing Company, I realized that dreaming wasn't enough. I needed to understand profitability and strategic financial planning.

One simple but powerful lesson I implemented: The 1% Profit Account. Every month, I put 1% of gross income into a separate account never to be touched. For example, if you earn $5,000, you deposit $50. You won't miss it, but over time, that account grows into a powerful visual reminder of your profitability.

How do I know Ultimate Music Theory has generated millions in sales? Because I track it through my 1% Profit Account and disciplined financial practices. Most music teachers don't struggle because they lack passion. They struggle because they lack a financial plan for success. Inside the UMTC Elite Educator Program, we teach these financial strategies so you can build a sustainable, profitable music business and create your freedom lifestyle.

Remember: Focus creates direction. Financial planning builds security. When you master both, you transform your teaching business and your life.

To break free from financial limitations, it's essential to explore different types of financial plans and recognize which ones keep you limited and which ones open the door to growth. Every challenge presents an opportunity to rethink and reframe your approach. The key is shifting your mindset from focusing on barriers to focusing on the solutions that allow your business to thrive, no matter what the circumstances.

Limited Financial Plans:

1. **Hourly Teaching Only: Teaching one student per hour caps your income based on the number of hours you can physically teach each week.**

2. **Undercharging for Services: Without a clear pricing strategy, many teachers undervalue their time and expertise, limiting their profitability.**

3. **No Diversified Income Streams: Relying solely on private lessons creates financial vulnerability if one income stream slows down.**

Growth-Oriented Financial Plans:

1. **Teaching Group Lessons: Shifting to group lessons, such as Ultimate Music Theory Club Classes, allows you to teach multiple students at once, maximizing income without adding teaching hours. For example, teaching six students at $45 each per hour generates $270/hr, compared to earning $50/hr from just one student.**

2. **Expanding Your Offerings: Diversify your services with workshops, six-week music camps, themed short-term programs, or pop-up classes for different ages and abilities.**

3.   **Scaling Through Digital Products:** Develop resources like eBooks, video lessons, or downloadable guides (composition workbooks, practice planners, repertoire guides) that can be sold repeatedly without extra teaching hours.

4.   **Implementing a Profit Plan:** Use strategies like the 1% Profit Account to build wealth steadily, ensuring your business remains profitable year after year.

By implementing growth-oriented strategies, you not only increase your income you also create more freedom to focus on what you love: inspiring students and living your freedom lifestyle.

Teaching group lessons, such as Ultimate Music Theory Club Classes, is one of the most powerful ways to build a sustainable financial plan. You increase your income per hour, free up time, and enjoy the rewards of watching students thrive in a collaborative, engaging environment. When you prioritize financial planning and embrace innovative teaching models, you create opportunities for both personal and professional growth.

So, are you ready to shift your financial plan and take your teaching business to the next level?

"To be successful, you have to have your heart in your business, and your business in your heart."

~ Thomas Watson, Sr.

Want to build a successful music business? In my journey from Musician to Educator to Author to Publisher to Course Creator to Podcaster to Producer to Business Coach and Serial Entrepreneur, I've discovered the FLOW System - an essential framework to achieve life goals and reach next-level growth.

The FLOW System

The FLOW System is designed to help you create both a business and a lifestyle that you love. You are about to discover the one essential framework every entrepreneur needs to build an extraordinary music teaching business that thrives with productivity and profitability.

The FLOW System stands for Focus, Learn, Operations, and Willingness. Each step aligns your business strategies with your personal goals. Now, let's put this system into practice with interactive exercises to help you create your own roadmap to success.

Step 1: FOCUS on what you want to achieve

What you focus your attention on grows. Where are you investing your time? Do you want to teach group lessons? What action steps do you need to take to make that happen? Focus on strategies that will elevate your teaching systems and take your business to the next level.

Your focus determines your outcomes. To build a successful music business, you must first define where you're focusing your time and energy. The strategies you devote your focus to, will shape your ability to achieve your life goals and implement your business plan with ease.

Write a clear Focus Statement that aligns with your vision for your business and lifestyle. Example: "I focus on growing my music teaching business by enrolling new students through group classes, improving my teaching skills, and expanding my online presence to increase profitability."

Now, write your own Focus Statement:

_____

_____

_____

_____

Step 2: LEARN what you need to grow

Learning means letting go of what is not serving you and embracing new strategies with an "I CAN" mindset. True learning happens outside your comfort zone: just like a rubber band, you need to stretch it, to be effective. Learn the systems, skills, and marketing techniques that will help you meet your ideal students with clarity and confidence.

Ask yourself: What do you need to learn, and who can guide you toward greater confidence in your business and branding? Continuous learning is the key to long-term growth and relevance.

Create a Commitment to Learn Statement that outlines your plan for growth. Example: "I commit to investing in my professional development by completing two music education workshops this year and implementing new teaching methods."

Now, write your own Commitment to Learn Statement:

_____

_____

_____

_____

Step 3: OPERATIONS are the foundation of your business

Managing your operations wisely ensures your teaching business remains efficient, effective, and profitable. It's not just about making money; it's about keeping it. Even large businesses fail when they operate without profitability.

Focus on two critical areas:

First, holding down expenses and increasing profitability: Optimize your resources to create smart, scalable growth.

Second, creating more time for leadership: Streamlining operations frees you to focus on new opportunities and scaling your business.

Set a SMART Goal for Operations that will strengthen your business operations. Example: "I will implement a new online scheduling system within the next 30 days to improve booking efficiency and reduce administrative work."

Now, write your own SMART Goal for Operations:

_____

_____

_____

_____

Step 4: WILLINGNESS unlocks success

Being willing to listen, stretch, and stay open to new opportunities sets you apart from those who only dream without action. Willingness is what transforms potential into progress.

Ask yourself: What are you willing to commit to in order to lead a meaningful, productive life of enrichment and prosperity?

Develop a Practice of Willingness, a daily habit like meditation, gratitude journaling, or intentional goal setting to keep you aligned with growth. Consider the difference:

- **Without meditation: You start the day rushed, stressed, and reactive.**

- **With meditation: You start the day calm, clear, and focused on what matters.**

Example: "I will begin each morning with a 10-minute meditation, focusing on gratitude and setting intentions for the day."

Now, define your own Practice of Willingness:

_____

_____

_____

_____

Your FLOW System brings together the essential elements of strategy, marketing, finances, and prosperity, helping you define your business purpose and ensure you're moving forward in the right direction.

By applying the FLOW System, you're building a business and creating a lifestyle that reflects your passion, goals, and highest potential.

Remember: Your success flows from Focus, Learning, Operations, and Willingness.

The Power of Extraordinary Support

I believe the one thing every entrepreneur needs to build an extraordinary music business with productivity and profitability is extraordinary support. Support comes in many forms: books, courses, coaches, friends, family, and so much more.

To create your extraordinary business, you need extraordinary support, or you can take ten years to figure it out on your own (but trust me, it's lonely, time-consuming, and there are no guarantees).

I owe all my success to the incredible support systems and people in my life: my husband Ray, my children and grandchildren, my amazing Ultimate Music Theory Dream Team, and my coaches and mentors.

I've read countless books, taken online courses, and watched hundreds of training videos, all with one goal: to move my business forward rapidly, expertly, and profitably.

It's why I created the Ultimate Music Teachers Academy, so you can access the same level of support through the FLOW System. With quick-start tools designed to put you on the fast track to success, you'll have the extraordinary support you need to GSD (Get Stuff Done).

Why set your goals to achieve success and implement the FLOW System? Why not?

Now that you've set your goals and implemented the FLOW System, it's time to craft your pitch to enroll students into your music teaching program. Here are five tips to help you create an irresistible offer and fill your studio with excited students:

Five Tips to Pitch Your Music Teaching Offer and Fill Your Studio

Tip #1: Know Your Audience Start by identifying who you're pitching to. Are you offering group music theory club classes, private beginner lessons, or exam prep for advanced students? Tailor your pitch to their needs and desires.

- **Note: Speak directly to the student's or parent's goals whether that's mastering theory or preparing for performance success.**

Tip #2: Highlight the Benefits Focus on the transformation students will experience when they enroll in your program. Let them visualize their success.

- **Note: Use examples like, "By the end of this program, your child will be able to read music fluently and perform with confidence."**

Tip #3: Create a Sense of Urgency Motivate potential students to act quickly with limited-time enrollment periods, early sign-up bonuses, or limited class spots.

- **Note: Offer a bonus for early-bird registration, like a free workshop or additional one-on-one session.**

Tip #4: Showcase Your Expertise Share your credentials and student success stories to build trust and credibility.

- **Note: Highlight achievements, such as students scoring 100% on theory exams or confidently performing challenging pieces, using testimonials.**

Tip #5: Offer a Clear Call to Action Make enrollment easy with a direct and straightforward call to action.

- **Note: Use clear language like, "Ready to start your musical journey? Sign up today and secure your spot."**

By applying these five tips, you'll craft a pitch that attracts students and helps you build a thriving music teaching business.

Financial Planning to Create Your Freedom Lifestyle

Set Your Financial Goals

Define Your Freedom Lifestyle: What does financial freedom look like for you? More time? Scaling your business? Consistent income? Short-Term and Long-Term Goals: Establish short-term (3–6 months) and long-term (1–5 years) goals. Example: "In the next year, I want to increase my income by 25% by offering group music theory classes."

Calculate Your Freedom Number

Figure out how much monthly income you need to comfortably support your lifestyle, including living expenses, business investments, and savings. Exercise: Write down your total monthly expenses, then determine your ideal monthly income. Break It Down: Once you know your target, calculate how many students or classes you'll need each month to reach it.

Diversify Your Income Streams

Private Lessons and Group Classes: Offer both to maximize income and reach broader audiences. Additional Revenue Streams: Add options like online courses, workshops, or downloadable teaching materials. Tip: Create passive income streams with teaching resources or premium coaching packages.

Plan for Business Expenses

Track Expenses Regularly: Monitor fixed costs (rent, materials) and variable costs (marketing, professional development). Budget for Growth: Set aside income for tools, marketing, and continuous education. Use simple tools like Google Sheets or software like QuickBooks, Xero, or Sage Intacct to stay organized and financially aware.

Develop a Pricing Strategy

Evaluate Your Rates: Are your fees aligned with your financial goals and the value you deliver? Offer Packages: Create monthly or term-based packages. Example: Offer a 3-month group class package at a slightly discounted upfront rate to increase cash flow.

Build Your Savings and Emergency Fund

Set Aside a Percentage: Save a percentage of income every month for emergencies and future opportunities. Aim for 3–6 months' worth of expenses. Tip: Set up automated savings transfers to make it easy.

Adjust Quarterly to Track Your Progress

Review income, expenses, and savings every quarter. Adjust your strategy as needed to stay on track toward your Freedom Lifestyle.

Financial Success Is a Journey

By following this financial plan, you'll create a business that brings you both joy and sustainability. Whether you're starting out or scaling up, these steps will empower you to take control of your finances and achieve your dream lifestyle.

When my client Mark Pfannschmidt implemented these strategies and connected them to a solid financial plan, he grew his teaching business profitability by 60%. That's the power of combining intentional financial planning with a clear vision for your success.

"It is the supreme art of the teacher to awaken joy in creative expression and knowledge."

~ Albert Einstein

Case Study:
UMT Certified Teacher Mark Pfannschmidt

Mark Pfannschmidt loved performing; he didn't love teaching. He knew from a young age that he wanted to be a musician. A talented violinist and pianist, he quickly rose to lead among his peers, determined to build a career on stage, not in a classroom. In fact, he once firmly believed that "those who can play, do and those who can't, teach." Teaching, in his mind, was something he'd never do.

But life had a different plan.

After graduating from college, Mark found himself competing at a whole new level where freelancing was unpredictable, and full-time orchestra positions were fiercely competitive. Like many professional musicians, he realized he needed a more stable way to support his passion.

That's when an unexpected opportunity arrived: a teacher friend asked Mark to take over her studio while she was away. His immediate response was, "No, I don't teach." But after a few persistent calls and a nudge from life itself, Mark agreed to give it a try.

Stepping into teaching without formal pedagogy training, just a deep understanding of music and a desire to help, Mark felt the weight of uncertainty. In the beginning, he often questioned himself, wondering if he was truly making a difference. At times, he felt like a fraud, unsure if he was qualified to teach at all.

But as time went on, something remarkable happened. His students were improving, not just technically, but artistically. They were practicing better, developing skills they once thought impossible, and reaching new milestones in their musicianship. Mark began to realize that much of what he was teaching was effective and powerful.

He found his "Why."

Teaching, he discovered, wasn't just a backup plan. It became a calling. The joy of watching a student master a dotted quarter note rhythm, shift smoothly on the violin, or develop the beginnings of a beautiful vibrato filled him with a new sense of purpose.

Helping students make musical choices with confidence and seeing their growth from tentative beginners to expressive artists was a different kind of stage, and one that he grew to love deeply.

More than three decades later, Mark still enjoys performing as a violist and pianist. But it's teaching that has become one of the greatest blessings of his life. His students and their families have brought him joy beyond anything he had imagined when he first stepped reluctantly into that studio.

Today, through the application of financial planning, business strategies, and professional development, Mark grew his music teaching business profitability by 60%, transforming his career and his life.

He captured the lead once again, not through performance alone, but through teaching and empowering the next generation of musicians to reach heights he once only dreamed of himself.

Read Mark's inspiring story in *The Power of WHY Musicians 5* Book Series.

Starting from Passion, Building from Structure

Growth doesn't stop; it evolves. And with every achievement, it opens new doors.

As musicians and educators, we often start, simply driven by love for music and the joy of teaching. But passion alone, without a clear business strategy, isn't enough to build a sustainable, profitable life.

I learned this lesson firsthand when I stepped into publishing, and my first proposal was turned away with a "no thanks." That moment taught me that creativity had to be paired with financial wisdom if I wanted to succeed.

The Importance of Coaching and Mentorship

Looking back, I realize how much time, money, and stress I could have saved by hiring a coach earlier. Mentorship shortens the learning curve, offering proven strategies that transform goals into reality. This is why I created the Ultimate Music Teachers Academy, to provide the extraordinary support and step-by-step guidance I wish I had at the beginning of my journey.

Building a Plan for Profitability

Having a vision is important. But executing that vision through smart financial planning is what fuels sustainable growth. When I wrote and published 20 Ultimate Music Theory Supplemental Workbooks, it wasn't just about creative energy, it was about focus, strategic planning, and financial discipline. Without a clear profit plan, those books might never have reached the thousands of teachers and students they serve today.

Creating Your Financial Roadmap

Financial planning isn't just about tracking income. It's about ensuring the heart of your business beats strong and steady. It means reading the fine print, understanding your revenue sources, and proactively designing a business that supports your life, not one that drains it.

Lessons in Profitability

If I could whisper advice to my younger self, it would be to focus on profitability from day one. Surround yourself with mentors. Use time-blocking to create space for both business and creativity. And remember, visibility creates opportunity.

From Passion to Profit

Today, Ultimate Music Theory supports thousands of educators and students worldwide. Our Dream Team continues to expand with creativity, commitment to growth strategies, financial planning, and leadership.

Turning passion into profit is not about sacrificing your love for teaching, it's about nurturing that love into a thriving business that can sustain you for a lifetime.

The Paradigm Shift

Teaching is an art. But running a music teaching business is also a science and a calling. By balancing passion with smart business management, you unlock your full potential to inspire, uplift, and leave a lasting legacy.

By following the Business Booster Formula and committing to your financial planning journey, you're building your Freedom Lifestyle.

You're creating the time, income, and opportunities to live with purpose, impact lives through music, and build a business that sustains your passion for years to come.

It's time to move from inspiration into action because your music, your message, and your students are waiting for you. Now, let's dive into your next step in creating financial freedom.

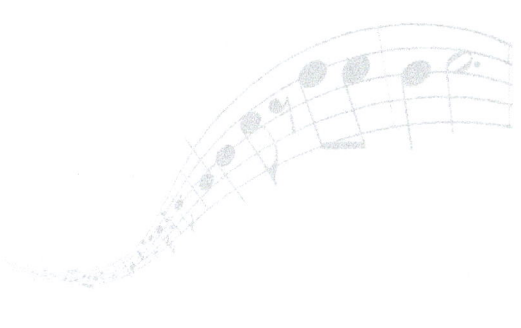

⌢ *Fermata* (Pause to Ponder): Three Steps to Financial Planning

Financial freedom begins with taking intentional control of your finances. Every successful business stands on a foundation of clear goals, sustainable growth, and constant reflection.

Step #1 Define Your Financial Goals

Your financial goals must be specific, measurable, and aligned with your long-term vision.

How can you define your financial goals more clearly?

_____

_____

What specific financial milestones do you want to achieve this year?

_____

_____

How will achieving these goals bring you closer to your Freedom Lifestyle?

_____

_____

Step #2 Plan for Sustainable Growth

Success isn't about working harder—it's about working smarter.

What financial systems can you put in place to ensure steady, sustainable growth?

_____

_____

How can you diversify your income streams to build resilience?

_____

_____

What steps can you take today to manage expenses more efficiently?

_____

_____

Step #3 Commit to Regular Financial Reviews

Consistency is the heartbeat of success.

How often are you reviewing your income, expenses, and progress?

_____

_____

What adjustments could you make right now to stay aligned with your goals?

_____

_____

How will you continue refining your financial strategy as your business grows?

_____

_____

"As with music, your financial success is a composition—a masterpiece built step by step with focus, strategy, and perseverance."

~ Glory St. Germain

Your journey toward financial freedom is about building a business and composing a life where you teach, inspire, and live with passion, purpose, and prosperity.

By embracing smart financial strategies today, you're creating a ripple effect that will echo in the lives you impact for generations to come.

♪ Your Coda Notes ♪

_____

_____

The 12 Key Strategies include online Ultimate Music Teachers Bonus Resources.

TEACH MUSIC CHANGE LIVES

Financial Planning to Create Your Freedom Lifestyle

Dive deeper into **KEY STRATEGY #9** - get your
Ultimate Music Teachers
FREE Bonus Workbook to refine your pitch for profitable,
purpose-aligned teaching.

Go To: UltimateMusicTeachers.com/guide

 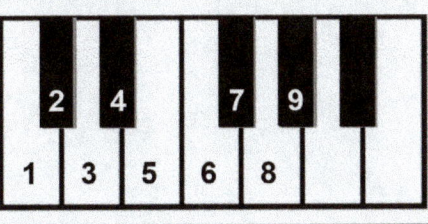 

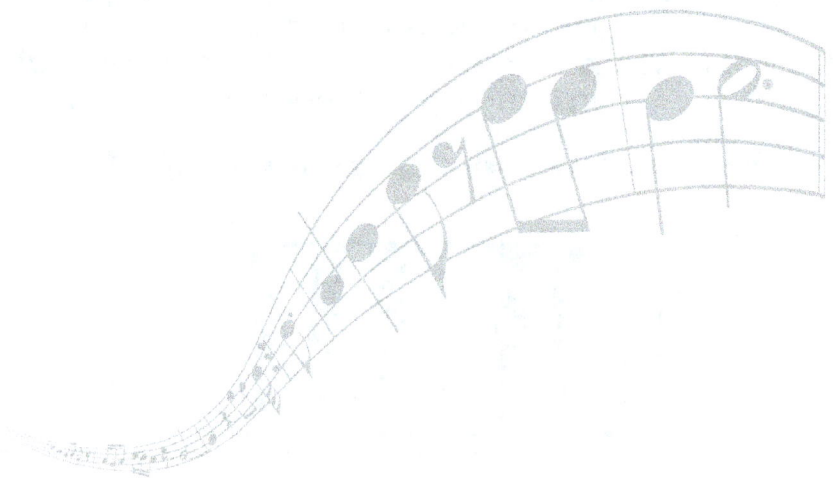

Key Strategy #10
PLAYING THE SYMPHONY OF YOUR WORK-LIFE BALANCE
Texture

"Music heals in ways words cannot, it feeds the soul, mends the heart, and opens us to the beauty of life's deepest emotions."

~ Glory St. Germain

Can music heal a broken heart or a devastating loss? What gives our life its texture? It's not just the highlights; it's the layered moments. The quiet pauses, the aching dissonance, the gentle harmonies that hold us together when everything else seems to fall apart. And sometimes, the most profound texture in our life comes from the deepest losses and the love that remains.

I lost the love of my life.

The texture of our life is like the texture of music, woven with highs and lows, crescendos and decrescendos, dynamic variations, articulations, and rhythms that can leave us breathless or even overwhelmed.

As I write these final chapters, the texture of my own life has taken a profound turn. You've read about the love story of meeting my incredible husband and our symphony of a loving marriage, our children, our life together, traveling the world, and sharing our passion for music. Together, we truly created a work-life balance and lived the freedom lifestyle, weaving a musical texture into our lives like no other.

Christmas has always been a joyous, musical occasion for us. Born on Christmas Day, it has been an extra special time of celebration, bringing our family together for the traditions of music and our family jam.

Last Christmas, however, was one I never expected to be our last together. Ray, who had been battling Parkinson's for some time, went into the hospital on Christmas Day, December 25, 2023, with complications. Four days later, he was transferred to a long-term health care center, never to return home again.

Music was Ray's life, and mine too. Many musicians, family, and friends came to play for him, lifting his spirits and reminding him of the joy he had given to so many. Even as his health declined, Ray still longed to sing, though his body struggled. Music has a way of uplifting us when we are low and supporting us when words fall short.

Six months later, on June 7, 2024, Ray was honored with a Street Naming ceremony. The news read, "Ray St. Germain, a Winnipeg-born Métis country music legend, performed a song alongside his family and fans Friday as the street in the St. Vital neighborhood where his childhood home is located was given the honorary name Big Sky Country Way, after St. Germain's award-winning national network television show, which ran for thirteen years."

Despite being wheelchair-bound and barely able to speak, when the time came, Ray wanted to sing, not just any song, but his signature showstopper, "It's Now or Never." The crowd erupted in a standing ovation. That day marked his last public performance.

Ray passed away a few weeks later, on June 25, 2024, exactly fifty years to the day that we first met. My life changed forever that day. The love of my life now lives on in my heart and the memories of our incredible life together. Thankfully, I can still hear his voice every day through the many albums he recorded, and the television shows he left behind that are now on YouTube.

I share this personal story, not to make you sad, but to uplift you with the profound power of music. You have chosen an extraordinary profession. You are not just teaching music lessons; you are giving your students and their audiences a life-changing experience.

You are part of something much bigger. Ray wrote a song called, "If You See the Same Bird, You'll Know That It's Me," and in fact, he returned to me as a hummingbird, twice. (But that's a story for another time.) To experience the power of his voice, you can listen to Ray's music inside your Ultimate Music Teachers Free Resources to hear and feel for yourself the impact of his musical legacy.

Everyone experiences loss, change and stress in their life at some point. Sometimes it feels like an overwhelming dilemma, but only if we let it. Life's challenges often remind us of the importance of creating a work-life balance, not only in the face of major crises or life events but also in the everyday rhythms of our lives.

When a crisis strikes, whether it's the loss of a loved one, a health challenge, or another life-altering event, our carefully woven balance can feel as though it's unraveling. These moments test the strength of the systems and support we've put in place. They remind us of the value of leaning into the healing power of music, the love of our community, and the inner peace we cultivate through intentional practices.

Yet work-life balance isn't just about navigating monumental events; it's about finding harmony in the small, daily choices we make. The texture of our day-to-day lives, our routines, priorities, and interactions create the symphony of our existence. By managing these rhythms thoughtfully, we can sustain balance even amidst life's crescendos and decrescendos.

Let's take a closer look at how you can nurture balance in both dimensions: staying grounded and resilient during times of crisis and crafting the rhythms of everyday life with intention. Whether you're facing a moment of profound change or seeking to maintain harmony in your daily routine, the principles of balance and texture offer a path toward a more fulfilling and meaningful life.

Overcome the Overwhelm – Three Strands to Untangle

Overwhelm can weave its way into every aspect of our lives, creating tangled strands that blur the boundaries between our personal, family, and professional lives. Whether it's the guilt of feeling like you're neglecting your family while teaching, the stress of trying to support others because you can't say no, or the weight of trying to meet your own high expectations, overwhelm has a way of creeping in and taking over. But it doesn't have to stay that way.

Let me share with you how I learned to untangle the overwhelm in my own life, strand by strand. Through three pivotal moments in my journey as an educator, a mother, and an individual. I discovered how to shift my perspective, embrace empathy, and find grace. I shared these lessons in one of my TEDx Talks. These moments taught me how to live with joy, purpose, and passion while creating balance across the three strands of my life.

The first strand: Professional Overwhelm.

At a coffee shop meeting with fellow music teachers, I sat silently, afraid to raise my hand and ask questions, paralyzed by imposter syndrome. But as I watched others shifting uncomfortably, I realized they shared the same fears. I took a deep breath, raised my hand, and asked the first question and then another. Far from ridicule, my questions unlocked a ripple of relief, community, and courage. That day, I shifted from comparison to connection and untangled the first strand. May I invite you to untangle your professional overwhelm by embracing community over comparison?

The second strand: Family Overwhelm.

There was a door that separated my home from my music studio. One day, after barking hurried instructions to my daughter as I rushed into teaching mode, she quietly said, "Mom… when you come through this door, can you be the teacher on this side too?" Her small voice taught me a huge lesson: empathy shouldn't stop at the classroom door. That day, I opened the empathy door in my family life and untangled the second strand.

May I invite you to untangle your family overwhelm by listening with empathy and love?

The third strand: Personal Overwhelm.

Sitting by my jewelry box, staring at my mother's old pearl necklace, I felt the crushing weight of unrealistic expectations. And then, it felt as if my mother's voice whispered: "Live each day with grace." Not perfection. Not pressure. Just grace, one small step, one precious moment at a time. That day, I left the jewelry box open as a reminder: life is a collection of small pearls, not one perfect strand. I untangled the third strand, accepting grace over overwhelm.

May I invite you to untangle your personal overwhelm by embracing grace and self-acceptance?

You have a choice: to live with Joy, Purpose, and Passion by untangling your professional, family, and personal strands one beautiful moment at a time.

The world is your oyster. Which strand will you untangle first?

The heartbeat of every great teacher is fueled by Three Magic Keys that unlock extraordinary possibilities, enriching the texture of your teaching and nurturing your life-work balance.

THE 3 MAGIC KEYS FOR YOUR LIFE-WORK BALANCE

Everyone experiences stress. Sometimes, it feels like an overwhelming dilemma, but only if we let it. To live your dream and capture the lead in achieving your goals, consider using the Three Magic Keys to drive the texture of joy and productivity into your life. These keys can dramatically impact how you feel about yourself, your goals, and your outcomes.

The Magic Key of A: Attitude

The first magic key, whether you choose A Major or a minor is up to you. A is for Attitude. In life, just as in music, you can choose a bright, major feeling or slip into the minor tones of negativity. To drive positivity into your life, you need a #PMA: Positive Mental Attitude. The way you deal with situations is a direct reflection of your attitude.

Think about your relationships and your goals. You have a choice: Show up with gratitude, positivity, and resilience even when life gets messy or let negativity take center stage. The Key of A reminds you: a positive attitude is the rhythm of success.

The Magic Key of B: Beautiful State

The second magic key, whether you choose B Major or b minor, it's your call. B is for a Beautiful State or a Bleak State. When life feels bleak, you can either stay stuck or #TurnItAround.

Transformation starts with the simple decision to shift your energy. A kind word, a moment of empathy, a playful laugh: you have the power to turn bleak into beautiful, for yourself and for others.

How do you play "Turn it Around"? You always have the power to transform any situation. When encountering someone in a bleak state, you face a choice:

You can either let frustration take over and just focus on the task at hand, or you can actively #TurnItAround by applying your Positive Mental Attitude.

They will thank you for turning their day around. Maybe they're carrying major burdens you can't even see, and you might be the bright moment they need to keep going.

You have the key to turning their state from bleak to beautiful and renew their faith that good things can still happen for all of us. You become not just a teacher of music, but a teacher of hope.

The Magic Key of C: Certainty

The third magic key is the Major Key of C, which stands for Certainty in Communication, delivering your message with clarity, focus, and the mindset of always aiming for #SolutionsOnly. Just like the Major Key of C in music, which resonates with a clear and confident tone, strong communication requires that same decisiveness and purpose. In the world of music, we value interpretation; in conversation, we must value clear understanding.

Conversely, the Minor Key of C adds a different layer to communication. In music, the Minor Key of C evokes reflection and complexity. In communication, a 'Minor Key' mindset invites us to notice subtle emotional nuances, the unspoken feelings behind the words. This deeper awareness leads to richer, more empathetic connections.

However, the Minor Key can also reveal a danger: complaining. While expressing underlying emotions is important, complaining for its own sake rarely solves anything. It drains positivity, slows momentum, and keeps us stuck. Effective communication in the Minor Key means tuning in to deeper emotions but always steering conversations toward constructive action and meaningful understanding.

The true art is balancing the direct clarity of the Major Key with the emotional depth of the Minor Key. Together, they unlock a more holistic, heart-centered way to connect and lead. When the written word is all we have: emails, texts, Facebook messenger, etc., we must choose words carefully, so they are not misunderstood. #SolutionsOnly. (And yes, sometimes a well-placed smiley face or emoji helps set the right tone.)

When speaking to someone on the phone, smile while you talk. They may not see it, but they will feel it. Your heart can be heard. Remember: You have the choice. You are the creator of your destiny. Choose your communication tempo wisely.

Live by the 3 Magic Keys to Drive Positivity into Your Life:

- **Success comes with Attitude (#PMA)**

- **Living in a Beautiful State (#TurnItAround)**

- **Communicating with Certainty (#SolutionsOnly)**

May your Three Magic Keys; Attitude, Beautiful State, and Communication unlock your highest potential and orchestrate the rich texture of your life. Just as texture in music emerges when melodies, harmonies, rhythms, tempo, and timbre intertwine, the same principle shapes our lives and our work.

For some, that texture may at first feel disjointed or overwhelming just as it once did for UMT Certified Teacher Shauna Hunter. Her journey of overcoming imposter syndrome and discovering her confidence shows how reshaping the texture of your life can lead to transformative success.

"Simplicity is the final achievement. After one has played a vast quantity of notes and more notes, it is simplicity that emerges as the crowning reward of art."

~ Frédéric Chopin

Case Study:
UMT Certified Teacher Shauna Hunter

Shauna Hunter once believed she was "just another piano teacher." Imposter Syndrome weighed heavily on her heart, convincing her that she had nothing special to offer.

Despite having been trained by a renowned Belgian concert pianist, she often doubted her worth. She had no fancy degrees hanging on the wall, only an overwhelming belief that she was destined to remain average. Being a music teacher doesn't automatically mean you have the confidence to see your own value.

For Shauna, the turning point came when she chose to invest in herself. She pursued professional development, earning her Royal Conservatory of Music teacher certification and completing the Ultimate Music Theory Certification Elite Educator Program achieving First Class Honors with Distinction.

This shift didn't just elevate her teaching skills; it transformed her life. Shauna grew her income by 50%, expanded her confidence, and began running her teaching studio with clarity, vision, and heart. Her success was not just financial; it was personal. She found her voice, her purpose, and her power.

Then life delivered an unexpected challenge. Shauna was diagnosed with breast cancer. Forced to scale back her teaching hours for treatment, she faced her own mortality and found a deeper perspective.

Through her healing journey, Shauna discovered that life is precious, and every hour must be spent well. She realized that teaching was not about credentials or income anymore, it was about building relationships, inspiring students, and using music as a force for healing and hope.

She listened to music throughout her therapy, feeling its power lift her spirit when everything seemed dark. It was during this time that she redefined her purpose: to teach each student with empathy, to adapt her methods to individual learning needs, and to nurture their dreams with compassion and creativity.

Shauna embraced new learning, connected with music teachers around the world, and found extraordinary support through the Ultimate Music Teachers Membership and weekly coaching calls.

Through this community, she didn't just grow her business, she grew herself. Shauna's story beautifully illustrates the transformative power of perseverance, resilience, and personal growth.

Her journey reminds us that the texture of our lives woven with ambition, family, and fulfillment can shift dramatically when we embrace new perspectives and take intentional steps toward balance.

Just as Shauna redefined her teaching and self-belief, you too can overcome the overwhelm and orchestrate your life into a symphony of joy, purpose, and prosperity.

Shauna Hunter's inspiring journey exemplifies her commitment to excellence and ongoing professional development. Her passion for empowering fellow educators and unwavering dedication to nurturing teacher growth led her to join our UMT Dream Team as our UMT Teacher Support Coach, where she continues to inspire, guide, and uplift music teachers toward their highest potential.

Read Shauna's inspiring story in *The Power of WHY Musicians* 5 Book Series.

Now let's pause to reflect on the Three Steps to Overcome the Overwhelm, with the texture of work-life balance in professional, family, and personal goals.

⌒ *Fermata* (Pause to Ponder): Three Steps to Overcome the Overwhelm

I believe there are three critical elements to achieving work-life balance and reducing overwhelm:

Step #1: Cultivate Professional Growth

Professional overwhelm often stems from imposter syndrome, lack of direction, or feeling disconnected from your goals.

To untangle this strand, focus on cultivating professional growth through intentional development, such as joining a teaching community, learning new techniques, or investing in certifications like the Ultimate Music Theory Certification.

How can you take one bold step to invest in your professional development?

_____

_____

What specific action will help you align your teaching with your long-term vision?

_____

_____

How can you build a support system of like-minded educators to reduce professional overwhelm?

_____

_____

Step #2: Strengthen Family Connections

Family overwhelm can feel like a constant tug-of-war between your roles at home and your business. Creating boundaries and open communication can help harmonize these two worlds.

What small changes can you make to balance family time with work commitments?

_____

_____

How can you use empathy to understand your family's needs and strengthen relationships?

_____

_____

What meaningful family rituals can you create to foster connection and reduce stress?

_____

_____

Step #3: Prioritize Personal Well-Being

Personal overwhelm often comes from neglecting your own needs while focusing on others. Prioritizing self-care and personal growth is essential to achieving balance and fulfillment.

How can you incorporate moments of grace and mindfulness into your daily routine?

_____

_____

What personal goals or passions have you been putting off that you can prioritize now?

_____

_____

How will you take small, consistent steps to nurture your mental, emotional, and physical well-being?

_____

_____

The texture of your life professionally, with your family, and personally is unique to you. By redefining your approach, you have the power to untangle the strands of overwhelm and weave them into a rich, harmonious symphony of balance and joy.

How will you use these three simple steps to overcome the overwhelm in your life?

Mastering work-life balance allows you to build a sustainable business that reflects your values, inspires your students, and empowers you to thrive with purpose and profitability. Let's keep composing your symphony of success.

*"When you dare to reshape the texture of your life,
you unlock the strength to transform overwhelm into
opportunity and doubt into confidence."*

~ Glory St. Germain

♪ Your Coda Notes ♪

_____

_____

The 12 Key Strategies include online Ultimate Music Teachers Bonus Resources.

TEACH MUSIC CHANGE LIVES
Playing the Symphony of Your Work-Life Balance

Dive deeper into **KEY STRATEGY #10** - get your
Ultimate Music Teachers
FREE Bonus Workbook to create the texture of a life
and business you love.

Go To: UltimateMusicTeachers.com/guide

 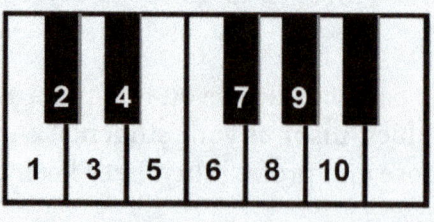 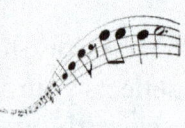

Key Strategy #11
TEACHING BUSINESS MONEY MINDSET BLUEPRINT
Form

"Success in music and money comes down to FORM. Focus, Opportunity, Revenue, and Mindset. Master it, and your business will sing in prosperity."

~ Glory St. Germain

Taylor Swift didn't become a global icon by luck. She became one by formulating her own powerful strategy. She focused relentlessly on her craft, saw every challenge as an opportunity, negotiated for her own revenue rights, and fiercely protected her mindset. That's not just stardom, that's structure. That's form.

So, what about you? Are you structuring your teaching business with the same level of clarity, confidence, and purpose? Because the truth is, you don't need to be famous to be financially free, you just need the right form.

Form took on a whole new meaning for me. One day I decided to sit down and take a look at my finances (not a pretty picture). I saw that my income did not match my rising expenses. I saw that there was no plan to pay off my credit cards, my overdraft, or even invest in a savings account. At that point, I knew something had to change drastically. I needed to form a plan, a business plan, to get serious about my teaching business.

As a teacher, I loved analyzing form in music when introducing new pieces. In musical terms, form represents the structure of a composition, the way different sections interact to create a cohesive and engaging piece.

Whether it was binary, ternary, rondo, or sonata form, understanding the organization, repetition, contrast, and development within music helped my students grasp the beauty and logic behind the pieces they played. In fact, all music has a specific form and without that structure, it would just be random measures. Teaching form was my favorite element.

But it wasn't until years later that I realized form applied just as much to my teaching business as it did to music. Being a great teacher, helping students excel, inspiring them to love music, didn't automatically mean I was successful in money management. Teaching and financial success were two completely different skill sets, and in the business department, I was struggling to find the right rhythm.

I needed to redefine my approach and apply **F.O.R.M.** in a whole new way:

Focus I had to shift my mindset from "just teaching" to running a business. This meant getting clear on my financial goals, pricing my lessons appropriately, and structuring my studio for long-term success.

Opportunity Growth wasn't going to happen by accident. I had to create opportunities, expanding my offerings, marketing my studio strategically, and stepping into new teaching formats that would allow me to scale.

Revenue Sustainability mattered. I realized that simply adding more private students wasn't the answer; I needed a repeatable, scalable income stream. That's when I started teaching Music Theory Groups, and everything changed.

Mindset Most importantly, I had to reset my money mindset. Instead of viewing finances as stressful or overwhelming, I embraced the idea that money is a tool that empowers growth, impact, and possibilities.

By mastering FORM in both music and business, I was able to transform my teaching studio from a passion project into a profitable, sustainable, and fulfilling career. Now I want to share these principles with you, so you can orchestrate your own financial success, one strategic note at a time.

FOCUS: Your Compass for Success

A common mistake we see in business is starting without first communicating and aligning strategic goals. Skipping this crucial step can leave your teaching business adrift, like a ship sailing without a course, hoping to land somewhere great but drifting wherever the winds take you.

Where is your focus in your music teaching business right now?

Before you map out your destination, let's take a little trip down memory lane. Think back to when you first decided to become a music teacher.

Was it because you couldn't imagine doing anything else?

Because you wanted to share the magic of music?

Or, let's be honest, was it because you thought, "How hard can it be?

I love music, kids are cute, and I get to work from home in comfy clothes."

Then reality hit: negotiating with an eight-year-old who confidently insists their left hand is their right hand; decoding a teenager's version of "practice" ("I totally practiced, in my head."); realizing that 30 minutes of lessons per week doesn't magically substitute for consistent practice at home; and convincing students that music theory is actually a secret superpower? Good luck with that!

Yet here you are still showing up, still teaching, still loving it (even on days that require an extra-large tea and a pep talk).

It's time to get crystal clear on what you're building. Clarity is power and with the right focus, your business can grow in harmony with your goals. Here's how:

1. Define Your 'Why'

Before you map out where you're going, reflect on why you chose this path:

- **Why did you start teaching music?**
- **What impact do you want to create?**
- **What excites you the most about teaching?**

This isn't just about teaching notes, it's about your purpose. Maybe you're passionate about helping students unlock creativity or creating a new generation of musicians who love learning theory instead of fearing it.

Your 'why' is your fuel. It's what gets you out of bed even when Johnny the Human Metronome is your 8 AM student who plays at exactly one speed, *presto.*

2. Create Your Vision Statement

Once you reconnect with your 'why,' the next step is to put it into words. A Vision Statement is your North Star, a short, powerful phrase that guides your decisions and keeps you aligned when distractions arise (like redesigning your website for the seventeenth time instead of actually marketing your lessons).

Example: "I empower students to discover their love of learning music through engaging, joyful, and inspiring lessons."

Drill into that vision by asking yourself "what does that look like for me"? Maybe your passion lies in:

- **Teaching theory creatively (no more "musical broccoli" lessons.)**
- **Fostering a love for confident performances**
- **Helping students creatively compose their own music**

Whatever drives you, put it into a concise, meaningful statement that you can return to whenever you need motivation or when you're questioning why you taught composing (because who wouldn't love to hear "The Ballad of Mr. Whiskers" written by an enthusiastic ten-year-old?).

3. Visualize Your Future

Now, let's dream BIG. Close your eyes (unless you're making a snack between students then maybe just squint thoughtfully, because teachers + snack breaks = real life, right?) and imagine your ideal teaching life five years from now:

- **Who are your students? What skills are you cultivating?**

- **Are you teaching privately, group classes, creating courses or all three?**

- **How does your teaching impact your income, lifestyle and sense of fulfillment?**

Write it all down. Take action. Turn your dream into your direction.

OPPORTUNITY: Open the Box of Possibilities

Opportunities don't always arrive with drumrolls and spotlights, sometimes they show up in a passing comment from a parent, a collaboration with a fellow teacher, or a simple idea sparked by a student. Success is built through connection: your students, families, teaching peers, and community are your greatest resources. Every relationship you nurture opens new doors, referrals, partnerships, creative programs, and support when you need it most (like when a student insists on playing "Jingle Bells" in October, again). Collaboration is not competition. There are enough students for everyone (this isn't "Music Teacher Survivor").

By staying open to possibilities, seeking creative partnerships, and bravely stepping into new opportunities even when you're nervous, you transform your teaching business into a thriving, joyful career. If opportunity doesn't knock, build a better door or launch that group class, send that bold email, or finally convince parents that yes, music theory is life changing. Open the box of possibilities and watch your dreams take center stage.

Ask yourself:

- **Who's already in my circle that I can connect with more deeply?**

- **Are there other teachers I could partner with for workshops or events?**

- **What small, simple steps can I take to strengthen my network today?**

REVENUE: Expand Your Growth and Scale Your Business

Let's be real, most of us didn't become music teachers just for the money, but passion alone won't pay the bills (or buy that dream piano/guitar/mic). The good news? Expanding your revenue doesn't mean working harder, it means working smarter.

Start by adding new income streams like group classes, workshops, online courses, or fun merch (hello, "Practice Makes Perfect" tote bags). Raise your rates to reflect your expertise, you wouldn't expect your favorite coffee shop to keep 1990s prices, so why should you?

And finally, automate your systems: use online scheduling, automatic payments, and email templates to save time and energy. Small shifts add up fast, a $5 lesson increase or a new group class could grow your income by thousands annually. Ask yourself: What new income stream could you launch in the next 90 days?

Where can you raise your value and rates with confidence? Which task could you automate today to create more freedom tomorrow? Your dream lifestyle isn't a fantasy; it's just a few smart moves away. You're building a thriving, profitable, and sustainable teaching business.

Now, go make it happen. Your bank account will thank you and so will your future self, preferably while sipping something fabulous on a beach.

MINDSET: The Key That Unlocks It All

- **I had focus, I knew my goals.**

- **I had opportunity, I connected with my community to grow my studio.**

- **I had revenue goals, big, life-changing goals.**

And yet, something was still holding me back.

What was it? Mindset.

Not the business plan. Not the strategy. Not even a student meltdown over the Circle of Fifths homework. It was me.

You've heard the saying: "If you think you can, or you think you can't, either way, you're right." Well, at that moment, I was firmly in Camp "I Can't."

The biggest AHA moment? Realizing that to reach the next level in my business and my life, I had to change. Not my teaching style. Not my logo. Me.

When I shifted my mindset, everything changed. I stopped waiting for the "right time" and became the right person who made things happen.

Here's your quick Mindset Reset:

Change Your Self-Talk:
Ditch Nervous Nellie who whispers, "I'm not good enough," and channel Powerhouse Parker who proudly says, "I'm learning. I'm growing. I'm unstoppable." (And if Netflix calls while you're growing? Politely decline. Your future self will send you a thank-you note.)

Recognize Your Strengths and Own Them:
What makes you a rockstar teacher? (Hint: It's not about playing Bach upside-down at 200 bpm.) Maybe you make theory fun, ignite students' creativity, or inspire shy kids to shine. Write down three of your superpowers, then lean all the way in.

Set Your Money Mindset for Success:

Write down the exact income you want each month. Write down how many hours you want to work. Now, connect the dots:

What needs to shift in your business model to make that vision real?

What bold action can you take today to close that gap?
(And no, "waiting for a sign from the universe" doesn't count unless that sign says, "Raise Your Rates.")

Your mindset can either fuel your journey or leave you stranded with a flat tire, so choose wisely. The life, business, and impact you're dreaming of are the direct result of cultivating a bold mindset and taking consistent action.

"The moment you shift your mindset to possibilities instead of limitations, you become unstoppable."

~ Glory St. Germain

Your mindset is your guiding star as it determines:

- **How you set goals.**

- **How you react to challenges.**

- **Whether you see obstacles or opportunities.**

Just like you tell your students, learning never stops. The teachers who keep growing are the ones who thrive. That's why I created the UMTC Elite Educator Program, to give you the support, the roadmap, and the community to grow faster and with greater confidence.

You've now mastered the essential FORM to build a thriving, profitable teaching business:

Focus is your compass that aligns every decision with your goals. Opportunity is your bridge to connections, community, and unstoppable growth.

Revenue is your rhythm, ensuring your business remains profitable and scalable.

Mindset is your conductor, orchestrating your success through bold, intentional thinking.

This is your ultimate Set List for thriving and flourishing in your teaching business. Now, apply this same Mindset Mastery to inspire your students. Because just like a captivating performance, building a powerful student mindset is intentional; it grows through focused practice, steady encouragement, and purposeful mindset shifts.

The Five Elements of a Practical Lesson: Teaching the Student Mindset Transformation

Your business success isn't about how many students you have, it's about how successful your students become. The better they learn, grow, and gain confidence, the greater your reputation, retention, and referrals.

The secret? A structured lesson strategy that teaches music and mindset transformation.

The Set List Mindset

Students who feel successful stay motivated, practice more, and inspire parent loyalty. That's why building lessons with a "Set List Mindset" is so powerful. It strengthens bonds, sets clear goals, and makes learning feel rewarding.

Here's how to structure a one-hour lesson with five transformational impact steps:

One: Teach New Material First. Students are sharpest at the beginning of the lesson. Spend the first ten minutes introducing new concepts, focusing on one clear takeaway. Check for understanding because that blank stare? It's real. And if all else fails, a music joke never hurts: "Why did the piano player keep banging his head against the keys? He was trying to play by ear." (I know, keep my day job.)

Two: Connect Theory to Practical. Theory shouldn't feel like musical broccoli. Spend ten minutes applying theory through scales, sight-reading, and ear training. When students see theory as the secret weapon to making music easier, they stay engaged, and frustration (and quitting) is less likely.

Three: Review Progress from Last Lesson. Use the next ten minutes to review assignments. Celebrate wins, address challenges, and give clear, specific next steps. Instead of saying, "Keep practicing," say, "Work on bars 9–16, focusing on left-hand dynamics." Vague practice plans = vague results.

Four: Focused Lesson Practice. This. Is. Huge. Set a ten-minute timer and have students practice their pieces during the lesson. Stay silent unless they need your guidance. If the ten-minute solo practice is interrupted, assist them, then reset the timer and start again. If they can't practice ten minutes independently now, they won't do it at home. This locked in ten-minute practice during lesson time builds real-time confidence, and fewer "practice battles" at home, which means happy parents.

Five: Build Their Set List. End each lesson by adding to their Set List, a repertoire of 10–20 polished pieces students can perform anytime. Include Happy Birthday, seasonal favorites, personal picks, and classics. When students have a ready-to-play Set List, they don't just say, "I take lessons", they say, "I am a musician."

The Set List Mindset helps students:

- **Build musical independence**

- **Connect theory to real-world playing**

- **Feel confident performing anytime**

- **View themselves as real musicians, not just students**

And when your students confidently pull out a piece at a family gathering or when someone says, "Play something" and they actually can play, that's when the real magic happens.

Teaching is more than technique and a few performance pieces, it's about teaching life skills. Confidence. Focus. Ownership. We step into the role of Powerhouse Parker to lead the way, so our students step into being Successful Sammy. Because in the end, it's about inspiring a lifetime of music and confidence.

Let's teach, inspire, and create the next generation of thriving musicians. And if someday your student sight-reads at a wedding with the confidence of a rock star? You'll know exactly where they got it from. Because you teach music and change lives.

The Professional Set List

I can still see it clearly: musicians arriving early, gear set up meticulously, tuned and ready to go. In my husband Ray's world, thirty minutes early was on time. Professionalism wasn't just about playing well, it was about preparation, respect, and presence.

Ray wasn't just a singer or a guitarist; he was an entertainer. He could read a crowd with uncanny intuition, adjusting his show in real time to create unforgettable experiences. Standing ovations weren't luck, they were the result of mastery.

At the heart of it all? The Set List.

Each show began with a planned Big Show Set List: a carefully curated lineup that built emotion, momentum, and connection. Yet Ray's true genius was his adaptability. If he sensed a shift in the audience's energy, he pivoted seamlessly because great musicians don't just play songs; they play the moment.

Each band member received only the essentials: song titles and keys. Preparation was expected. Adaptability was non-negotiable.

That level of readiness shaped how I see musical evolution today. A Student Set List, those early polished pieces aren't just for recitals; it's a training ground for the habits of professionalism: preparation, flexibility, and performance under pressure.

What happens when you go "Off" The Set List

Funny you should ask. My husband Ray was performing, captivating the crowd as always, when a super fan shouted, "What's the first song you ever wrote?" Without missing a beat, Ray grinned and replied, "I wrote a rock and roll song called *She's a Square.*" The fan called back, "Can you play it?"

Now, most musicians would hesitate, this wasn't on the set list, and the band hadn't rehearsed it. But not Ray. Without a second thought, he turned to the band and said, "It's a little blues in C, watch me for the changes." Showtime.

Ray counted in the tempo, struck the first chord, and the band fell right in effortlessly. How? Because they knew the form. They trusted the framework they had mastered: the 12-bar blues, the I-IV-V progression, the groove, the instinct.

No sheet music. No panic. Just professionalism and presence. And yes, as always, he earned his signature standing ovation.

She's a Square holds a special place in Canadian music history. Released in 1958, it became the first rock record produced in Winnipeg to reach the national charts, heavily inspired by Elvis Presley's style. Ray's uncanny vocal resemblance to The King earned him the nickname "Winnipeg's Elvis." In fact, Ray wrote a book called "I Wanted to be Elvis, So What Was I Doing in Moose Jaw".

A full circle moment.

The Set List Mindset: A Full-Circle Moment

As I reflect on our family's journey, I see how the Set List Mindset shaped each generation. From a young age, our children curated their own Set Lists, polished pieces that built their musical identity. What began as a tool for lessons became a second-nature practice of preparation, confidence, and adaptability. Our son David performed numerous shows with Ray, learning how the Set List Mindset worked on tour.

And now, I see it continuing, the ripple effect of what we teach as music educators going far beyond the lesson room. The Set List Mindset is about preparing for performances and being ready for life-changing opportunities when they arise.

And that's exactly what happened for our youngest daughter, Sherry St. Germain.

In her twenties, Sherry was invited to perform in the *Viva Elvis* Cirque du Soleil show in Las Vegas, a full-circle moment of preparation meeting destiny.

Picture it: Sherry, floating down from the sky, playing piano center stage at the Aria, belting out *One Night with You* in pure Elvis style. It was a moment of magic and mastery, born from years of daily practice, stage presence, and relentless refinement.

From the moment she climbed onto the piano bench at age two, to countless rehearsals with her father, to studying with masters in classical and jazz, Sherry's foundation had been built strong. Every step tested her confidence, but she was ready. When destiny called, she didn't hesitate. She soared.

On opening night, as the music filled the theatre, I turned and saw proud tears streaming down Ray's face. His daughter, his legacy, was carrying forward the music, the spirit, and the dream. It wasn't just a performance. It was a living testament to preparation, passion, and the power of stepping fully into your moment when it arrives.

The Set List of Your Life

As music teachers, we may not always see the long-term effects of our work but every lesson, every note, every word of encouragement plants a seed. Some students will go on to perform on the world's biggest stages. Others will carry their love of music into their daily lives, enriching their families and communities. Either way, the impact we make lasts far beyond the lesson room.

The Set List Mindset isn't just about preparing students for their next recital. It's about equipping them with the confidence, skills, and readiness to step into any opportunity that comes their way.

Because one day, just like Sherry, they'll be center stage in their own lives, ready to shine.

As teachers, we sometimes forget the profound impact we have. Many of my students have gone on to become professional musicians, carrying the habits they built in lessons into their careers and into every stage, recording studio, and community they touch.

Remember Connor? His Set List began when he was a young student, performing pieces in order, growing comfortable with structure, and learning the power of preparation. That practice became his norm. And now? That same mindset continues to guide his professional performances today.

A Set List isn't just a collection of songs. It's a mindset. It's a commitment to being ready, to showing up prepared, and to embracing the responsibility of music.

Give your students every opportunity to become Successful Sammy, because the habits they build now will shape not just the musicians they become, but the people they become.

From Hairbrush Mic to Global Stage: The Evolution of a Dream

I can still picture myself as a young girl, alone in my bedroom, posters of superstars on my walls, hairbrush microphone in hand, belting out Beatles songs into the mirror while inventing dance moves no one had ever seen. I was living the dream. Little did I know the climb over countless obstacles had just begun.

The stage was calling me. I always dreamed of being on the big stage, playing keyboards and singing in a band. My grandpa used to say, "If you wish upon a star and believe with all your heart, your dreams will come true."

And isn't it funny? When you're a kid, you believe anything is possible. But as we grow, self-doubt creeps in, whispering that maybe dreams are only for other people.

One day, I saw a newspaper ad: Superstar Band Seeks Female Keyboard Player. At seventeen, my heart skipped a beat, this was my moment. I was already teaching piano and running a small music studio. I had years of "hairbrush microphone" training. How hard could it be? The night of the audition, I stood backstage, with a music bag in hand. The lights, the energy, it was everything I had ever wished for. But as I watched the other girls audition, all so talented, so radiant – that little voice of fear took hold. Suddenly, my dream felt fragile. Without playing a single note, I quietly walked out the back door. I thought I had lost my one shot. But sometimes, "failure" is simply a pivot, a gentle nudge toward a bigger destiny.

Over time, I realized my dream hadn't vanished. It had evolved. I wasn't meant to perform. I was meant to create something even bigger: a way to help students and teachers around the world unlock their own stars. I went on to create the Ultimate Music Theory Workbooks, Teacher Training Courses, Business Coaching Programs and speaking on global stages I never could have imagined. I remember the moment it all came full circle. Years later, I found myself standing on a different stage, not behind a keyboard, but in front of hundreds of music educators. This time, there was no walking away. This time, I picked up the microphone, not to sing, but to speak. It was then I realized: This was my true stage. Not to entertain, but to empower. Not to chase applause, but to spark transformation.

Listening to the struggles of fellow educators inspired me to create teacher training programs. Because I knew firsthand: teachers didn't have to struggle alone. I had taken the hard road, so others could have a map. In life, we all have a choice: To dream big and keep climbing, or to let doubt steal our destiny. Maybe the stage I once imagined wasn't my final destination. Maybe my true spotlight was always shining, not behind a keyboard, but within me, as a speaker, a mentor, an author and educator.

And in my heart, I know this: the true star in our family has always been my husband, Ray. His "marshmallow voice" still melts my heart, alongside the music of our children David, Sherry, Catherine, Ray Jr., Chrystal and grandchildren Jeff and Catie, all carrying forward his legacy of love, music, and passion.

Global Music Teachers Summits

In 2021, I founded the Global Music Teachers Summits, bringing expert speakers together to connect with thousands of music educators worldwide. These summits sparked real conversations, the ones essential for true professional growth.

From this movement, a bigger dream unfolded. Many of these musicians became international best-selling authors through my publishing company, Gloryland Publishing. (Yes, there really is a home in Gloryland.) Together, we released five books in *The Power of WHY Musicians* series, featuring 125 inspiring stories of perseverance and passion. It hit me then: We don't just pivot—we evolve.

One dream led to another: educator, course creator, speaker, podcaster, author. A single star became a constellation. One of my biggest dreams was to become a TEDx Speaker, to share my message with the world. That wish came true, twice. (And maybe three times by the time you read this, never stop dreaming.)

From the girl with the hairbrush microphone to the global speaking stage, the journey was real. (No, the hairbrush didn't make it to the TEDx stage, but the dream sure did.) And now, I wish upon a star for you. As your Ultimate Music Teachers Business Coach, my greatest joy is helping you reach your dreams, build a thriving music business, and shine brighter than ever. Because dreams don't disappear, they evolve. And so do you.

Your next chapter has the power to be your brightest yet. At one of our Global Music Teachers Summits, I met an incredible music educator, Leanna Minnick. Her story of resilience, passion, and transformation touched my heart and inspired musicians around the world. Today, I'm honored to share a glimpse of her journey with you.

"Success in the music industry isn't something that you wait for or hope for. It is something you create, day after day."

~ Simon S. Tam

Case Study:
UMT Certified Teacher Leanna Minnick

How does someone with hearing loss who endured the pain of countless earaches as a child, taught herself to read lips, and faced overwhelming communication challenges, find healing through music? How does that same person go on to master piano, violin, and accordion, earn a degree in music composition, and become an internationally recognized educator? The answer: Mindset.

Through every move, from being born in Canada, to living in New Zealand, to settling in America, the one thing that stayed constant for Leanna Minnick was her unwavering passion for music.

As a young student, Leanna sat in the front row of every class, teaching herself to lip-read and excelling in school and music academics. She carried that same determination into her teaching career, looking into the faces of her young students as she shared her love of music, determined to be the best teacher she could possibly be.

It wasn't until years later, at a State Fair with her young children, that Leanna's life would change. Curious, she stepped into a booth offering free hearing tests. As she listened through the headphones, she was stunned. She heard sounds she had never heard before, sounds most people take for granted. She asked the audiologist in disbelief, "Does everyone hear what I'm hearing right now?"

It was at that moment that Leanna fully realized the depth of her hearing loss.

Still, she pressed forward. In 1990, while attending the University of Utah as a music major, Leanna received her first set of hearing aids. The world opened up.

For the first time, she could hear the sound of rustling leaves, a moment she described as deeply emotional, connecting her to Beethoven, whose story of triumph over deafness had always inspired her.

Music became not just something she heard, it was something she *felt* in her soul. Leanna shared that this is why she loved playing the accordion so much: because she could face her audience, see their smiles, and feel their appreciation even if the sound wasn't fully there.

Through all the challenges her deafness brought, Leanna's heart for teaching only grew stronger. She understood, at a profound level, the responsibility teachers have to instill a love of music in every student. Her deafness did not define her limitations, it defined her resilience, her innovation, and her empathy as a teacher.

To date, Leanna Minnick has become a UMT Certified Teacher and Elite Educator and served as my Executive Assistant at Ultimate Music Theory. Her life's journey is a testament to perseverance, excellence, and the beautiful truth that music is not just heard, it is seen, felt, and lived.

Read Leanna's inspiring story in *The Power of WHY Musicians* 5 Book Series.

Your teaching business is a powerful vehicle for impact, growth, and financial success.

Let's pause to reflect on the Three Steps to Shift Your Money Mindset for Business Profitability focusing on FORM, the Set List, and the Evolution of Your Teaching.

⌒ *Fermata* (Pause to Ponder): Shifting Your Money Mindset for Growth

Your teaching business is more than a passion, it's a powerful vehicle for impact, financial success, and personal fulfillment. Like a well-crafted musical composition, true business profitability follows form: structure, vision, and the right mindset.

Here are three essential steps to shift your money mindset for business profitability:

Step #1: Implement the FORM Framework

Focus, Opportunity, Revenue, and Mindset are the foundations for translating your passion into profit. When you apply FORM strategically, you stop working harder and start working smarter.

How can you refine your daily actions to better align with the FORM strategy?

_____

_____

Which area of FORM (Focus, Opportunity, Revenue, Mindset) needs the most attention in your business?

_____

_____

What action will you take this week to bridge the gap between passion and profitability?

_____

_____

Step #2: Strengthen Your Business with the Set List Mindset

Just as a musician prepares a Set List to be performance-ready, you must create a repeatable system of revenue streams like group classes, workshops, or online programs to build consistency and confidence in your income.

What "Set List" of income streams will help you scale and serve more students?

_____

_____

How can you package your lessons, courses, or experiences to create recurring revenue?

_____

_____

What revenue generating idea have you been putting off and what's your first small step toward launching it?

_____

_____

Step #3: Embrace the Evolution of Your Teaching and Business

Growth is not about perfection, it's about progress. As your business evolves, so must your pricing, your offerings, and your belief in your own value.

How can you refine your teaching or studio model to create more impact, income, and freedom?

_____

_____

Are your current pricing and offerings aligned with the value and transformation you deliver?

_____

_____

What new skill, certification, or mentorship opportunity will accelerate your next level of success?

_____

_____

Your mindset is the conductor of your success. When you align strategy with purpose and embrace the evolution of your role as both educator and entrepreneur, you unlock limitless possibilities for yourself and for every student you teach.

When you apply FORM, build your Financial Set List, and embrace the Evolution of Your Teaching, you create income, and you create impact. Your future isn't somewhere far away. You're building it, one powerful decision at a time.

"When you embrace the evolution of your mindset, you unlock the limitless potential to transform your business, your teaching, and your life."

~ Glory St. Germain

♪ Your Coda Notes ♪

The 12 Key Strategies include online Ultimate Music Teachers Bonus Resources.

TEACH MUSIC CHANGE LIVES
Teaching Business Money Mindset Blueprint

Dive deeper into **KEY STRATEGY #11** - get your
Ultimate Music Teachers
FREE Bonus Workbook to form the foundation of a
profitable teaching business.
Go To: UltimateMusicTeachers.com/guide

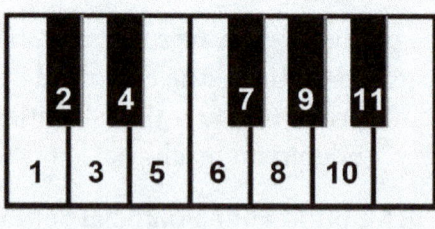

Key Strategy #12
YOUR PROFIT-FOCUSED ULTIMATE LEGACY
Analysis

*"It's the joy of giving, the power of teaching, and
the gratitude of music that fuels a profit-focused legacy."*

~ Glory St. Germain

From J.S. Bach to Beyoncé, two of the most influential musicians in history didn't just perform, they *taught*, they *mentored*, and they led with *purpose*.

Bach, often called the "teacher of teachers," composed for family and students, creating a generational legacy grounded in love and education. Beyoncé, mentored by David Lee Brewer, now empowers creators worldwide through BeyGOOD and fierce ownership of her artistry.

These icons prove a timeless truth: when you teach music, you change lives.

A dream became reality for me when a simple sticker changed everything. When I wrote my first *Ultimate Music Theory* workbook, it was meant only for my students. But as teachers discovered it, their enthusiasm revealed it was more than a resource, it was the beginning of a legacy. Legacy isn't reserved for the spotlight.

It's written in the lessons we pass on, the students we inspire, and the passion we pour into every note. It's not just what we leave behind, it's what we build while we're here.

One defining moment stands out: when I shared my teaching chapter on modes with my mentor, the late Joan Passey. Joan was a concert pianist, master educator, and a force in the Canadian music community. She was strict, disciplined, and not one to offer easy praise. I braced myself as she reviewed my work, and then, she nodded. She said words that still echo in my heart: "This section alone is worth the price of the book."

Time seemed to stand still. My passion for teaching had transformed into my purpose. And then came a gesture I'll never forget. Joan reached for her stickers. She placed a yellow poodle sticker on the page. To anyone else, it was a small thing. To me, it was a standing ovation at Carnegie Hall.

That sticker became a symbol: excellence, passion, and a relentless pursuit of impact.
I still have it and every time I see it, I'm reminded that when we teach, we don't just pass on knowledge; we create something that lives on.

That moment sparked an analysis of my life, my teaching, and my business. Gratitude, continuous learning, and intentional growth became the foundation of a business that evolved from teacher to author to speaker to coach.

As musicians, we know the value of analysis. When we study a musical score, we consider melody, harmony, rhythm, structure, form. Every detail contributes to deeper understanding and so it must be with our businesses.

What is the message we are creating? What is the legacy we are building?

Legacy isn't only in the notes our students play, it's in the mindset, habits, and values we instill. Great teachers empower others. My teacher Joan empowered me and in that yellow poodle sticker moment, I realized: Legacy isn't where we end up. It's every lesson, every connection, every seed we plant along the way.

As educators, our *Analysis* isn't just a performance plan, it's a blueprint for our future.

Now, let's explore the Five Core Strategies Profit-Focused Teachers Need, your guiding principles to scale your business, create financial freedom, and give back with gratitude.

Five Core Profit-Focused Strategies

One: Focus on ROI for Financial Stability
A sustainable teaching business doesn't run on passion alone; it runs on smart financial decisions. Focus on your ROI (return on investment) and cash flow so your income grows in tune with your impact. Every expense and opportunity should either build your studio, your skills, or your savings. (Because let's be real, teaching is way more fun when your bank account isn't singing the blues.)

Two: Align with Your Students for Maximum Impact
The fastest way to grow your studio is by helping your students succeed. Create a clear learning journey with goal setting, mission statements, and personalized practice strategies. When students feel understood, supported, and celebrated, they stay longer and so does their enthusiasm. (Translation: fewer conversations about quitting when soccer season starts.)

Three: Make Your Message Unforgettable
In a sea of music teachers, your unique message is what makes you unforgettable. Clarify how you teach, why your method matters, and what transformation students can expect. When you inspire parents and students with a message that resonates, you don't have to chase enrollments, they come to you. (Because "We make music theory FUN" beats "We offer standard lessons" every day of the week.)

Four: Turn Interest into Enrollments
Inspiration without enrollment doesn't build a business. Build a simple, strategic system that moves potential students from "curious" to "committed." Think of it like composing a great piece of music, you need a clear intro, a strong melody (your offer), and a finale that makes them say, "Where do I sign up?" (Bonus points if your onboarding process doesn't require a PhD in website navigation.)

Five: Implement Systems to Scale and Succeed

If success feels chaotic, it's time for systems. Automation, scheduling tools, and streamlined processes free up your time and energy so you can teach, grow, and breathe easier. The secret isn't doing more; it's doing things smarter. (Because no teacher dreams of spending Saturday night chasing late payments when they could be practicing Chopin or binge-watching feel-good movies.)

Mastering these Five Core Strategies turns your teaching passion into a sustainable, scalable business; one that fuels your dreams, your financial freedom, and your lasting legacy. Let's explore how to design your ultimate Freedom Business Blueprint.

Blueprint for Success: Designing a Profitable Teaching Business

You wouldn't build a house without a blueprint, so why build a business without one? A strong business blueprint isn't a luxury, it's essential for creating a sustainable, profitable studio that supports both your passion and financial success.

As music teachers, we're masters of preparation, lesson plans, recitals, practice strategies, etc., but when it comes to running a business, many fall into the "just winging it" trap. Operating on good intentions alone leads straight to overwork, underpay, and burnout.

A profit-focused blueprint ensures that your studio grows intentionally not by accident. It helps you:

- **Clarify your vision (so you know where you're going).**
- **Define your pricing & offers (so you don't trade time for pennies).**
- **Create a business that fits your lifestyle (instead of your business running you).**

Because here's the truth: your time is your most valuable asset. Managing it wisely means building a business that thrives and so do you.

Your Business Blueprint: Let's Map It Out.

Step 1: Define Where You Are

Take a clear-eyed look at your current business structure.

- **Are you fully booked? Teaching groups, privates or both?**

- **What's working? What's draining your time and energy?**

- **What's the biggest challenge you need to solve right now?**

(If you're spending more time chasing payments than making music, that's a red flag.)

Step 2: Define Where You Want to Go

Picture your dream teaching life 30, 60, 90 days from now.

- **How many hours do you want to teach each week?**

- **What's your ideal income?**

- **What teaching format aligns with you? Online, in person or hybrid model?**

(Because if "teaching from a beachside cabana with a coconut in hand" is your vision, then we need to start structuring that now.)

Step 3: Design How You'll Get There

Now it's time to connect the dots between your reality and your dream.

- **Are you setting rates based on your value or on what everyone else charges?**

- **Which model maximizes your income without overloading your schedule?**

- **Where can you automate systems, streamline and save time?**

If your current model feels like "survival mode" instead of "freedom mode," it's time to design a smarter, scalable plan.

Your Blueprint, Your Business, Your Success

Every successful teaching business begins with a blueprint, a clear plan that aligns with your passion, strengths, and vision.

Below are three inspiring business models to help you design a profitable, purpose-driven career.

Models are based on 20 hours of teaching weekly.

Private lessons at $50/hour.

Group classes of 6 students at $45/hour each = $270/hour.

Artistry at $500/hour.

Business Model #1: Private one on one Lessons

Best for: Teachers who love deep, individualized instruction.

100%

100% private lessons = $4,000/mth

Key Insight: Great for personal connection, but limited scalability without raising rates or expanding services.

Business Model #2: Private and Group Teaching
Best for: Teachers ready to expand impact and income.

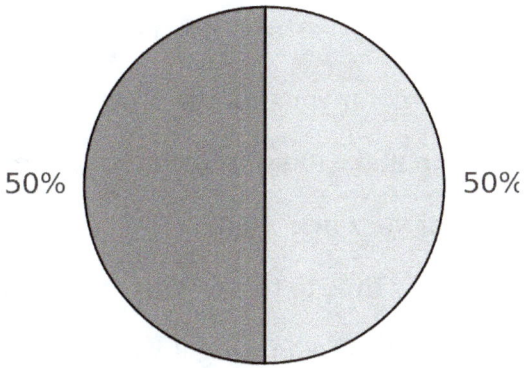

50% private, 50% group = $12,800/mth

Key Insight: Same 20 teaching hours making $8,800 more monthly income by adding group classes.

Business Model #3: Private, Group and Musician Artistry
Best for: Musicians, creatives who love teaching, performing, composing, recording, and/or speaking.

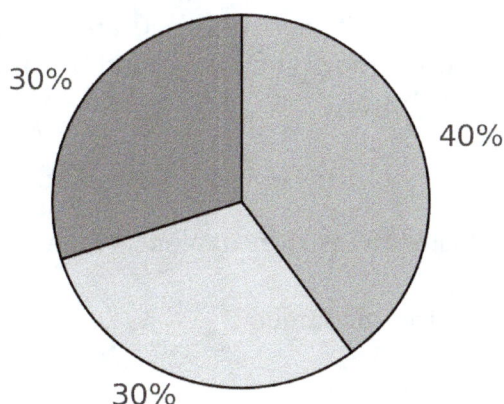

30% private, 40% group, 30% artistry = $21,840/mth (and growing.)

Key Insight: This model creates an unlimited opportunity to increase revenue. Diversifying with artistry fuels creativity, builds authority, and adds powerful new income streams.

Which model resonates with you

Your business should work for you, not the other way around.

What's one shift you can make today to move toward profitability?

What's one bold goal for your next 90 days?

How will you protect your time to thrive without burning out?

Teachers who plan, win. Those who wing it wear out.

Now, what's the blueprint you're building?

How to Get the Most Out of Coaching and Accountability Partners

As musicians, we naturally have accountability built into rehearsals and performances. The same principle transforms your teaching business: having a coach and accountability partners accelerates your success.

Busy schedules and "I'll do it later" mindsets are dream-stealers. A coach keeps you focused, moving forward, and building momentum when life gets overwhelming.

Why Every Music Teacher Needs a Coach

You would never master an instrument alone, you had a teacher, a mentor, a guide.
Business growth requires the same.

A great coach helps you:

Clarify Your Vision; know exactly what you want and how to achieve it.

Stay Accountable; replace "someday" with action today.
Learn Proven Strategies; cut years off your learning curve.

Gain Confidence; lead, teach, and grow with certainty.
Achieve Profitability; create a business model built to thrive.

Could you figure it all out alone? Sure. But why take the long, bumpy road when you can fast-track your success with clarity, confidence, and a proven path?

Inside the Ultimate Music Teachers Academy, you don't just gather information, you ignite transformation. The real question isn't "Do you need a coach?" It's "How fast do you want to succeed?"

Next up, let's explore how to create the right morning ritual because success starts before your first cup of coffee.

Create the Right Morning Ritual

Science shows we are most creative right after waking up yet 80% of people grab their phones and instantly lose their focus. Instead of diving into emails, texts, and social media (hello, distraction city), use those precious first moments of your day to fuel your goals and creativity.

Try this 3-Minute Clarity Exercise. Grab a notebook. Set a timer for 3 minutes. Answer this:

- **What do I want my business to look like in 90 days?**
- **What opportunity am I ready to pursue?**
- **What one decision can I make today that moves me forward?**

No editing. No overthinking. Just flow. Because clarity is for successful entrepreneurs and it's non-negotiable.

Create the Right Profit Plan

Most teachers calculate profit backward: income minus expenses and hope something's left. Smart businesses flip that: Profit first.

Quick Exercise:

Calculate Your True Hourly Rate: Total monthly gross income. Subtract all expenses (teaching, admin, marketing, memberships, rent). Divided by total work hours (teaching, prep, emails, marketing, etc.). Is your true hourly rate where you want it to be? If not, it's time to shift.

Shift to a Profit-First Mindset: Price your services with profit built in from the start. Inside the UMTC Elite Educator Program, we teach the 7 Master Keys for Wealth helping teachers increase income, manage expenses wisely, and create financial freedom without overwhelm. Because running your business on the "Toothpaste Method" (squeezing out every last dollar) isn't sustainable.

Heather Revell, UMTC Elite Educator, shared: "The Profit First Principle is excellent. Thank you, Glory. I've put it in place today. It makes so much sense to work Profit First rather than 'Toothpasting' my finances, haha. I appreciate your wisdom."

Goals, Gratitude and the Path to Profitability

What's the secret behind my clients' success? Clarity of goals, a mindset of gratitude, and the power of implementation. By continuously developing their skills, implementing strategies from the UMTC Elite Educator Program, and staying committed to growth, they've created lasting success in their teaching businesses. And you can too.

When you set clear, specific goals and infuse them with gratitude and positivity, something incredible happens: opportunities flow toward you. Your teaching becomes more impactful, your students thrive, and profit naturally follows.

But here's where many teachers get stuck: setting vague goals.

Saying "I want to be a better teacher" isn't enough. Growth comes when you define what "better" looks like, map out how to get there, and take consistent action toward that vision. Ask yourself:

- **What skills do you want to develop?**

- **What kind of impact do you want to make on your students?**

- **How do you want to be recognized in your teaching community?**

When you focus on growth through gratitude, you create an unstoppable cycle of positivity, possibility, and profitability.

Two Essential Teaching Mindsets for Success

First, Goal-Setting with Purpose and Action. Your goals must be clear, intentional, and actionable. Set them with focus, accountability, and a step-by-step plan because when you combine desire, determination, and dedication, anything is possible. What specific goals will drive your teaching business forward?

Second, Gratitude as a Success Multiplier. Gratitude isn't just a feeling, it's a way of thinking, leading, and teaching. It shapes your confidence, strengthens student relationships, and opens doors to new opportunities. What are you most grateful for, and how can you amplify gratitude in your teaching and business?

"Profitability comes from loyalty, productivity and a character base from which to work."

~ Zig Ziglar

Now, let's take that abundance mindset and apply it directly to your teaching business:

The Power of Productivity and Profitability

Productivity: teaching success depends on efficiency, structure, and intentional time management. What strategies will you implement to maximize your impact without overworking yourself?

Profitability: your financial freedom, lifestyle, and long-term success are driven by running a profitable business. What's your plan to ensure consistent growth and revenue?

The truth is, when you focus on productivity and profitability with a heart of gratitude, your business will grow and thrive.

> *"Gratitude for the present moment and the fullness of life now is the true prosperity."*
>
> ~ Eckhart Tolle

The Hummingbird's Message: A Legacy of Love and Gratitude

Music has been the heartbeat of my life but its meaning deepened in ways I could never have imagined after my beloved husband Ray passed away.

You've heard me share stories of Ray, his unwavering encouragement, his music, his larger-than-life presence. He cheered me on through every word of this book. I only wish he were here to see these final pages come together, because this book, this journey, is dedicated to him.

Ray wrote a song called *"If You See the Same Bird, You'll Know That It's Me."* Originally written after his father passed, it became a requested favorite on his radio show, a message of comfort for anyone missing someone they loved. After Ray passed, that song took on a whole new meaning for me. I wondered: Would he send me a sign? Would I know when it came?

I thought maybe a blue jay, his favorite bird. But life, and love, had different plans.

A few months after his passing, I stood quietly in my daughter's backyard in Las Vegas, facing a tall palm tree. I spoke out loud into the sunny morning air, wondering if Ray could hear me. And then, out of nowhere, a tiny hummingbird appeared, hovering just inches from my face.

Perfectly still. Perfectly present.

I had never seen a hummingbird up close before, and yet there he was, staying with me for what felt like an eternity. Tears filled my eyes. I whispered, "Honey, is that you?" And still, the hummingbird remained, listening.

Later that day, I returned to the same spot. And once again, there he was, this time perched lightly on a twig, tilting his head as if to say, "I'm still here." It was a moment of overwhelming peace, connection, and gratitude. It reminded me that love is never lost. It only changes form.

A few days later, the ultimate confirmation: standing in the kitchen, coffee in hand, patio doors wide open, I looked up and there he was again. Ray the Hummingbird, hovering at the doorway. Not outside. Right there, between the worlds.

Checking on me one last time.

Music has shaped my life from the very beginning:

- **My father's first songs on his hummingbird guitar.**

- **My husband's loving message through his song, *If You See The Same Bird You'll Know That it's Me*.**

- **The melodies, harmonies, and rhythms that connect every chapter of my life.**

My first Christmas without Ray, I listened to our family Christmas album with new emotions. Our song *"I'm Missing You This Christmas"* carried a deeper meaning now, yet somehow, also a profound gratitude.

Music is memory.
Music is love.
Music is legacy.

And gratitude is the ultimate key to living a life filled with memory, love, and legacy.

As we reflect on the impact of music in our lives and in our students' lives we realize that true analysis leads us to passion, purpose, and ultimately profitability as musicians and educators.

For one of my clients, UMTC Elite Educator Shirley Wang, reflection brought a life-changing realization.

"The mind is everything. What you think, you become."

~ Buddha

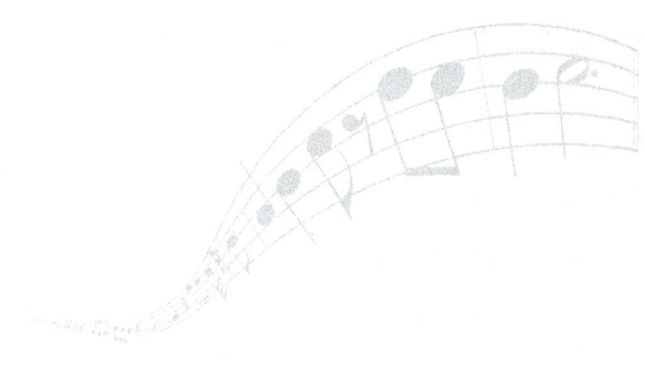

Case Study:
UMTC Elite Educator Shirley Wang

Shirley Wang's journey began in Taipei, Taiwan. At fifteen, she moved to America, speaking little English, navigating a world of change and challenge. Yet, her passion for music and her gratitude for every opportunity never wavered.

In 2012, Shirley made her solo debut at Carnegie Hall, standing in the spotlight most musicians only dream of. With over 2,700 seats spanning five levels, she was living her dream. Then came an even bigger offer: a lucrative full-time operatic contract.

Yet something didn't feel right. Rather than jumping at the opportunity, Shirley did the unthinkable, she paused and analyzed her future.

She realized the music she was being asked to sing didn't align with her artistic vision or values. After many sleepless nights, she declined the offer and followed her passion for creative, themed concerts blending storytelling, opera, piano, show tunes, traditional Chinese music, and other world languages.

Then came another life-altering challenge. In 2018, while kayaking, Shirley contracted Lyme Disease, a debilitating illness that caused severe brain fog, exhaustion, and muscle coordination issues. Singing and playing piano became a daily struggle.

As she put it:

"It was as if a storm had come through and made a real mess of my previously peaceful house. But somehow, I knew, after sweeping with a broom, wiping down with rags, and some straightening up, I would again have a tranquil home. Albeit it may be different with some re-arrangements. I rested in this 'knowing'".

Through her healing journey, Shirley learned to let go, live mindfully, and reconnect with her purpose. She changed her diet, prioritized rest, sought out alternative treatments, and ultimately found a doctor who helped her heal.

Inspired by the teachings of Thích Nhất Hạnh and fueled by her unwavering love for music, Shirley returned to the stage, not the same, but transformed.

"As a result of my health struggles, my voice is different, my body feels foreign, and my whole person has changed. But I am grateful for the healing and the power of music. I look forward to new performances, in new cities, states, and continents."

Today, Shirley continues to inspire audiences around the world, blazing brightly through her music, her resilience, and her unwavering gratitude.

"Music itself is magnificent. In music, I see God. Only when I am living, breathing, and making music do I experience God fully. Music has chosen me."

Shirley's story is a powerful reminder that success isn't just about reaching a destination, it's about choosing the path that aligns with your heart, even when it's the harder road. She could have chosen the conventional career path, but instead, she designed a life and career that reflected her true values, creativity, and spirit.

Read Shirley's inspiring story in *The Power of WHY Musicians* 5 Book Series.

As music educators and entrepreneurs, we, too, hold the power to shape our journey, pivot when needed, and build a sustainable, fulfilling career in music.

It starts with clarity, courage, and the willingness to take action.

Think about this and write your answers below.

- **What legacy do you want to create through your teaching?**

- **How will you align your business and passion to build a profitable, purpose-driven career?**

- **Are you ready to embrace your own journey to success, just like Shirley did?**

Your music, your business, and your impact matter. The time to build your Profit-Focused Legacy is now.

"Gratitude transforms the ordinary into extraordinary, turns teaching into passion, business into purpose, and opportunities into profitability."

~ Glory St. Germain

My Legacy Statement

Music has been the heartbeat of my life woven into every moment, every lesson, every note played and taught. For over 50 years, I have guided thousands of students, composers, performers, and educators, helping them develop their musicianship, confidence, and artistry on international stages.

From my first days at the piano to writing the Ultimate Music Theory Series, my journey has always been about more than just teaching, it has been about empowerment, transformation, and leaving a lasting impact.

But my mission didn't stop there. My passion for teaching evolved into a calling to serve educators, coaching and mentoring music teachers to build thriving, sustainable businesses. Through the Ultimate Music Teachers Academy, I now have the privilege of supporting thousands of educators worldwide. A legacy isn't just what we leave behind, it's what we create in every moment we teach.

It's in the students who find confidence through music.
It's in the teachers who build thriving businesses.
It's in the generations of musicians who carry forward the knowledge and passion we share.

My mission is to elevate music educators to provide the strategies, tools, and mindset shifts that allow them to teach with passion, purpose, and profitability. Because when teachers succeed, music thrives.

This is my legacy: a movement of dedicated educators who believe in their value, embrace their expertise, and build financially empowering, purpose-driven, profitable teaching businesses. And now, it's your turn.

Let's pause to reflect on the Three Steps to Build a Profit-Focused Legacy through analysis of your business and how to take it to the next level.

⌒ *Fermata* (Pause to Ponder): Three Steps to Analyze Your Purpose, Your Passion and Your Profitable Business

Step #1: Your Lasting Legacy

A legacy is crafted through daily intentional action and lifelong impact. The music you teach today lives on in the hearts of your students forever.

What do you want to be remembered for as a music educator?

_____

_____

How will you structure your business to ensure your impact lasts?

_____

_____

What action can you take today to solidify your legacy in the music industry?

_____

_____

Step #2: Gratitude Manifests Success

Gratitude is a magnet for abundance. What you appreciate, appreciates.

How can you implement a daily gratitude practice to elevate your mindset?

_____

_____

What challenges can you reframe as opportunities for growth?

_____

_____

Who shaped your teaching journey and how can you express your gratitude?

_____

_____

Step #3: Music Impacts Life

Music connects, heals, and transforms. You are teaching life skills.

How has music transformed your life and how can you share that passion?

_____

_____

What strategies can you use to foster a lifelong love of music in your students?

_____

_____

How can your teaching expand the global impact of music education?

_____

_____

Your Business, Your Legacy, Your Future

Your music teaching business is more than a career; it's a masterpiece in the making. Just as a beautifully composed piece of music requires form, structure, and interpretation, your business requires strategy, planning, and constant refinement.

A profit-focused business expands your capacity, allowing you to create more, serve more, and live more.

Money becomes a creative force, fueling opportunities, sustainability, and transformation in your life and in the lives of those you teach. Remember: Analysis is an ongoing process.

Just as we analyze music to uncover its beauty, we must analyze our business to amplify its impact. Set your monthly, quarterly, and yearly profit goals with the same commitment you bring to your lessons. Because when you teach with purpose, plan with clarity, and build with profitability, you create a legacy that inspires generations.

Congrats, YOU are an Ultimate Music Teacher. TEACH MUSIC CHANGE LIVES. With Love and Gratitude, Glory St. Germain.

Your passion brought you here. Your purpose will take you further. Your profitable legacy starts now.

♪ Your Coda Notes ♪

The 12 Key Strategies include online Ultimate Music Teachers Bonus Resources.

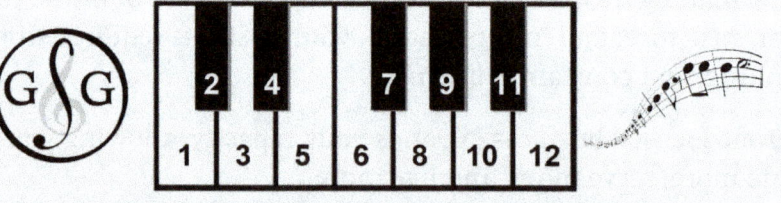

TEACH MUSIC CHANGE LIVES
Your Profit-Focused Ultimate Legacy

Dive deeper into **KEY STRATEGY #12** - get your
Ultimate Music Teachers
FREE Bonus Workbook to reflect through analysis and
rise to your next level.
Go To: UltimateMusicTeachers.com/guide

Your passion is your purpose.

Your business is your bridge.

Your legacy begins today with every note you teach, every life you touch, and every dream you dare to believe in.

ULTIMATE MUSIC TEACHERS ACADEMY

This is an open invitation to musicians and music teachers everywhere who feel called to contribute to the world of music education.

If your heart beats to the rhythm of impact and inspiration, and you're ready to give back in meaningful, impactful ways, now's your moment to become more than "just a music teacher."

Step into your role as an Ultimate Music Teacher, an empowered educator and joyful entrepreneur dedicated to enriching lives through music and implementing the 12 Keys to Unlock the Ultimate Music Teachers Success Strategies, so you can Teach Music and Change Lives.

Teach with Passion, Purpose and Profitability.

Learn more about the Ultimate Music Teachers Academy at:

UltimateMusicTeachers.com

GIVING BACK WITH GRATITUDE

Ultimate Music Theory, founded by **Glory St. Germain** in 2008, began as a comprehensive program designed to simplify music theory for students, making it accessible, engaging, and unforgettable for musicians of all ages.

This educational foundation grew into the **Ultimate Music Teachers Academy**, a global platform supporting educators in building thriving teaching businesses through the power of music and fulfilling the mission to *Teach Music and Change Lives*.

At **Ultimate Music Teachers**, we're also passionate about giving back. A portion of all profits from *Teach Music Change Lives* is donated to **El Sistema USA**® a nonprofit organization supporting a binational network of programs across the United States and Canada.

Together, we share a commitment to expanding access to high-quality music education that empowers youth and strengthens communities through creativity, collaboration, and opportunity.

Inspired by the original El Sistema founded in Venezuela in 1975 by José Antonio Abreu and championed by conductor Gustavo Dudamel, El Sistema USA now includes over 140 member programs, 6,000 teaching artists, and 25,000 students across North America.

Rooted in the philosophy of *"Music for Social Change"*, El Sistema uses ensemble-based learning to provide free or low-cost instruction, particularly to students in under-resourced communities.

Their impact reached new heights—literally—on September 13, 2024, when Polaris Dawn Mission Specialist Sarah Gillis, SpaceX engineer and accomplished violinist, became the first person to perform a violin solo in space.

Aboard the Dragon spacecraft, she played *Rey's Theme* by John Williams, launching a global campaign in support of music education.

Her performance, titled *Harmony of Resilience*, featured a stunning collaboration with youth musicians from El Sistema programs around the world, including Venezuela, Brazil, the U.S. (Boston String Academy), Sweden, Uganda, and Haiti.

This first-of-its-kind concert, transmitted via SpaceX's Starlink, united Earth and space through the universal language of music.

Through educational training, student leadership programs, research, and advocacy, **El Sistema USA®** and its international partners prepare expressive, resilient individuals who grow not only as musicians, but as confident, compassionate citizens who enrich the world around them.

Together, we're building a future where every child has access to music education that inspires possibility, nurtures potential, and connects hearts across cultures, communities, and even galaxies.

This movement reminds us that music transcends boundaries, uniting us across generations, cultures, and even the cosmos. It is with this same spirit of unity and generosity that I share this closing note with you.

I warmly invite you, budding musicians and educators alike, to explore Ultimate Music Theory and our Ultimate Music Teachers Academy. Discover our innovative workbooks, comprehensive courses, Ultimate Music Theory App, insightful Ultimate Music Teachers podcast, and our engaging YouTube channel.

At Ultimate Music Teachers, we inspire you to unleash your superpowers to teach with Passion, Purpose & Profitability.

"Goals set with accountability and tools for mastery of execution are the greatest motivation for achievement."

~ Glory St. Germain

ACKNOWLEDGMENTS

To the thousands of music teachers and musicians around the globe that have connected with us on social media, our Ultimate Music Theory YouTube Channel, UMT App, UMT Podcast or attended one of our events or enrolled in our Ultimate Music Teachers courses or UMT Membership—from the "girl who Dreams Big" with a heart full of gratitude, you are the reason I wrote this book.

Your support and desire to be more, do more and ultimately teach more with passion, purpose and profitability is why I do what I do. I cannot wait to hear how these 12 Keys have impacted your life both personally and professionally.

Thank you to my husband Ray for believing in me and sharing a life of love, music and family. I will treasure our memories forever.

Thank you to my wonderful children Sherry, David, Ray Jr., Cathy & Chrystal and grandchildren for all the love, laughter and memories we continue to make.

To my entire UMT Dream Team: Shelagh, Joanne, Leanna, Shauna, Jessica, Danika, Kyle, Randy, Miriam, and children David and Sherry, I couldn't have done it without you. Thanks for being part of the amazing journey. I'm so proud and grateful to all of you.

Special thanks to Sage Lavine, my Women Rocking Business coach for starting me on my writing journey, Carolyn Dawn Flynn, my book writing coach, Wendy H. Jones, my line editor and Shauna Hunter, my copy editor, and Michael O'Donnell for interior design.

Special thanks to Jack Canfield for your passion as a musician, teacher and success coach in helping me finish my book. Steve Harrison and Patty Aubery for sharing your insights in navigating the publishing industry and your dedication to authors sharing heart-felt messages with the world.

Thanks to my coaches, mentors and accountability partners through the years who gave me the greatest lessons in teaching with passion, purpose and profitability.

Thank you to all my clients and UMTC Elite Educators for sharing your vision to grow your music teaching business so you can TEACH MUSIC and CHANGE LIVES.

ABOUT THE AUTHOR

Glory St. Germain ARCT RMT MYCC UMTC is the Founder & CEO of Ultimate Music Theory, TEDx Speaker, and International Bestselling Author of over 60 music education books, including the global anthology series, *The Power of WHY Musicians.* As host of the Ultimate Music Teachers Productivity and Profitability Podcast, Global Music Teachers Summits, and expert music business coach, Glory empowers educators worldwide to build profitable, passion-driven studios.

Creator of the Ultimate Music Theory Certification Course & Elite Educator Program, Glory provides teachers with essential strategies to elevate their income, amplify their impact, and achieve personal fulfillment. A passionate NLP (Neuro-Linguistic Programming) Practitioner, composer, and seasoned educator with decades of experience teaching Piano, Theory, and Music for Young Children, Glory deeply understands the power of mindset to transform outcomes. Committed to Enriching Lives Through Music Education, Glory advocates for a Positive Mental Attitude (PMA), believing that mindset shapes our personal and professional success. She continues to inspire educators through workshops, coaching, and international speaking engagements. Glory lives her life with gratitude, passion, and purpose.

Explore the inspiring world of music education at_ **UltimateMusicTeachers.com** and **UltimateMusicTheory.com** where passionate educators unite to elevate teaching and transform lives. This harmonious journey is reshaping the future of music education one note, one student, one inspired teacher at a time.

CONNECT WITH GLORY

Every concept taught and every chord played contributes to a global symphony of transformation and impact. You are now part of this movement. Your passion, your purpose, and your teaching have the power to shape lives and inspire generations.

As you continue your journey, know that I'm here to walk beside you and to support, celebrate, and spark new possibilities with you.

Let's stay connected! I invite you to explore our live events, inspiring blog, and the Ultimate Music Teachers Academy, filled with courses, coaching, and a community of educators just like you who teach with passion, purpose, and profitability.

Because when we teach music, we change lives.

Here's to your success,

Glory

Connect with me:

Website: TeachMusicChangeLives.com
LinkedIn: Glory St. Germain
Facebook: Ultimate Music Teachers
Instagram: @UltimateMusicTheory
YouTube: Ultimate Music Theory